JUST ENOUGH C/C++ PROGRAMMING

GUY W. LECKY-THOMPSON

THOMSON

COURSE TECHNOLOGY

Professional ■ Technical ■ Reference

Important: Thomson Course Technology PTR cannot provide software support. Please contact the appropriate software manufacturer's technical support line or Web site for assistance.

Thomson Course Technology PTR and the author have attempted throughout this book to distinguish proprietary trademarks from descriptive terms by following the capitalization style used by the manufacturer.

Information contained in this book has been obtained by Thomson Course Technology PTR from sources believed to be reliable. However, because of the possibility of human or mechanical error by our sources, Thomson Course Technology PTR, or others, the Publisher does not guarantee the accuracy, adequacy, or completeness of any information and is not responsible for any errors or omissions or the results obtained from use of such information. Readers should be particularly aware of the fact that the Internet is an ever-changing entity. Some facts may have changed since this book went to press.

Educational facilities, companies, and organizations interested in multiple copies or licensing of this book should contact the Publisher for quantity discount information. Training manuals, CD-ROMs, and portions of this book are also available individually or can be tailored for specific needs.

ISBN-10: 1-59863-468-2
ISBN-13: 978-1-59863-468-6
Library of Congress Catalog Card Number: 2007906522
Printed in the United States of America
08 09 10 11 12 TW 10 9 8 7 6 5 4 3 2 1

Publisher and General Manager, Thomson Course Technology PTR:
Stacy L. Hiquet

Associate Director of Marketing:
Sarah O'Donnell

Manager of Editorial Services:
Heather Talbot

Marketing Manager:
Mark Hughes

Acquisitions Editor:
Mitzi Koontz

Project/Copy Editor:
Kezia Endsley

Technical Reviewer:
Keith Davenport

PTR Editorial Services Coordinator:
Erin Johnson

Interior Layout Tech:
ICC Macmillan Inc.

Cover Designer:
Mike Tanamachi

Indexer:
Katherine Stimson

Proofreaders:
Gene Redding
Sara Gullion

THOMSON
COURSE TECHNOLOGY
Professional ■ Technical ■ Reference

Thomson Course Technology PTR,
a division of Thomson Learning Inc.
25 Thomson Place
Boston, MA 02210
http://www.courseptr.com

This book is dedicated to my parents.
Thanks for the encouragement and early programming start (see anecdote)!

Author's anecdote: In the early 1980s a father and son sat down in front of a state-of-the-art home computer, equipped with a pencil, paper, programming book, and nothing more than the faintest idea about programming.

They did, however, have an idea revolving around an animated Christmas card that would display graphics of a tree and include the names of the guests invited to a Christmas party. Maybe it could even play a seasonal tune.

Over time, they looked up only what they needed to know to achieve their goal. They studied individual commands that seemed appropriate. They put together a working program, complete with music, and set it up as a background installation at the Christmas party. The guests were suitably impressed.

That experience—learning just enough to do the job—shaped the author's outlook on programming ever since. You don't need to know everything about a language if you know enough to achieve your programming goals.

So, thanks Dad, for being my first programming partner!

Acknowledgments

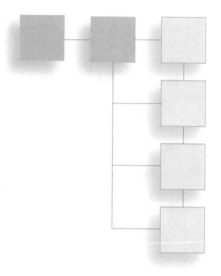

Although my name is on the cover of this book, these things are rarely ever the work of a single person. My family, as ever, has been supportive, and I'm particularly grateful to my wife, Nicole, for putting up with my occasional rants during the final editing. Speaking of which, I also have to thank Kezia Endsley and Keith Davenport for keeping me on the linguistic and technical straight and narrow; their combined editing prowess helped to shape this book into what it is. Mitzi Koontz also deserves a mention, along with the rest of the publishing and support team.

Finally, thanks to my children, Emma and William, for the reality checks. It's always refreshing to know that, for some people, the world does not revolve around publishing deadlines.

ABOUT THE AUTHOR

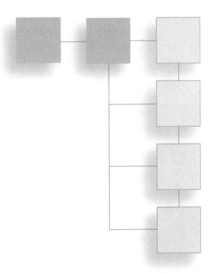

Guy W. Lecky-Thompson holds a BSc. in Computer Studies from the University of Derby, UK and has written articles and books on a variety of subjects, from software engineering to video game design and programming.

A technical all-rounder, he brings all aspects of his professional life and personal views to his writing, injecting personality into technical subjects. In his books this often translates into giving the reader the vital information, cutting away anything that isn't immediately relevant or useful.

When not writing books, Guy enjoys family time, video gaming, writing opinion pieces, and creative programming.

CONTENTS

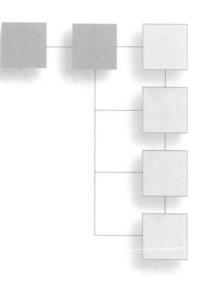

INTRODUCTION

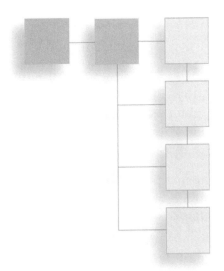

Welcome to *Just Enough C/C++ Programming*, which aims to provide you with just enough information on the subject of C/C++ in hand to be useful in the real world. The main principles of *Just Enough C/C++ Programming* are to give you:

- An understanding of programming.

- Small increments of information on an as-needed basis.

- Quick and easy reference should you need it.

- Examples from real applications.

The goals are to help you get started as quickly as possible, and build useful programs within a short space of time. You can start at the beginning (and for a newcomer to the world of programming, this is advised), or you pick up the book when needed and use it as a reference guide.

In Chapter 1, "Getting Started," you will see exactly what the tools of the trade are, and learn some basic concepts related to the programming process. This chapter sets the scene for the whole book, and gives you some useful paths through it, depending on your own needs.

Chapter 2, "Programming Recap," contains a programming primer; if you're new to programming, this chapter is invaluable. Even if you have some programming experience, I advise you at least skim through Chapter 2 to be sure that you are starting from the same point.

Chapter 3, "C Program Structure," covers the various concepts that make up a typical C program. This gives you an immediate appreciation of what the code might look like, and how the C program is constructed. It is important that you understand the basic structure and layout, because the story moves along very quickly thereafter.

The first part of that story is Chapter 4, "Data Types and Variables," where you consider how information is stored in a program. This is followed by Chapter 5, which includes an introduction to Console I/O—ways to get information from the user and display it on the screen. At this point, you'll know enough to write genuinely useful applications.

You'll then take a look at decision making in Chapter 6, to extend the usefulness of the techniques you've already learned. You'll learn how to selectively perform tasks based on the outcome of preceding tasks, which is vital in programming. The complement to this is the loops chapter (Chapter 7), which covers the mechanisms available for task repetition.

The book takes a small timeout from the language aspects at this point, to cover standard libraries in Chapter 8. This chapter also serves as a good reference if you ever need to look up a definition for one of the library functions.

Having read Chapter 8, you'll be fully equipped to begin writing applications; however, you still need to look at command-line processing (Chapter 9) and user-defined functions (Chapter 10) before you'll be able to write complete applications. These two chapters provide, on the one hand, a detailed explanation of how programs process incoming arguments, and on the other, how you can create functions within your programs.

Having looked at a language aspect, you'll then put it to use in Chapter 11, about file I/O, which deals with ways to process files and perform external data storage. This is followed by the complex data types chapter (Chapter 12), which shows you how you can create your own templates for storing information.

The last C language topic is pointers, covered in Chapter 13, which is an advanced programming topic, but necessary for understanding the bridge into C++. Before considering C++ itself, you'll take a look at pre-processor directives in Chapter 14, which detail how you communicate with the program charged with taking your code and turning it into an application—the compiler.

Chapters 15–18 then discuss the extensions to C that make C++ a useful language.

The C++ standard libraries echo the C standard libraries chapter in providing a good reference while presenting some very useful routines for a variety of tasks. You'll then move on to something called the *STL*, a template library with pre-defined data types and algorithms for processing complex data types.

Finally, I'll sum up the book, and give you some direction as to how you can go about using all this information, in Chapter 19. Chapter 20 provides a list of all the various useful Web references. At this point, you can begin programming for real, and I'll give you some useful proving grounds to hone your talents.

The first thing that you should do is read Chapter 1, and then decide if you have the equipment that you need to get going. Then decide which category of reader you fall in to—academic, private interest, bedroom programmer—so you can plot a path through the book that will bring you the most reward.

It is unlikely that any reader can absorb everything the first time around, which is why there is quite a lot of reference material in this book. It is, however, important to use the source code from the companion Web site (go to www.courseptr.com and click on the Downloads button). That way, you can try the variations suggested as you go along. Trial and error is a great learning tool; and it will help you get a better appreciation of C and C++ programming.

What's On the Companion Web Site

Go to www.courseptr.com and click on the Downloads button to access the code from this book. The companion Web site contains, chapter by chapter, all the complete programs that are listed in the book. Where multiple files are necessary, they are in sub-folders of the chapter folder. All code is in C or C++, and has been test-compiled with the Borland BCC32 command-line compiler environment.

To use the code from the companion Web site, you must have at your disposal a computer running the following:

- Microsoft Windows (95/NT/98/2000/XP)

- Linux (all)

- Apple Macintosh (all)

Your computer should also have a suitable development environment if you want to compile the source code.

CHAPTER 1

GETTING STARTED

Before you start to look at how programs are created, what they can and cannot do, and how you are going to set about writing them, you need to look at a few general points of order. The key to *Just Enough* is in not overcomplicating the process, so I have tried to make the preliminaries as painless as possible.

Once you have worked your way through this chapter, you will have all the information you need to make some informed choices about the tools you need in order to make the most of this book.

Conventions Used in This Book

There are some conventions that I use consistently to help you identify various parts of the text—be they code samples or a kind of enigmatic shorthand for indicating how a piece of code is supposed to be used. This stems from the fact that you need to know:

- Syntax: How the code is to be used.

- Semantics: Where the code is to be used.

In other words, I'll provide a kind of generic template description that shows you how to write the single piece of code, as well as showing you how it is used alongside other bits and pieces of programming. Each important facet of C code will be presented in this way.

To distinguish something that you should type in and be used as code, we use a specific font. Whenever text is shown in a fixed `font`, like this, then it is a piece of C/C++ code, or part of a program. Complete fragments will also be indented.

Sometimes I'll need to show, in the generic template for a piece of code, some items that are either:

- Optional: The programmer can choose to include them.

- Mandatory: The computer expects them to be there.

On top of this, values can be chosen either by the programmer or from a list of allowed values, and I need a way to indicate this, too. So whenever I want to indicate that you can choose a specific value from a list of possible allowed values, you'll see a list separated by the pipe symbol, |. For example:

```
One | Two | Three
```

Here, you can use `One`, `Two`, or `Three`. I will, however, usually enclose the list in one of two sets of symbols in order to indicate whether the value is optional or mandatory. To show that the value is mandatory, I enclose it in chevrons:

```
< One | Two | Three>
```

This code line indicates that you can choose from any of the values in the list, but one must be present. Conversely, if I want to indicate that you can choose a value but don't have to include any, I enclose the list in [and] symbols, as follows:

```
[ One | Two | Three ]
```

Here, you can choose from these values, but you don't have to choose any value. This might sound like an unnecessary complication, but it can be very useful and is much easier to understand once you look at some concrete examples.

If there is no list to choose from, you're free to enter the value of your choice, with some restrictions that will be explained when the code is introduced. It will usually look something like:

```
< number >
```

This indicates that you can choose any number, but that you must choose one since the chevrons indicate that this is a mandatory value. On the other hand, you might see:

```
[ number ]
```

This indicates that while any number can be chosen, its presence is optional. Notice that the number is in *italics* to show that it is a value chosen by the user. You can also indicate a specific constant value (one that does not change and is imposed on the programmer) that should be used by specifying a list with a single item:

⟨ 1 ⟩

This indicates that you must place the digit 1 in your code, whereas the following indicates that you can choose to use 1, or not, depending on your needs:

[1]

This last example is not very widespread in the code examples but is included here to complete the picture. It is more common to see a specific required value specified as part of the generic template itself, as a constant value, without any indication as to whether the programmer has any choice over its inclusion.

How to Use This Book

This book is designed to have a long shelf life, and as such, the way that it is used will change as you gain experience. The book is also designed for non-programmers as well as technicians who have also had some exposure to programming.

Different readers will have different needs, so there are different paths through the material, depending on individual circumstances:

- Beginner: No exposure to programming.

- Some Knowledge: Some exposure to programming, with non-C languages.

- Intermediate: Understands the basics, can create programs.

- Learning Reference: Ongoing study.

- Professional Reference: Off-the-shelf solution seeker.

Of course, as you gain confidence in programming, you may well find yourself moving from one of the categories to another more advanced one. In fact, by reading and understanding this book, you will add to your experience and knowledge and will find it valuable as a reference even after you have become a bona fide programmer.

Although the book has not been written in a specific order for each reader, I can give you some guidance as to how to approach the book given your own background and needs. Furthermore, as a course text, I can define a path that deals with the issue of programming first, the C language second, and problem solving and programming third.

Readers with no agenda and enough time to dedicate to reading and understanding can just read the book from cover to cover and try out the code pieces as they go along. However, some readers will benefit from more structure, and so I give you some guidance that will help group similar topics together.

Study Areas

To help private individuals and course developers, I have grouped the chapters according to three study areas:

- Programming and C Language: The basics of programming in general and C in particular.

- C++ Language: The additions to C that make C++ really useful.

- Applied Topics: Topics that show how C/C++ can be applied and require knowledge of programming to understand fully.

Some topics can be skipped, depending on personal requirements, and I have left the pure reference areas to one side for the time being. In the context of a C programming course, the course developer can use the reference material as self-study materials and as preparation for practical assignments.

Programming and C Language

This study area will give you a good grounding in useful C, without being concerned with the more esoteric program structures or advanced in-depth dissection of the language. In this section, the book is more concerned with using the tool in practice than learning how to sharpen it.

- Programming Primer: A primer in programming, without reference to specific languages, but dealing with the entire family of procedural programming languages.

- C Program Structure: The generic structure of C programs, and the various pieces that have to be assembled in order to make one.

- Data Types and Variables: How you store data in C programs, and how to get it back again.

- Decision Making: Ways to decide which instructions should be followed and which can be ignored.

- Loops: How you can perform the same task over and over again and know when to stop.

- Complex Data Types: Storing data that is defined by the user, rather than the language.

- Pointers: A way of referencing information without being concerned as to what that information might actually be. You know that the box exists and how big it is, but not what is inside it.

C++ Language

This is not a book about C++ and how to write *good* C++ software. It is a book about using the bits of C++ that make it truly useful as an extension of C rather than a language in its own right. Having absorbed this information, you can explore the rest of the C++ language over time, and any C++ book will make much more sense after having played around with these examples for a while.

- C++ in Practice: Covers the extensions that are part of C++ that make it useful for C programmers.

- Templates and the STL: You'll look at ways to extend the C and C++ standard libraries in a more powerful and transparent way, as well as look at some standard data structure and algorithm implementations designed to make your life as a programmer easier by giving you a starting point.

Applied Topics

Once you understand the basics, you're ready to move on to some applied topics. This section allows you to go from the beginning to the end in a short space of time and reinforce your learning through doing.

- Console I/O: Covers ways in which users can receive information on the screen and ways in which the program can receive information from the users via the keyboard.

- File I/O: A detailed look at how you can read data from and write data to files.

- From C to C++: Learn about various useful entry-level features to C to learn the bare essentials of C++.

Reference

These reference sections make easy quick references in the future when you find you need to solve a particular programming problem.

- C Standard Libraries: A collection of useful data manipulation and system functions.

- Command-Line Processing: Ways to receive information from the users when a program runs.

- Preprocessor Directives: Useful macros and techniques for making programming more flexible and making programs easier to maintain.

- C++ Standard Libraries: Similar to the C standard libraries, with some useful extensions.

Choosing the Right Tools

The C language has been in existence for so long that there is a whole gamut of tools available for programmers. While the choices are vast, they break down into two basic categories:

- Integrated Development Environments (IDEs)

- Separate Tools

The IDE contains everything that you need to get started right away. Although there is usually a number of intricacies in the setup that you need to deal with, these IDEs have the virtue of being complete environments. Generally, these are large downloads that take a lot of space, and a certain investment is required sometimes before they work as advertised.

The separate tools require downloading three basic tools, separately:

- Editor

- Compiler

- Linker

However, before you rush into downloading an IDE, it is worth remembering that most operating systems come with an editor of some kind—be it Notepad for Windows users or an Open Source equivalent for Linux users—and that a compiler usually comes with a linker.

Essentially, an editor is used to edit the source code (instructions for the computer), a compiler turns that from readable text into something the computer understands, and the linker turns *that* code into an application. The process is called *building an application.*

Editor

The more sophisticated the editor, the more efficient the programming experience will be. A simple text editor, like Notepad, can be used to enter all the examples in this book.

However, better editing environments also come with something called *syntax highlighting,* which will change the color of text that has special meaning in the C language. This is a great help when editing source code because it makes it very easy to spot keywords within the rest of the text.

A programmer's editor, such as the ones built into most available IDEs, has some special features beyond syntax highlighting. For example, most C IDEs (environments specifically for C programmers) offer some form of inline editing help such as auto-completion of text and little context-sensitive help balloons that remind the programmer of the language syntax.

The downside of an IDE is that it is often restricted to a specific language. So you might need one for C programming, one for HTML design, one for creating plain text documents, and so on. There are some popular editors that offer a good halfway point between this restriction and offering IDE-style benefits. There is a list of these in the Web references section of the book, and updates will be available on the accompanying Web site.

Compiler and Linker

The first thing to note is that most commercial software vendors (Microsoft, Borland Inprise, and so on) now offer free versions of their commercial compilers. This is great news for the programmer because it means that you can obtain a free IDE with an editor, compiler, and linker of commercial quality.

However, not all compilers are created equal, and besides, any Linux users reading this will have access to an excellent compiler, called gcc, as part of the operating system. Windows and Apple Mac users are not so fortunate, and in order to try to cater to as wide an audience as possible, you'll see a complete list of places to obtain a compiler in the Web references chapter (Chapter 20).

Debugger

One of the advantages of an IDE is the integrated debugger. A debugger allows the programmer to follow the code as it executes, in order to spot where there might be an error. Programmers make mistakes, and the nature of computer code is such that sometimes the mistake is not immediately obvious from looking at the static source code.

Debuggers exist for standalone tools, some of them very powerful, but beginner programmers will benefit, in large projects, from an IDE-based debugger. For learning purposes, a debugger is not a real benefit, because the programs aren't long or complex enough to benefit from one.

There are also some tricks I'll cover that show you how to debug without a debugger, but keep in mind that more complex programs will need a debugger. They allow you to stop and start the program in different places at will and examine what it is doing in between.

Inside Your Computer

You know now about editing, compiling, and linking. Before you can begin to learn about programming, you have to understand a little about how the computer works in general and some differences between platforms in particular.

All computers follow the same pattern. They have much the same capabilities, regardless of make or model, and the only aspect changing is how well they perform. All computers have the following parts:

- Processor: Follows instructions and processes data

- Memory: Temporary working storage

- Hard drive: Permanent storage

- Display: Visual feedback to the users

- Keyboard (and mouse): Input from user

All of these need to be controlled by the program. In reality, however, control is maintained by the operating system (Windows, MacOS, Linux, and so on), and the user program is allowed to run within fairly strict and robust conditions.

Different operating systems have different capabilities and different architectures (the way the pieces are put together), and different machines have different capabilities and architectures. A program compiled on a Windows PC will not run on an Apple Mac. A piece of software created on the Mac cannot be run on a Linux system.

However, the C code that was used to create the application can be compiled under each of these operating systems and machines to yield a program that will run. Whether it does exactly the same thing and achieves the desired results on each platform depends on the skill of the programmer, the operating systems in question, and a number of other factors.

The lowest common denominator for the Windows and Linux operating systems is the command-line interface. They might have graphical front ends, but they both offer access to the command line to run programs that interact with the users through simple text display and keyboard entry.

With the advent of MacOS X, Apple also provided a command-line interface, and so all three platforms now have the capability to offer programmers the chance to learn programming without worrying about the graphical front end.

This is important because the C language that is specified by ANSI has some standard libraries that offer this level of interactivity. These are standard for all platforms, largely thanks to the efforts of the compiler developers. So you can create a piece of code that can be compiled and run on all three platforms, making the job of teaching C that much easier.

If programmers want to step outside of this box to write applications that have a graphical user interface (GUI) or that use the sound capabilities of the machine or invite the users to interact through a mouse, joystick, or other means, they need to find a library that supports that functionality.

A *library* is just an interface for programmers to a specific functionality not provided by the language standard. Each non-standard component of a system (operating system or hardware) needs a library before you can do anything with it.

Programming for Windows, MacOS, or X Windows is firmly outside the scope of this book, as is creating graphical applications or anything else outside the command-line interface. However, much can be achieved with the command line, and entire books exist on those other topics.

Using Open Source Resources

Part of the reason that this book exists is to help the next generation of programmers make better use of the growing body of Open Source software. *Open Source* just means that the source code is available to anyone to use, re-use, and learn from, with some specific agreements in place to govern exactly how it can be used.

Once you understand how to write C/C++ code, several important doors open to you. First, you can read and understand other people's code, which is important in continuing your programming education. Second, you can recompile applications for your own platform to make use of other people's achievements.

Most importantly, however, you can take (within license restrictions) code from all kinds of different projects and libraries and glue it together and create something entirely new. This concept of gluing code together to make an application saves a lot of time and effort.

Licensing restrictions aside, it is polite to remember where the code has come from and give credit where credit is due. Some licenses on source code dictate that the resulting application must also be Open Source under the same license as the original code, and it can be difficult to reconcile some of these restrictions when entire libraries are being re-used.

Programmers can also (and are expected to in certain circles) contribute to the Open Source code that they have borrowed. In other words, if you improve code, remove errors, or otherwise change code, in certain circumstances you should place it back into the Open Source arena.

It is the combination of sharing and enhancing that many people credit with keeping Open Source alive.

Open Source collections are also good places to find tools that can be used to create programs, usually without any restrictions. These can include code generators that can take a representation of an application and create source code that can be used to form the basis for that application.

There are also Open Source test harnesses that are useful for testing application code. Testing is one of those programming activities that are both necessary and occasionally frustrating, and predefined test harnesses can help make it less so.

Finally, as mentioned, there are plenty of Open Source tools for editing, compiling, browsing, and maintaining code.

Recap

Now you know the tools that you will need and how they will be applied. You should also know which category you fall into and what order to attack the contents of the book: Beginners might need to read everything carefully, whereas those with slightly more exposure to programming need only pick out those bits that they find relevant to them.

The computer is no longer a mystery, nor is the sorcery behind programming itself, but I have covered a lot of ground quite quickly. It is all vital to you progressing with the rest of the book—there are concepts that most technicians take for granted but that others might need to look over once more.

With all this preparatory information absorbed, you can now start the task of learning how to program in general, and how to program in C in particular.

CHAPTER 2

PROGRAMMING RECAP

This chapter contains is a rapid recap of general programming topics with the aim to prepare non-programmers for the concepts ahead. If you are already familiar with the concept of programming, it might be best to scan the chapter's topics and read only those that are of specific interest to you before continuing to the rest of the book.

What Is Programming?

A *computer program* turns a collection of components into a useful machine, capable of taking information, processing it, and putting the results on the screen. Everything that enables the computer to do something or that allows the user to interact with information is the result of a program.

Programming refers to the technique used to:

- Determine how the computer should achieve a task that the programmer would like it to.

- Create a set of instructions that reflect the steps required to achieve the desired result.

A specific mindset is useful in creating computer programs: the ability to break a problem down into a discrete set of steps and then devise a solution that takes the machine from a starting state to the end state, or solution. Most programs are sets of small solutions to discrete problems that are the steps on a longer journey to achieving the end result.

Most programming tasks exist to take information of a specific format and then process it in a given way that transforms it into something different. Along the way, this information may be stored, printed, or otherwise manipulated, depending on the goals of the computer program.

A word processor, like the one that was used to write this book, takes text and arranges it in a useful manner. It provides a facility to store the text and use it to create something new—a book or a printout of the text, for example. Some programming team has spent years creating a word processor that can be interacted with, by breaking down the functionality into a series of solutions.

If you think of programming as cooking, the program is like a recipe. The ingredients are the input information, and the final dish is the output information. The chef is the computer, following the instructions (recipe/program) and using other tools in order to help transform the input data (ingredients) into their desired output form (a meal).

Creating the recipe requires a set of skills, such as knowing what has to be done and in what order, how long each step will take, what the various control parameters are, and so on. Creating a program requires a similar set of skills in order to devise a solution that is efficient and complete.

Like cooking, programming is also often the result of trial and error. You might know that something should work, in the same way that a chef often can tell that certain ingredients will work well together. You can also know that there are tried and tested solutions to given problems; this is similar to the wealth of information available to chefs in the form of recipe books.

The point is that, like chefs, programmers often reuse all the existing knowledge, add something new, and create an original work. Whether it does exactly what the programmer intended is often found out only once the program has been written. The proof of the pudding is in the eating.

So part of the programming process requires something called *testing*. This can be seen as a parallel to the chef cooking a new (original) meal or dish for his family first, to see if all the instructions, parameters, and ingredients are correct. As the proof of the recipe is in the eating, the proof of the program is in running it and checking the results.

To do this, you have to know what the expected results are; you have to be sure of what you want to do in the first place. This brings you full circle to that part of programming that is understanding enough about the problem domain and the effective solutions that you can devise a way to get from the starting state to the ending state.

This process is called *design*. Entire volumes have been written on the subject of design in programming, and this is not the place to discuss it in depth. However, as you go through the process of learning how to program, I will cover bits and pieces of the design process as it relates to the problem you are trying to solve at the time.

Programming, Testing, and Debugging

Although the design might seem perfect and cover all eventualities, the nature of a computer program is often such that it goes wrong unexpectedly. You might hear the phrase *the intangible nature* of software, meaning that it cannot be touched physically, and the only evidence that it exists is by the results that you can observe from its actions.

This sounds quite abstract, and it is. Programming is an abstract skill, involving problem solving, some creativity, and lateral thinking. The results are often more concrete, ranging from the benign to the critical. Computers control aircraft, but they also provide entertainment and manage nuclear reactors.

The tangible nature of the results and the scope for error between design and implementation (the actual programming bit) mean that *testing* is vital. Even the simplest program must be tested to make sure that the actual result is what the programmer expects.

You'll look in more detail at how different kinds of program can be tested as you discover the C language. Most of the simple techniques revolve around observing effects, or allowing values from the program to be displayed so that they can be verified while the program is running.

An aid to this kind of verification is something called a *debugger*. A bug is simply an error in the software package or program—a niggling mistake that causes it to behave in a manner that is either unpredictable or unwanted. Getting rid of bugs is called *debugging*.

The debugging process often requires that you look at each decision point in turn in a program and try to imagine what you have done wrong. Assuming that the original design was correct, the first thing you have to do is step through each piece of code and decide whether it accurately reflects the design.

You have a few choices about how you do this. Hand execution is by far the most painful, but it is a good exercise for beginning programmers because it opens up the possibilities of both learning and practicing. You will be doing some hand execution as you go along.

However, it is more efficient to use a debugger. This is a little program that watches your program as it executes and lets you look inside to see what is going on. This way you can watch as the values change and detect errors in the same way as you can with hand execution, except that you are only involved as an observer.

Most IDEs come with a debugger, and there are debuggers available for most compilers that are not part of an IDE. However, for simple programming, and for those who do not wish to tangle with a debugger right now, I have many tricks to teach you that you can use to help detect and correct errors without using a debugger.

Procedural Programming

There are different kinds of programming languages, using different approaches to creating software. Some dictate that a program is a discrete set of steps that can only be executed in a top-down fashion. Other languages perform evaluation on a mathematical basis. Some allow programmers to break the problem domain down into a set of interacting objects, and others just allow programmers to organize code into modules that are unable to interconnect or interact.

This book approaches the C language as a *procedural* language—it has a specific execution sequence, and interruption is allowed only if the programmer indicates that such an interruption is part of the instruction sequence. Such interruptions can be a pause for the users to enter some data, for example.

A recipe is a good example of a piece of procedural programming. Driving a car is not—if you drove a car by following a sequential set of instructions from start to end, you would not be terribly successful; you could not be interrupted by an event outside of your control. The odds that you would arrive at your destination would depend on what happened between the start and the end.

The only way you could actually determine whether you would be successful would be through testing. Testing would show you where your program needed to allow interruption in order to be successful; however, you would likely wreck an awful lot of vehicles in the process.

Nevertheless, the act of driving can be broken down into a set of sequential steps. Even the process that must take place if an interruption occurs (a cat running in front of the car, for example) can be broken down into steps; a routine. So, the driving program will be a set of routines allowing you to effectively drive the car from point A to point B.

In addition, when driving, you might encounter a condition that you cannot deal with, such as a flat tire. When cooking, the recipe could run awry and render the ingredients into an inedible mush due to a cooker malfunction. Although neither of these events can necessarily be foreseen, both can (with varying degrees of sophistication) be avoided and even rectified by the creation of a specific routine (or handler) to deal with them.

These events are, in procedural programming terms, equivalent to a programming bug, or system malfunction, where something the program does causes the system to behave in a way that is unexpected, or where the user does something you did not anticipate. If you can test for crashes, you can take steps to avoid them.

If you can detect unexpected events or the result of them, there are also things you can do, in programming terms, to rectify, or repair, any damage that they do. This applies equally to users doing something wrong, such as the system taking an unexpected turn, perhaps as the result of another program, or because of the users themselves.

There is always the possibility, as with anything else, of a situation arising that will require that the computer be restarted. A good programmer will try to limit this kind of behavior, as it may have far-reaching consequences for the user.

So, a procedural programming language is one in which the traditional flow is top-down—a series of steps to follow. However, you can arrange the program into mini-programs, or routines, each of which can be invoked, or run, depending on circumstances.

Clearly, there will also be a routine that is in general control—in terms of driving an automobile, it is the central interruptible driving routine that can call other routines to perform tasks according to conditions. However, most of the time, it is watching for events, deciding what to do next in the general scheme of things, while following instructions to get from A to B.

Program Flow

As mentioned, the computer progresses through the program one instruction at a time, from top to bottom. If this were the only path through a program, it would severely limit the program's efficiency. You would need to run many different programs to arrive at a given result.

To bake a cake, you would need many different recipes, in different books: one book to tell you how to make icing, one to tell you how to break eggs, another to tell you how to whisk the ingredients into a cake mixture, and yet another to tell you how to use the oven.

This is not efficient because the person doing the cooking would have to be constantly changing books, finding recipes, and generally following sets of unconnected steps. It is much more efficient to have a single recipe. However, if you could only follow the recipe from top to bottom, one step at a time, it would be a long and tedious reading process.

So the flow of control through a program or a recipe can be changed. If a recipe requires that the cook break five eggs, separating the yolk from each, it does not need to describe that process five times. Instead, it will describe it once and tell the cook to follow the process five times, with five eggs. So rather than having the following:

Break egg 1.

Break egg 2.

Break egg 3.

Break egg 4.

Break egg 5.

You just have the single statement:

Break 5 eggs.

Similarly, a computer can be told to perform a set of instructions a certain number of times. This method of program flow control is known as a *loop*. There are different kinds of loops used for different purposes, largely depending on the condition that you are trying to achieve. A counted loop assumes that you know in advance how many times you need to perform the actions to be looped.

If you do not know in advance how many times you must do something in order to achieve the correct final result, you might know what the final result should *look like*. So there are other kinds of loops that allow you to perform the instructions until a given condition is met. This would be equivalent to the part of the recipe that tells the cook to beat the egg whites until they are fluffy.

Now, different eggs, different whisks, and different cooks will all require different lengths of time to achieve perfect fluffiness, so it is not useful to tell the cook to beat the eggs a hundred times. You might be able to tell the cook that it could take about five minutes, but the real test is the end condition of fluffiness. The same approach is sometimes needed in programming.

You say that you test for a condition, and when that evaluates to *true*, you stop the loop. This is sometimes called an uncounted loop to differentiate it from a counted loop. There are different kinds of counted loops in C programming, which you read about in Chapter 7.

Of course, there are also tasks that repeat in different recipes at different times, as well as multiple times in the same recipe. If you have a task, such as separating the yolks and whites from eggs prior to beating them, that you do often, it might be convenient to store that process definition somewhere as a set of steps.

You could then call upon that process whenever you needed to separate yolks and whites—perhaps prior to beating the egg whites to fluffiness. In programming terms, this little mini-program is called a *routine, procedure,* or *function.* It happens that in C programming, you call it a *function.*

Having defined the egg-separation function you can reuse it in many different programs, making it much more useful and saving time in the future. To make it really useful, though, it needs to be able to be called upon with varying input and output values.

So instead of calling the function five times to separate five eggs, you might just want to look at the eggs that you have (say, five) and call the function with the basket of eggs as an *input parameter.* The function would then count the eggs (or you could tell it the size of the basket) and separate the eggs for you.

The output would be a bowl of separated egg whites and another of yolks.

As a bonus, you could also use this function as part of a more general function that turns eggs into a fluffy mixture. You just need to break it down into steps, figure out which other *functions* it might call, and give it the eggs. You would then receive back a bowl of fluffy whites and a small collection of yolks.

With these three possibilities—counted loops, uncounted loops, and functions— you have just enough control over the program to be able to achieve complex tasks in an efficient manner. You can do one thing many times or the same thing until something else tells you to stop and wrap up the whole lot and call it whenever you need it.

If you need to do one set of steps a certain number of times, frequently at different points within the program, you need only create one piece of code and then use the *flow of control* to make sure that the steps are performed at an appropriate frequency.

Decision Making

A special kind of program flow control allows the programmer to execute steps of a process based on the outcome of a condition test. In much the same way that an uncounted loop can be stopped when a certain *condition* is met, you can also define a set of steps as being executed only if a condition is met.

This might sound a little superfluous, but it is a fundamental part of programming. Without the ability to selectively execute parts of a program, the programmer's task is made very difficult, as you have to try and plan the program in such a way that it is entirely predictable.

Anyone who has worked with food or computers knows that this is nearly impossible. In fact, most of the things that we do in life are a summation of lots of little decisions. In writing this book, I made many decisions, some good, probably some not so good.

The editor also made more decisions, some good, some of which were questioned by the author, technical reviewer, or reader. The result is a better book. The result of being able to make decisions while cooking that are a reaction to what is going on in the kitchen will make a better meal.

Before you can actually make any decisions, however, you need some way to store the result of what you have been doing so you can test it against things that you *do* know in advance and can test for. You need to be able to retain a context of everything that has gone on that you cannot control to compare it against what you can.

Data Storage

A vital part of any program is the ability to hold information transiently or permanently. That is, the information can be held for the duration of a program or just for the length of time that it is needed.

Think back to Chapter 1, where we looked at a computer in terms of processing power and storage. Part of that storage—the bit that is emptied when you turn off the machine—is called *memory*. The information that you need to process during the lifecycle of a program is stored in memory.

Anything you might need once the program has finished needs to be put somewhere else—usually on the hard drive of the computer.

Within a program, you can allocate areas of computer memory to hold the information that you need. It might help to think of computer memory as a big expanse of pigeonholes, or slots in a postal sorting office. Each one has a name, so you can refer to it, and you can put information in and take information out—like writing on bits of paper.

These slots are also color coded, giving you a clue as to what the nature of the information might be:

- Numbers

- Words

- Characters

- Something user-defined

- And so on

One restriction that programming languages puts on the programmer is that only the same kind of information can be put in the slot as matches the color scheme. In other words, you cannot put a string in a slot designed for a number; its *type* does not match.

In programming terms, the named color-coded slots are called *variables*, and the color code is known as a *type*. C is a strongly typed language, so each variable of a specific type can only hold data of that type. As you will see later on, there are a few tricks you can use to define your own types as well for storing complex information.

The term *variable* also gives a clue as to the nature of the data. Whether the variable lasts for the duration of the program or just while it is being used, it is designed to contain a value that can be changed. This is different from something known as a *constant*, whose value cannot change.

Variables are a form of temporary storage—once the program stops running, the information contained in the variables is lost unless you store it permanently somewhere else. You can also store information permanently on the computer's hard drive (or a CD-ROM or other writable media).

Knowing how to store data permanently is necessary for any program that needs to import or store data. Try to imagine a program with no possibility to refer to a previous state, and it becomes clear that most programming projects will need external storage. All of the classic applications (word processors, spreadsheets, HTML editors, and so on) need the facility to write data down permanently somewhere.

Typically, external storage is provided by the computer language, and all ANSI-compliant C programming environments provide several functions for doing this. They are, however, not part of the language itself, as in other languages such as BASIC.

So in C programming, you can store variables natively using facilities offered by the language, but because external storage is a facility that varies from system to system (platform to platform), you need to call upon the operating system. Hence, built-in support is not provided, but instead, ANSI implementations provide *libraries* for interfacing with the system.

One of those *libraries* handles files, and I will cover the other libraries in due course. The important point to take away right now is that external storage requires external support because it might change from platform to platform.

Parts of a Language

The ability to declare variables is part of the facilities offered by the language, as is assigning a specific type to each one. The *declaration* of a variable is usually a statement within the language that is comprised of the type plus variable name. You say that you have declared a variable of a given type, and from that point on, that variable can only contain data of the given type.

A variable name usually follows certain conventions. For example, it cannot be comprised solely of a number because it might be confused with a constant numeric value. Similarly, it cannot contain spaces because that would make it two individual words, which could be misconstrued. Programming is a precise exercise.

Another constraint on the naming of variables is that they cannot conflict with other parts of the language such as keywords. A variable name cannot be the same as a keyword because that could also be misconstrued. Keywords offer the built-in functionality to support data types and flow control.

Data types, variables, and keywords are parts of every programming language, including C. They are the building blocks used to construct solutions to programming problems, including a set of standard worker functions, or libraries.

There are several standards, ANSI being one of them. The ANSI libraries that are provided with most C implementations deal with math functions, standard ways to allow the user to interact with the system, as well as specific libraries to enable programming with graphics, sound, and other hardware extensions.

It all starts with understanding the building blocks, or parts of the language. They also enable users to define their own extensions to the language. If another piece of hardware comes along that needs to be interfaced with, then it can be catered to. That includes the functions, data types, and user-defined data required to represent the interface to the programming language.

As long as these user-defined extensions do not conflict with the language implementation, anything can be used. User-defined solutions cannot, therefore, replace reserved words or keywords, but they can extend the functionality.

Naming these extensions is a careful exercise. You need to respect the keywords and other reserved words in the language, or the compiler will become confused. A side effect is that you cannot try to replace these reserved words with your own functionality, but your own implementations can extend the language by offering alternatives.

One other side of programming languages is operators—they are used to combine keywords, data types, variables, functions, and other parts of the language in a way that allows the programmer to perform a variety of comparisons and assignations. The majority of C operators are numerically based.

Operators have a parallel in the real world. Simple everyday tasks such as making sure you have enough cash in your wallet to pay for your groceries involve manipulation of operators, even if you didn't know it.

For a start, you need to total up the expected cost based on your previous shopping trips. Adding these together uses the addition operator; the *total* is modified by adding an item's price to it. Then you need to check that the total is less than the money you currently have; the *less than* comparison is an example of another operator.

In other words, operators provided by the language provide a way to compare numerical values, add them, multiply them, divide and subtract them, as well as assign them to variables. A simple understanding of logic and math can help in this regard, as you shall see.

For now, all you need to be aware of is that these operators exist. Operators can be used to modify variables, and the value used to modify them cannot be of a different data type. So you cannot add a string to a number, or a decimal to an integer, or a function to a memory address.

Compiling and Linking

So far, you have read about the various parts of the language and are equipped with an editor and a basic understanding of what programming entails, but you have not looked into what actually goes on under the hood. It is worth having a passing knowledge of what happens when you take a piece of text and turn it into a program, because it can help you understand the programming process and help you learn the language of C.

A programmer understands C code. A computer, helped by the operating system (DOS, Linux, Windows, and so on), understands machine code. We need a way to get from one to the other, and there are two basic ways to achieve this.

The first is to use an interpreter. Like translating from one language to another, an interpreter translates a computer language written by a person into actions that the computer understands. This, however, is not very practical or efficient.

So we use a compiler to validate the code that the programmer has written and then convert it into a step-by-step process. Machines work in a step-by-step fashion, at the highest level of granularity. In other words, a machine can work only with very simple statements, but programmers prefer to work with complex statements that can achieve much more in a single statement.

This makes programming more efficient. If you had to write programs that were understandable by the computer, you would have to do the work of the compiler, something the earliest programmers had to do but that programmers are now shielded from.

This is only the first step in the process. The second step, *linking*, takes all the little fragments of code and puts them all together in such a way that the complete set of instructions can be followed from beginning to end. A C program will consist of many different, separate source files, and compiling them generates many different, separate *object code* files.

The linker and library together will make these into one complete, contiguous set of instructions, all provided by the programmer.

Still, however, there is something missing—recall that external libraries provided by third parties interact with hardware, the operating system, the user, and so on. It is up to the linker to also put these *precompiled* libraries together with the rest of the code to make the application.

To use the cooking analogy, a recipe tells the cook how to bake a cake. There are certain techniques that the cook will be aware of that are not mentioned in the recipe but that, if the cook had to tell someone else how to bake the cake, he would have to add to the instructions.

Even the cook might come across parts of the recipe that he has not encountered before and has to look up in other recipe books—these are libraries. Even if a recipe is concocted from various sources, there might be bits missing that need linking with other sources to be able to make a coherent whole that can be followed by a cook.

However, there will also be things that are not explicitly mentioned in the recipe that the cook knows how to do. These are the equivalent of the bits and pieces of the language that are inherent to it—bits and pieces shared by all the cooks. The recipes are the programs, and the systems are the people doing the cooking—some will need more help than others.

Both the compiling and linking stages are required before the program can be executed, and the output of the linking process is an application, or executable. There are also a few operations that need to be applied to the executable that makes it run effectively on a given platform.

Although the output of the compiler might not differ from platform to platform, the executable will certainly be different, depending on the platform. Object code, the in-between step from source to executable as output from the compiler, might be the same on all platforms. The executable itself, however, will be different, as different platforms need different support.

It is worth taking a look at the executable format just to complete the circle and make sure that you fully understand what you are getting yourself into.

Executable File Format

An executable file, or application, is the end result of the programmer's hard work. Whether it acts as the programmer intended is immaterial; the compiler and linker will do their best to *build* the application from the source code and libraries provided by the programmer.

This executable file is worth knowing about in a little more detail. Each one contains three vital areas: startup (or bootstrap) code, the program and data segments, and cleanup (or shutdown) code. The places where the application lives are called *segments*, which are just locations in the computer's internal storage, or memory.

The computer reads the startup block (from the program segment), which tells the operating system (Windows, DOS, MacOS, Linux, and so on) about the application and where to start the execution itself. This point will usually be later on in the program segment.

You have probably started reading this book from the start—and at some point, you came across something that made you realize that you could skip ahead. You have looked at the book and chosen an *offset* to start at, a number of pages from the beginning.

Any startup code exists purely to set the application in context for the operating system, telling it the amount of stack memory it might need, where the actual offset into the code starts, and passing any external information into the application. You might have done this in the past; any time you start a program from the command line, you usually give it some starting data to work with. This can be a flag, option, or filename.

Depending on the operating system, there might be other tasks required, such as detailing any other resources and setting the local memory (or stack) that the program needs for its variables. You probably have some paper somewhere that you will take notes on when reading the book—that's your own personal local memory. Some people might be able to hold everything in their heads while they read; that's also local *stack* memory.

However, most of that fixed storage will be in the data segment. A result of generating the code and environment from the source code, the data segment contains reserved space for all the data needed by the program to perform the task it has been set.

The code segment contains the instructions on how to operate upon that data in order to achieve its objective. It has specific starting and ending points, and the flow initially prescribed by the programmer dictates how the program is processed within the data segment.

It is the operating system that maintains a pointer into the code and a set of temporary values for comparison and decision making. This is not the place to discuss the internal format in detail; however, you should understand that there is still some interpretation at work to process the compiled program and data.

When the interpretation has finished, the shutdown code is invoked. This may not exist on all platforms, but it is there to make sure that the system is left in the same state that the program found it in. In other words, it tidies up the kitchen, washes the tools that have been used, and closes all the cupboards.

All platforms have their own specific executable file format and additional data segments or resources, depending on their priorities and goals. In WIMP (Windows Icons Mouse Pointer) environments, a slightly different paradigm is in place than the one developed in the course of the examples in this book.

Windows (or MacOS or X Window) programming is a different topic, and a whole book on its own. Understanding C programming is vital in understanding how to write applications for different platforms, but when you're just learning, it's better to stick with the traditional command-line interface.

External Files (Header Files)

The final piece of the programming jigsaw puzzle involves the external files (or libraries) which you need to allow the application to interface with the system. These cannot exist in isolation, because the compiler and linker do not necessarily have any knowledge of the operating system or anything else that the programmer wishes to interface with.

So you need to provide definitions that tell the compiler what the library functions look like and how the programmer is allowed to interact with them. This allows the compiler to check that the programmer has used the library functionality correctly, on the one hand, and provide a way for the linker to know how to link the library objects with the other application code.

The C language also permits the programmer to break down the program into smaller units and compile them separately. Each unit can be shared with other application developers or used within the project under development. They can be referenced via the header files, meaning that they also do not need to be recompiled if the source has not changed since the last build cycle.

If you think back to the recipe analogy, recall that there are some common tasks used in a number of recipes that are not repeated each time in the source. These are like libraries and need only be referenced through the index, but never rewritten.

However, the instructions, in their compiled form, often need to be available at the time that the program is built (that the executable is linked). Usually, these will be in separate files (source or object code) and can be woven into the application during the linking process.

There are specific files called *header files* that are used to describe what these little pieces of reusable code in external files contain. The header file is useful to the programmer to know how a specific function should be called, what data it can accept, and if there are any special pieces of information defined specifically for this feature.

I will cover these in detail later on.

There is one last detail. Libraries can be linked into the application; in a real sense they become part of the application, like photocopied recipe notes glued onto other recipe pages. They can also be accessed at runtime, allowing the libraries to be updated without rebuilding the application, like new tools and techniques for beating eggs, baking cakes, and so on.

The first technique is known as *static linking,* and the second is known as *dynamic linking.* Examples of dynamic linking include using DLLs in Windows programming, or dynalink libraries in Linux applications.

Recap

A program is a set of instructions that are human readable and are turned by a compiler into something that the computer can use to perform a set of tasks. The linker then takes the compiled version, combines it with any supporting functionality created by a third party, and produces a file that can be directly executed by a computer.

Each program comprises a set of instructions that specify somewhere to store temporary information, instructions to manipulate that information, and ways to display the result. In doing so, you can define your own functions, repeat steps one or more times, and perform data value comparisons to selectively execute code.

The act of producing a program that fulfills a specific task is called programming. In order to ensure that it is doing the correct task, the program needs to be tested. Adequate testing is a vital part of the programming activity.

Libraries provide additional functionality and can be supplied by:

- The compiler provider

- The application developer

- Operating system vendors

- Hardware vendors

- Open Source solutions

These libraries need to be defined externally and linked with the application at compile time or used dynamically at runtime. In both cases, the build process must include header files to be able to ascertain exactly how these libraries should be interfaced.

This ability of a language enables reuse of existing code, thus reducing workload, and increases the stability of applications by allowing hardware, software, and operating system vendors to create the best solutions for their platforms.

All of the above needs to go into creating a program. It is a combination of:

- The programmer's solution to a problem.

- The expression of that solution in a programming language.

- The flow of control and data within the application.

- The operating system supporting the execution.

- The external libraries used to enhance the application.

If any of these are not correctly understood and leveraged, the application will not work as intended, and finding the error is a sometimes frustrating but important part of the programming process.

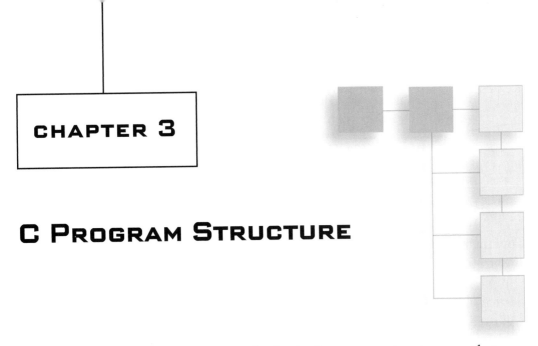

CHAPTER 3

C PROGRAM STRUCTURE

The aim of this chapter is to cover the basic C program structure, so that you become familiar with the main parts of a program.

After reading this chapter, you should take away a very clear overview of the different parts of a C program and be well equipped to read, if not completely understand, a simple piece of C code. There is such a piece of code at the end of the chapter that contains all the elements described in the chapter's text.

The Entry and Exit Points

A computer begins to execute a C program with the main function. It is in this part of the code that you set up the program context and begin the tasks that are required of the application. Some small programs will contain only a main function and others might contain the main function as a place to start and stop the application, with the bulk of the work done elsewhere.

In any C program without a main function, the program will not compile or be able to do anything useful. The exact declaration of the main function will vary from platform to platform, but for the purposes here, the standard declaration is used. This is because you are writing C programs that will work anywhere that the ANSI standard is supported with a command-line interface.

The correct way to declare the main function is this:

```
<return type> main ( [argument list] )
```

Remembering the conventions from the opening chapter, this example means:

- The `<return type>` is required but supplied by the programmer.

- `main` is a keyword, part of the language.

- Parameters are supplied in brackets.

- The `[argument list]` is optional and supplied by the programmer.

Looking at these items one by one, you can define the *return type* as a value that the program will provide to the operating system. The keyword `main` lets the compiler know that this is the entry point to the program—that it can be run. Source files can include only functions, but they are not complete programs and will need at some point to be linked with some source code that contains a `main` function.

The *argument list* will be empty in the majority of programs that are written as part of the learning experience. However, to give some insight as to what they are used for, imagine that you are using the command line (DOS, Linux, and so on), and you type the command:

```
dir *.*
```

This produces a directory listing. The `dir` command can be seen as a command-line program whose sole purpose is to display a list of files. In order to do that, it needs to know what files it should display, and you provide that as a *parameter* or *argument*. In this case, it is `*.*`; or all the files.

This parameter is fed to the `main` function of the `dir` command through the argument list.

For a program that returns nothing and has no arguments, the basic form for the `main` function declaration is as follows:

```
void main ()
```

The use of the `void` keyword indicates that the `main` function does not return a value, and the empty brackets tell you that there are no parameters. This program does not need any command-line data, nor will it inform the operating system of the result of its processing.

Because this is bad manners (rather like the guests not complimenting the chef), this book will usually try to return some kind of meaningful information, encoded as a number. This number is then useful to the operating system to know the *exit status* of the program.

So the standard basic form of the `main` function declaration becomes:

```
int main ()
```

This is the declaration that you'll see most often in the short programs presented in the book.

The declaration tells the computer that the `main` function will return an integer value, indicating the result of its processing. Although that integer will remain constant in the meaning that you attach to that return value, different operating systems will attach different meanings to it. As a general guide:

- Less than 0: Some kind of error

- Exactly 0: Processing was successful

- More than 0: Some user-defined positive information

As a programmer, if you stick to this convention, you are likely to have the correct outlook for interaction with most operating systems. As an aside, programs in this book always use this basic format for reporting the success or failure of a piece of code, in order to facilitate the testing process.

As an example, when you have a small program that is designed to count the number of words in a text file, there are various things that could go wrong. Some of these problems you can test for:

- File not found

- Not a text file

- File empty

You can then attach a meaningful result code to them, such as –1, –2, and –3, with anything else indicating success. This way you allow the operating system to know the result.

Of course you are also going to display the result on the screen, to a file, or however else you have decided that the user needs to receive the result and not just use the return value to convey that information. The real use of the return code is to allow users interfacing with the operating system at a higher level to know the result.

Again, an example will illustrate this. Suppose you have a daily batch job (for DOS users a batch file, for Linux users, think of a cron job in a shell scripting language) that runs a series of programs. Because it is unattended, there is no user watching to see the result.

However, you would probably like to be able to alert a user if something goes wrong with the job, and this could be an email or cell phone text message.

To do this, you need a way that the batch job can tell the success of the programs that it needs to execute in order to perform the required tasks. If it is, for example, a system backup that runs at night, you might want to be alerted if it fails for some reason.

This information is usually conveyed through the return code (or error level) of an application and can be used in a batch script to test for success without knowing what (if any) other output has been catered to.

Declaring Variables

Chapter 2 introduced the concept of values stored in memory, with a global view of data types.

Recall that a variable is a named place where the program can store information, and that each place can store only one kind of information *type*. This is true for strongly typed languages—like C—where the compiler will complain when two types are not compatible.

In other words, square pegs cannot be put in round holes, but they can sometimes be persuaded to fit with some side effects. A small square peg will go into a large round hole, but there will always be a risk of it falling out and some superfluous space that serves no real purpose.

On the other hand, a large square peg will fit into a smaller round hole only if you are prepared to shave off some information. The two types of fitting are compatible, but there might be some side effects.

That is the best way to look at variables and types in C; some types are more compatible than others. There are also some tricks that you will learn to achieve the fitting of different shaped pegs (data) into various shapes and sizes of hole (types).

The int keyword used above, in the analysis of the main function and its return value, is an example of a type. Recall also that it is an *integer* number.

The next chapter is devoted to data types and variables, so all that you need to know for now is that the integer data type stores decimal numbers—1, 42, 375658, and so on—and is referred to by the keyword `int`. There are some limits on the size of the integer; these limits are discussed in Chapter 4.

In C, there is a standard way to *declare* variables. All variables must be declared before use, another feature of strongly typed languages. If you've experimented with other programming languages, you know that (in Visual Basic for Applications, for example) you can often just assign a value to a variable, and the compiler figures out the type from that assignment.

Not so the C language. This might seem like a hindrance, but it is a blessing in disguise because it prevents a variety of errors such as:

- Duplicate variable names

- Incorrect/confusing data assignation

- Inappropriate operations on data

To declare a variable in C programming, you use the following generic layout:

`<type> <variable name>;`

Where `<type>` can be any of the built-in or user-defined data types (as you shall see in the next chapter) and `<variable name>` can be any allowed identifier. An allowed identifier in C has some specific naming restrictions:

- Cannot be solely a number

- Must not contain spaces or special characters

- Cannot be a keyword

These are restrictions placed on you by the system, with good reasons, most of them to do with confusing variables for other pieces of code or not being able to parse the code correctly. Parsing is done by a process known as *tokenizing,* where the entire source code is split into words and then processed.

If identifiers could include spaces, the program would not be able to tokenize the code correctly, as it would not know where the identifier started or ended. So not allowing certain characters is sensible and necessary for the tokenizing process to be successful.

To the list of imposed restrictions, let's add some best-practice naming conventions:

- Should reflect the data stored within

- Should be proper words

- Should be readable (correct capitalization)

Again, there are some good reasons for all of these. Because you mention the type of the variable only once, when it is declared, it is helpful to be able to tell from the name what kind of data is stored in it. Hence, calling a variable `counter` is better than just using a single letter n.

It also helps the reading process when you have a convention that allows you to be able to read faster. There are two solutions to this: use the _ (underscore) character or CamelBack capitalization.

An example of a good variable name might be:

```
int nReturnValue;
```

It contains proper words that describe what it is for and gives a clue as to what data might be stored inside the variable. The capitalization allows it to be readable. You could have used an underscore as well:

```
int n_return_value;
```

From either name, you can also have a good guess at the type of data that the variable is going to contain, with n signifying a [n]umber. In the declaration, it might be obvious, but later on in the program you might not remember how you declared the variable anymore, and rather than waste time looking for it, it is better to have a convention that lets you identify the type from the name.

For the sake of comparison, a bad example of a variable name might be:

```
int valuereturned;
```

This is harder to read at a glance, because the programmer has not capitalized the V and R correctly. It also gives no clue as to what the *value* in question might be. Even worse might be:

```
int vr;
```

This last is the worst kind of variable name—it does not give any information at all. There is a place for these types of variable names, and I will cover them later on, but by and large, for a variable that is going to be used often and at different places in the program, it is best to have a convention as described at the outset.

Variable naming is one of those programming issues that everyone has an opinion about and is a contentious issue in programming circles. In this book, I present a logical way of naming variables, by using a prefix to signify the kind of data (not the data type) that is stored within:

- n: An integer

- f: A floating-point number, such as 3.141

- l: A very big integer (also known as a long integer)

- d: A very big floating-point number (also called double precision)

- c: A character, such as a through z, 0 through 9, and special characters

- sz: A bunch of characters or a string, such as 'hello world'

If some of these seem a little strange right now, do not worry, all will become clear. The reason they are presented here is to give an idea about how the prefix-naming convention (sometimes called *Hungarian Notation*) looks. The precise difference between (for example) an integer and a very big floating-point number is discussed in the next chapter.

Operators, Comparison, and Precedence

The main core of any program is operating on data. When Chapter 2 covered programming, you learned that most programs exist to take data of one kind, process it, and store it as another kind. That processing can take several forms:

- Modification: Put this value in this variable.

- Comparison: Is this value equal to this value?

The C programming language provides several ways to do this for built-in types; there is a set of keywords and operators that allow you to process them in the language itself. This includes mathematical operators for numerical values, logical operators to test veracity (true or false, Boolean values), and so on.

However, you as the programmer have to provide solutions for user-defined and complex types that contain data that is not part of the language. In C, for example, unlike some other languages, strings are treated as a collection of characters—a complex type. So the libraries provided with the compiler need to support string handling, or you need to supply them yourself.

Luckily, standard ANSI-compliant libraries provide additional functions for comparing, for example, strings, and these are supplied with the compiler kit. These functions can save programmers a lot of time. You'll learn about these functions in Chapter 8, "Standard Libraries."

For now, concern yourself with the operators available for built-in types, which are the building blocks of the language. With them, you can build more complex statements to cope with other kinds of data.

Operators

The easiest way to think of an operator is as something that modifies the contents of a variable. It puts a value into the box, the peg into the hole, and so on. You say that you have *assigned* a value to the variable, and as long as the type is compatible, the result will be successful.

The compiler will catch errors of type compatibility, which is no guarantee of success, but it will, at least, prevent the most glaring of errors. Standard numerical types, integer (whole numbers), and floating point (decimal numbers) have the following associated built-in operators:

+

−

/

*

=

Readers will recognize the addition, subtraction, division, and multiplication operators as well as the equals sign. The equals sign is for assigning a value, whereas the other operators actually combine two values, yielding a result that depends on the values they are used with.

Thus, the following adds 1 and 1 and puts the result in a variable:

```
nVariable = 1 + 1;
```

The result, predictably, is that `nVariable` will contain the value 2. Other operators will produce similar results, with a few provisos, depending on the type of the variables and values being used. For example, a division operation involving two integer types will yield an integer. Thus, you might have the following mathematical statement:

```
1/2 = 0.5
```

This is not true in C programming—if you divide the numerical integer 1 by 2, you get zero, because the result has to be an integer. I will go back over this in the next chapter, when I look at the other available data types, but now is a good time to point out that the result of the operation is dependent of the type of data being operated on, and it might not always be what you expect.

This should become clearer as you combine other elements. For example, you can also add two variables, using code such as:

```
nVariable = nVariableOne + nVariableTwo;
```

Now, the type safety begins to make a little more sense. You can only get out what you put in, and if you put in two variables that are integers, the computer would have to do too much guesswork to get anything out of the equation other than an integer.

It is the equivalent of the computer refusing to shave the corners off a square peg to put it into a round hole where you might have wanted it to choose a larger hole instead. That is the programmer's decision.

You can also combine constant and variable values to create complex compound statements. For example, you might want to divide a number by a variable divisor:

```
nVariable = 100 / nDivisor;
```

A good example of such an operation that is frequently used is the complex single-line statement used to calculate a percentage. My math teacher once explained this as requiring four values—three we know, and one we do not. You typically know the maximum value (say, `nMaxValue`) and the maximum percentage (100) and want to know the percentage that corresponds to a test value (`nTestValue`).

The statement to achieve the desired result might look like this:

```
nPercent = (100 * nTestValue) / nMaxValue;
```

Here, the C code and mathematical theory dovetail very well, and the result will be an integer between 1 and 100 for various values of nTestValue and nMaxValue. Of course, if the test value is higher than the maximum, the result will be bigger than 100.

The C language also offers some useful shorthand syntax for operators, either on their own or in combination with the assignment operator (equals sign). The post-increment and post-decrement operators allow you to modify a variable value very easily:

```
nVariable++;   // add one to nVariable
nVariable--;   // subtract one from nVariable
```

These are called post-increment and post-decrement because they modify the value after all other evaluations have taken place. In the two previous cases, they are the only parts of the statement, so the result is that only the operator is applied. However, were they a part of a longer statement, the result would be different, as you shall see.

In addition to these operators, the assignment operator (or equals sign =) can be combined with constant values to perform simple operations. At the most basic, you can use two discrete values:

```
nVariable += 1;      // add one to nVariable
nVariable -= 2;      // Subtract two from nVariable
nVariable /= 4;      // divide nVariable by 4
nVariable *= 100;    // multiply by 100
```

While the operand on the left side can only be a single entry, a variable on the right side can contain one or more variables or constants in almost any combination. The previous examples use a single constant, but we might have used any number of values and operators.

The right side will be evaluated before the combined assignment operator is applied, so the last thing that the fourth statement will do is multiply the result of evaluating the right side by 100. Now for some quick hand execution. Consider the following fragment:

```
int nVariableA, nVariableB;
nVariableB = 3;
nVariableA = 0 + nVariableB++;
```

If you take out a piece of paper and write down the following at the top, you can perform a hand execution of the code:

```
Step        nVariableA        nVariableB
```

At each line, you put a value into each column. The Step will go from 1 to 3, and the nVariable columns will contain a value. The first step is easy; it just declares two variables. The second is also easy: You can write a 3 in the nVariableB column.

However, when you get to the third step, you are expecting to carry out several operations. Remembering that the post-increment operator is evaluated last, you can then enter two lines, Step 3a and Step 3b, which will yield the result of the hand execution.

You should find that after this code has executed, nVariableA contains 3 and nVariableB contains 4. You might have assumed that nVariableA should contain 4, because nVariableB has been incremented, but because it was a *post*-increment, this is not the case.

So, nVariableA has been assigned to 0, and then nVariableB has been added to it and finally incremented.

On the other hand, if you had used a pre-increment operator, you could have incremented nVariableB before adding it to nVariableA, as follows:

```
nVariableA = 0 + ++nVariableB;
```

This is equivalent to the following:

```
nVariableB = nVariableB + 1;
nVariableA = 0 + nVariableB;
```

The use of pre- and post-operators is necessary and convenient. However, the longer example is infinitely preferable to the single-line combination of an assignment and a pre-increment operator.

You'll find that post-operators are fairly widely used but that pre-operators are almost never used in this book. This is clearer for the beginning programmer, but many C enthusiasts prefer brevity over clarity. C was created, in some respects, to be able to achieve a lot of processing in a single line of code.

A final note—the only pre- and post-operators that exist are increment (add) and decrement (subtract). So you'll never see:

```
nVariable**;
```

or

```
nVariable//;
```

The reason for this is that these symbols * and / have other, very important meanings that I'll discuss during the rest of the book.

Comparing Values

Besides operators for assigning and combining values, you also have a set of operators that are used to compare two values and yield a true or false result. Is 1 equal to 2? No (false). Is 100 divided by 1 equal to 1 multiplied by 100? Yes (true). The C programming language provides several symbols to help you test the veracity of an expression:

==   Is equal to?

>   Is greater than?

<   Is less than?

!=   Is *not* equal to?

The double equals sign == is used to distinguish the expression from an assignment, because you can actually test for the veracity of an assignment within an expression. Like using pre-operators, this is not advised for code clarity but is sometimes useful.

So were you to write code such as the following inside a test condition, it would evaluate to false:

```
1 == 0
```

You can also test variables, so that the following piece of code will evaluate to either true or false, depending on the value assigned to the variable:

```
nNumberToTest == 0
```

The opposite to the test for truth is the test for false. For this, you can use a separate operator !=, meaning not equal to. In other words, the following would evaluate to true:

```
1 != 0
```

By the same token, the following would be either true or false, again depending on the value of the variable:

```
nNumberToTest != 0
```

So far, you can test only discrete values against each other, but quite often you'll want to know whether a value is more or less than a certain test value. You can achieve this with multiple tests against a range of *scalar* (or discrete) values, but this method isn't terribly efficient.

Instead, you have two operators—greater than > and less than <—which enable you to test against a range of values without needing to specify them. So the following will both evaluate to true:

```
2 > 1
99 < 100
```

In the first case, values on the left side of the equation that are all greater than 1 will cause the expression to evaluate to true, and anything less than 1 will cause it to evaluate to false.

Conversely, values less than 100 on the left side of the second equation will cause it to evaluate to true, with values above 100 causing it to evaluate to false.

So what happens when the values are exactly 1 or exactly 100? You're welcome to test and find out later on. However, the language also allows you to explicitly test for this by combining the < and > comparison operators with the = sign:

```
nNumberToTest >= 1
nNumberToTest <= 100
```

In the first instance, any time that nNumberToTest is greater than *or equal to* 1, the expression will evaluate to true. In the second, any time it is less than *or equal to* 100, the expression will evaluate to true.

Essentially, in programming terms, everything boils down to a binary test, or to a sequence of binary tests. All values are true or false—do this because that is true. Do something else because it's false. The comparison operators explored here all contribute to the decision-making processes that you need and are the basic building blocks of the C language.

Precedence

In the C language, expressions are evaluated according to certain rules of precedence. In other words, with no other guidance, a long expression containing several values and operators is evaluated according to a collection of rules that evaluates pairs of values according to something called *associativity*.

The standard rules follow the mathematical rules that evaluate expressions in the following sequence:

- Anything in brackets

- Multiplication

- Division operations

- Addition

- Subtraction

- Less than, and less than or equal to

- Greater than, and greater than or equal to

- Equals and not equals

- Assignment

- Assignment with operators (+=, −=, and so on)

There are more than the ones listed here, which is why I suggest one simple rule—*Put everything in brackets when you're using multipart expressions.*

Recall that anything in brackets will be evaluated first. So if you want to calculate the percentage of something and use it to determine a proportion of something else, you should break the expression down into steps and bracket each one.

Using the cooking analogy again, let's assume you want to express the need to calculate how much flour you have and top it off with water so that the entire mixture weighs 1 kilogram. You would need to perform the following steps:

1. Calculate the percentage (the weight of flour versus the total weight needed).

2. Subtract it from 100 (you need 100% of the weight, and you already have x% flour).

3. Use the remainder to calculate the new value (whatever's left must be water).

Rather than trying to remember the precedence rules, you have two choices—create three lines of code, using variables to store the result of each operation in, or use a single expression, with each step in brackets.

The solution to problems such as this is usually left to the discretion of the programmer, but the best approach is to use brackets if the expression will not be longer than a single line and then break it up if it helps understanding. Code is made to be read as well as written, and anything that can make that easier is good.

Using brackets also helps to reduce coding errors, and breaking a statement up into several lines will help this even further. Relying on rules of precedence is likely to lead to implementation errors and make the code hard to read, understand, and maintain.

Containing Code Blocks

All executable code is contained within a *block*. A program will be comprised of many blocks—this book, for example, is comprised of many topics, each in its own little section. If you wanted to pick it up and use it as a guide to reading a C program, you might have to consult sections more or less at random using the index.

In other words, you write your program as you would a structured document. However, whereas a document follows a top-down convention (it can be followed coherently from start to end), the same is not necessarily true of computer code.

The main function, for example, might not even occur at the start of the program, and so you need some way to make sure that the statements that it contains are identified as belonging to that function and have a clear start and end. Each piece has to be a self-contained block that can be referenced independently of the code surrounding it.

To do this, you put the code to be executed between an opening brace and a closing brace. Taking the previous example and expanding it slightly, you might write a main function that looks like this:

```
int main ()
{
}
```

The opening brace { tells the compiler that what follows is a code block that belongs to the main function. When it encounters the closing brace }, it knows that the code block has finished. If there is no opening brace, the compiler will not compile the code and will return an error.

Likewise, if there is no closing brace, the compiler will generate an error. Even if the code (document) ends, the compiler will generate an error. Although this might seem pedantic—after all, the document has come to an end, so the block could be said to have closed implicitly—programming relies on the pedantry to be precise.

Variable Scoping

One important side effect of grouping statements between braces is that the code defined within the braces is relevant only to other code also between the braces. This is called *scoping* and is of particular interest when defining variables that can be used by the code.

Recall that variables are places to store information. *Local variables* are relevant right now, and *global variables* are relevant to the whole program. The scope of a global variable is the whole source file in which it appears.

However, a variable that is *declared* inside a code block may be used only inside that code block or any other code blocks that might exist within it. It is said to be *local*.

The variable cannot be used in other code blocks that are not contained inside the same code block in which the variable was declared. Local variables are in scope only for the length of time that the code block is being executed.

Code Sample 3.1: Scoping Variables in Code Blocks

If this seems a little hard to follow, consider the following:

```
void my_function
{
    int nSecondNumber;
}

int main ()
{
    int nFirstNumber;

    nFirstNumber = 1;   // In scope
    nSecondNumber = 2; // Out of scope
}
```

This code sample introduces a few items that should look familiar but that have not been covered in any detail. You will look at them later on, but for now all you need to concentrate on is the code blocks and variables.

Reading from top to bottom, you have a named code block called `my_function`, which is just a piece of code that you can call by name, in the same way that the operating system can call the `main` function when the program starts. It has a variable defined inside it, which is local to that function.

The next code block is the main function, containing several variables. One of those, the nFirstNumber, is local to the main function and will be in scope while it is being executed. The nSecondNumber, however, is only in scope when my_function is being executed.

Subsequently, the code sample will not compile.

As previously mentioned, you can also define variables outside any code blocks. These are called global variables and are, generally speaking, a bad idea. The value can be set and reset (updated) by any code statement within the source code file, and it makes it very hard to manage the values.

If globals must be used, it is polite to prefix the variable name with g_ so that you remember that it is a global variable and that those reading are also aware of this fact. Wherever possible, though, globals are best avoided.

However, if you were to change the code sample to place the nSecondNumber outside my_function, it would be in scope for all the code onside that file. If you were to leave the declaration of nSecondNumber in place in my_function as well as declaring it globally, something strange would happen.

Inside my_function, the local declaration of the variable overrides the global declaration. Different compilers will deal with this in different ways. Some will throw up a compiler error, others just a warning. If the code does compile, it will be hard to test and debug—global variables are a bad idea.

Comments

Documenting code is one of the most important parts of the programming process and takes very little effort to do well. The C language, like most others, provides a facility to write plain English in the code but specify that it should be excluded from the compiler process.

As a programmer, you are telling the compiler that these words are for you, not for the compiler, so please ignore them. Good comments detail what code does and why it was written. The more (good quality) comments, the better. There are three main reasons that extensive comments are a good idea:

- To refresh you when you read it again to make changes.

- To help future programmers looking at the code.

- To help when you come back to optimize.

One of the mistakes programmers make, both the inexperienced and the hardened pros, is to assume that the code is self-explanatory. Even if the programmer follows all the conventions of variable naming, this is unlikely to be the case.

Another mistake is in assuming that code will be written once and never re-written. Code that is written with this in mind from the outset is very rare, and programmers need to get into the habit of writing code for re-use. Commenting code makes this more achievable and efficient.

Bad commenting will mean that time is wasted trying to establish what the code does, why it is doing it, and how it could be done better. This usually leads to a complete rewrite, which wastes time and energy. Code that is reused is code that does not have to be written again, something that cannot be emphasized enough.

In C programming, comments can be single line:

```
// This is a single line comment
```

This line can follow C code, or it can be a line on its own. It cannot precede C code, because that would make the C code part of the comment. When the compiler encounters the double forward slash, //, anything from there to the end of the line is treated as a comment and ignored by the compiler.

Comments can also be multi-line:

```
/* The comment starts here
...continues on this line
...and ends here */
```

Any code outside of the /* and */ sequences will be interpreted by the compiler, and if it is not valid C code it will cause a compile error. Similarly, code that is contained inside the /* and */ will not be compiled, even when it is on a new line. This means that comments contained within /* and */ sequences will be removed before the remainder of the source is interpreted.

So the following will not compile correctly, although it will compile:

```
/* The comment starts before the code

int nAVariable;

... this is still inside the comments,
as was the code

... and the comment finishes here */
```

If you enter the previous code into a text file and try to compile it as is, you will find that the compiler does not complain. However, the compiler will ignore everything, *including* the `int nAVariable` code block.

Multi-line comments are useful but need to be used with care. It is sometimes quite easy to lose track of them if they are spread out too much. This is especially dangerous when commenting out large blocks of code for debugging purposes.

Defining Functions

A key part of C programming, as in many other languages, is the ability to break up a program into smaller chunks that can be called, usually by name, from within other code blocks. In C, this is done using *functions*.

Functions are pieces of named code—code blocks that are self-contained, called by name, can take parameters, and provide return values. Recall the first-ever function *declaration* you saw:

```
<return type> main ( [argument list] )
```

This generic definition is incomplete because it does not contain any C code to be executed when the function is called. To expand upon this declaration, you can add a function *body* to it, which will actually do some work. The general form for declaring an entire function is as follows:

```
<return type> <function name> ( [argument list] )
{
    // Code statements
    return <value>; // If we return something

}
```

As with variable naming that you explored earlier, the function name should be something logical, something that explains what the function does. As a general rule, creating shorter functions that fulfill specific purposes is better than trying to put a lot of functionality into a single code block.

This also helps re-use, as each function is designed to do a specific task, and the more specific it is, the more future uses you're likely to find for it. It also makes them easier to follow, which helps future maintenance.

Note also that the `return` statement allows you to return a value, if necessary, of the same type as specified in the return type of the function definition. If the return type is `void`, no return statement is required (or indeed, allowed).

You saw this with the definition of the return value of a `main` function used to indicate the success of the program to the operating system. Although the `main` function can only really return an integer status code, other functions, defined by the user, can return values of any built-in data type.

The code block itself is contained within braces, as is usual for C programs. Again, the compiler will require start and end blocks and an opening and closing brace, and without them the program will not compile. The error that the compiler returns, however, will not generally point out that the programmer forgot a closing brace.

Rather, it will treat all the code that follows the function declaration and opening brace as part of that function. This means that the error might manifest itself a long way after the function has been declared.

For this reason, it is a good habit to immediately open and close the braces for the code block as soon as the declaration has been written. That way, nothing will be forgotten.

The last part of the function declaration is the argument list, where you can pass values into the function. These values have scope only within the code block, and their values typically hold only for the duration of the execution of the function.

There are some refinements to these rules making it possible to alter values and pass them back to the calling code block, but for now, this gives you enough to be able to understand the concept of functions and argument lists.

You'll revisit argument lists along with a recap of these principles in Chapter 10, "User-Defined Functions."

Code Sample 3.2: Simple Skeleton Application

You now have enough information at your fingertips to create a simple program—one that compiles and can be run. It might not do anything, but just being able to get something to compile is often an achievement in itself.

To give you a fighting chance, however, I'll define a simple skeleton application that fulfills this criterion.

The following might be used as a starting point for C applications—it is well behaved and contains enough components to be useful. It does nothing except return a non-error value at present, but it does give you a good platform upon which to build future programs.

```c
int g_nReturnValue; // An integer variable

void SetDefaultReturnValue()
{
  g_nReturnValue = 0; // Set to a non-error value
}

int main ( ) // Entry point
{
  SetDefaultReturnValue(); // Set default return value

  return g_nReturnValue;
}
```

Notice the use of a global variable, g_nReturnValue, at the start of the code. Although I previously stated that global variables should be avoided, the prefix g_ reminds you that it is global. In this case, it does actually make sense.

If you were to use a non-global variable, you would not be able to update it from outside the main function, which does not make sense for a return value. By using a global variable, you can set the return code from anywhere.

The SetDefaultReturnValue function does exactly that—it places the value 0 in the return value, which you can assume is the status code for "everything is OK." This function is then called as the first action performed by the main function.

The final action that the program performs is to return the return value and terminate. This might not seem to be the world's greatest application, and it's not, but it does serve to help you with the next important part of the learning process—getting a program to compile and link and building the application.

Building the Application

This example assumes a few things:

- You have access to the companion Web site with the code on it (go to www.courseptr.com and click on the Downloads button).

- You have installed and configured a compiler.

Because I have no way of knowing at this point which compiler you're using, I'm going to give examples using the Borland C compiler, which is available free from Inprise (Borland) at http://www.turboexplorer.com/.

However, in most cases, and on most platforms using command-line compilers, the process is the same. For integrated development environments, the process is a little more complicated but easier in some respects. IDEs usually have a command on a button bar or in a menu to compile the current project.

When in doubt, consult the documentation that came with the IDE or compiler, in order to follow the steps from source code editing to application building. The terminology remains the same regardless of the platform.

The first step is to copy the c_skel.c file from the companion Web site onto the local hard drive in a logical location. Command-line users should navigate to this file in a suitable shell. On Windows, this is achieved by selecting Start -> Run.

The name of the command to run is simply cmd. If you're using an IDE, start a new project and open the skeleton C code file as the only file in that project.

Linux users will know how to get a command-line prompt, and MacOS users should start their equivalent (in MacOS X), or open the development environment that they are going to be using.

To compile the c_skel.c file, those in a command-line environment need to type the command that invokes the compiler and/or linker. For Borland C users, the following will achieve the desired result:

```
bcc32 c_skel.c
```

For users of environments that support the make utility, a makefile can also be used. A *makefile* is just a set of statements that explain to the make application the relationships between the source files.

If an application is built of many source files, a makefile is vital. However, with a single source file, it is not usually worth the effort to create one.

Users of an IDE will find that while makefiles are used, the IDE creates and maintains them. They can simply click the Compile or Build button or menu option and watch for the response from the compiler in a suitable message window.

For the sake of completeness at this stage, the makefile of the skeleton application will look like the following:

```
APP      = CSkel
EXEFILE  = $(APP).exe
OBJFILES = $(APP).obj
LIBFILES =

.AUTODEPEND
BCC32    = bcc32
ILINK32  = ilink32

CFLAGS  = -c -I"C:\borland\bcc55\include"
LFLAGS  = -aa -V4.0 -c -x -Gn -L"C:\borland\bcc55\lib"
STDOBJS =
STDLIBS =

$(EXEFILE) : $(OBJFILES) $(RESFILES)
        $(ILINK32) $(LFLAGS) $(OBJFILES) $(STDOBJS), $(EXEFILE), , \
        $(LIBFILES) $(STDLIBS), ,

clean:
        del *.obj *.res *.tds *.map
```

If this looks a little daunting, rest assured that most of it can be ignored and copied between projects. In essence, the file contains definitions of some parameters that can be passed to the compiler on the command line and automates this process.

The compile process is still the same—it turns C code into object code and then links all the object code to make the application. All the makefile does is tell the compiler which object files to make from which C code files and what the end application will be called and look like.

There are some specific definitions to understand:

```
APP           = <Application Name>
EXEFILE       = <Name of Executable File>
OBJFILES      = <Object files, for this project>
```

The make utility will try to compile the .c files that exist for each .obj file listed in the OBJFILES definition. The $(<definition>) statements will replace the value in brackets (and the $ sign) with the definition following the equals sign.

So for the specific makefile mentioned previously, the OBJFILES entry becomes:

CSkel.obj

Similarly, the EXEFILE definition becomes:

CSkel.exe

These values, along with the others, are then substituted into the make process to help build the file. The more .obj files that are requested, the more .c files there needs to be to build them. For now, that is just enough about makefiles to begin compiling the sample applications.

If the Application Fails to Build

There are many reasons why the application might not build. The first thing to check is that the compiler is properly installed. Second, entering the name of the application that compiles the program on the command line will tell you whether the software is actually available.

The code itself, if it is copied correctly from the book or taken from the companion Web site, should compile with no errors as is. It might not link, however, if linking is a separate application that also need to be installed and configured.

Recap

A C program has a very distinct structure. It has an entry point, called the main function, and a collection of user-defined functions. All the code could be contained within the main function, but this would lead to a very unmanageable block of code.

Subsequently, you break up the code into functions, of which main is just one. Each function should perform a precise piece of processing and should be obvious from the function name.

You can also specify variables, which are places to store data of a specific type. These are declared either at the top of the source code, making them accessible to every statement in the source code (global variables), or they can be declared within the braces ({ }) that contain specific pieces of code (local variables).

Local variables should be used wherever possible. Global variables, where used, should be clearly identified as such. It is also reasonable practice to try and prefix the variable name with a specific letter in order to indicate more closely what kind of data is stored in that variable.

You can pass data around the program through a list of parameters to each function, which also helps you to keep variables local. You can even pass parameters into the program from outside, using special kinds of parameters in the `main` function argument list.

When you exit the program, it is useful to return a value to the operating system, as this will help determine the success or failure of the processing. This return value, otherwise known as a status code or error level, can then be used by the operating system or in unattended scripts.

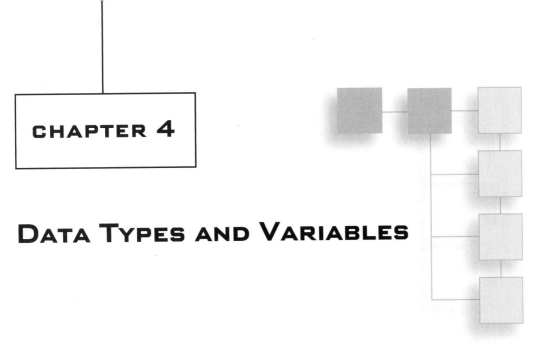

CHAPTER 4

DATA TYPES AND VARIABLES

The aim of this chapter is to present the concept of *data types* and *variables* in C programming.

After you read this chapter, you should be able to grasp the basic ideas behind *data modeling*, translating real-world items into a C representation. It is a skill that takes some time to master, but that's essential to programming in any language.

Because C is a strongly typed language, it is very important to remember that data types are vital to the correct working of a program. Luckily, this works to your advantage as far as basic correctness of the program is concerned, because the compiler will indicate areas where it detects a possible type conflict. In the worst cases, the program will not compile at all.

Basic Types

The C programming language provides the programmer with a set of data types for storing information and building up data types that are not part of the language itself. The former data types are called built-in types, and the latter are called user-defined types.

The three basic built-in types are these:

- Characters (char), such as a
- Integer numbers (int), such as 42
- Floating-point numbers (float), such as 42.42 or 1234.5678

The integer data types come in two flavors—signed and unsigned—which permit the programmer to specify values greater than and less than zero. In other words, positive and negative numbers.

All of these basic built-in types have a specific size (amount of memory required) and range of values that they can represent. The bigger the numbers, the more memory is required.

Beyond these three basic types, the C language also provides for complex data types such as *structures* (sometimes called *records* in other programming languages) and pointers. A pointer is simply a reference to a piece of information stored in memory. For example:

```
int * pnNumber; // a pointer to a number variable
```

This small piece of code is something I'll come back to in a later chapter. The essence, however, is that pnNumber *points to* a place in memory where you want to put int data: a number, or even a collection of numbers. After all, the pointer just tells the computer where the information starts. It could end anywhere, and this is both the power and drawback of using pointers.

The last basic data type to consider is the void type, which represents a non-specific data type. It is often used when a compile-time (declaration time) data type is not appropriate, and the type will be determined later on in the processing sequence. The main function (and other functions) also use void as a way of indicating that they do not return a value. This will be covered in great detail in later chapters.

Sizes and Ranges

The *size* of a data type refers to the amount of memory that it takes up. A bigger number will take more memory than smaller numbers. However, the smallest unit of memory available is a single byte, and sizes must be represented in multiples of bytes.

So a one-byte data type can store values that are limited to the number of variances that can be represented in a single byte of data. A character, for example, occupies one byte, allowing for up to 255 individual representations in the standard ASCII character set.

The actual amount of memory that a data type occupies can be established by using the built-in sizeof function. This returns a value that indicates the number of bytes occupied by the data type or a variable declared using that data type.

Without going into too much detail, C allows you to modify the data type by using the short, long, double, and unsigned keywords to change the range of values that can be stored in a specific data type. If you choose to make a type short or long, you will change the size of the resulting variable as well as the range.

Long modifiers are typically applied to numbers or pointers. A long pointer is equivalent to a far-off place in memory or a very large block of data. So if you need to store bigger numbers in a variable, you can make it a long variant.

Common ranges available for the built-in numerical and character types are listed in the following table:

Data Type	Size (Bytes)	From	To
unsigned char	1	0	255
char	1	−128	127
unsigned short int	2	0	65,535 (64KB)
short int	2	−32,768	32,767 (32KB)
unsigned int	4	0	4,294,967,295 (4GB)
Int	4	−2,147,483,648	−2,147,483,647 (2GB)
long int	4	−2,147,483,648	−2,147,483,647 (2GB)
float	4		
double	8	Architecture dependent	
long double	12		

Reading this table, you can see that a long int will require 4 bytes of memory and can store a value between −2 million and +2 million. For the same amount of memory, an unsigned int can store a value of up to 4 million but no negative numbers. This illustrates the difference between a signed value and an unsigned value.

However, floating-point numbers do not actually come in signed and unsigned variants; because of the way that they are stored, they are always signed. Things like accuracy and range are *architecture dependent*. You should check the documentation of the platform and compiler to know exactly what the limits are.

Although the values in the table are only indicative, most of the *scalar* types (those that have a single discrete value) have standard ranges associated with them. Non-scalar data types, where the value can be selected from a near-infinite set of values (such as floating-point numbers of an arbitrary accuracy) will have ranges associated with them that are architecture dependent.

Complex Data Types

The basic types are enough to process any kind of information. However, to represent certain real-world objects (such as addresses), creating a representative complex type is a more efficient way to construct the program code.

These complex types are known as structures, or `structs`, and allow the programmer to create a record containing several fields, each of which can be a basic type or another `struct`. Knowing how to break down the real-world objects into a series of complex data types is part of the skill set that you need to create useful programs.

The added flexibility comes with some caveats, however. A `struct` has no intrinsic value and therefore cannot be operated directly upon. In other words, the only value held by a `struct` is the value of each of its members (or fields).

This behavior can be illustrated by considering the assignment operator (=). For example, the following code allows you to assign a value to a basic data type:

```
int nValue;
nValue=42;
```

This results in the variable `nValue` containing the value 42. You'll read about variables in more detail in the last section of this chapter, but it is important to bear in mind that the assignment operator works only for built-in types.

A complex type (record) cannot be treated in the same way, and you need to provide some code to copy each field (member) of the `struct` from one place to another to achieve the same effect.

Casting

I have previously mentioned that data types and variables are rather like pegs and holes, and that it is sometimes possible to fit a square peg into a small round hole, losing some information, or fitting it into a large round hole, with some extra space. The programmer can make these decisions when writing the code, and this is called *casting*.

In C, a mechanism is provided by which a programmer can explicitly or implicitly cast a variable from one type to another. *Casting* is both useful and dangerous; it is strongly advised to only use explicit casting, and even that in recognized situations only. It is far better practice to select the correct type in the first place.

Generally speaking, casting is a number-to-number operation and can occur at the assignment level or the comparison level. Put another way, you can force a square peg into a round hole, and you can also compare a square peg and a round peg and find the similarities while ignoring some parts of the peg.

In programming terms, you can ignore the capabilities of a type and compare the actual value, even when the capabilities of the type of data that you are comparing it to are different. The value 42 stored in a 4-byte integer compared to a 2-byte integer is still 42.

The fact that you can get 4,000,000 variances in one and only 64,000 in the other does not really matter when they both contain 42. By a similar token, if you have a floating-point number 42.01, you can compare it with an integer 42 and arrive at the conclusion that they are both the same. You ignore the capability of the floating-point number to include decimals.

The same trick can also be done with assignments: You can put 42.01 into an integer and only have 42 stored. These are all implicit type casts and will be pointed out to the programmer at compile time as a possible error.

That is, implicit type casts will allow the programmer to compare a long integer with a short integer, and the compiler will merely generate a warning. The reasoning is that there might be a time where one representation contains a value that cannot be assigned to or compared with the other representation.

If one variable can contain anything up to around a number like 4,000,000 and another can only cope with values up to 65,000 casting from one to the other might lead to problems. For example, if you wanted to put 3,500,000 into the latter variable, it would not fit. Consequently, the compiler points these cases out by issuing warnings in case you are doing something that might have unintended consequences.

Your program might try to put a value greater than 64,000 into a 2-byte integer. The result is undefined, and an implicit cast likely to fail. Explicit casting, where the programmer provides the desired target type, can be performed between any of the numerical types:

```
int nValue;
double fValue;
fValue = 42.42;
nValue = (int) fValue;
```

Of course, the effect of casting is not the same as using a mathematical conversion such as generating a ceiling or floor (rounded up or rounded down) value. Often, the result will be something unexpected.

So explicit casting is better than implicit casting, but it is not reliable when you do not know the limits within which you are trying to work. If you cannot know that a specific number will be too big to be placed into a certain type, casting is going to be dangerous to the logic in the program.

Having said that, it is useful under certain circumstances to cast integers to floating-point types, perform a calculation, and cast them back to integers. This can be a great aid in retaining accuracy in complex formulae. Again, however, it should be used with caution.

The only cast that can really be recommended is when a piece of memory has been allocated with a void type. Recall that a void type can mean *nothing* when used with a function. In those circumstances, it means that the function has no return value.

A void pointer, however, is a pointer to a piece of memory that does not yet have a type associated with it. You'll read about cover pointers and memory later on in the book, but I will just introduce the concept of formatted memory briefly now so that I can finish the casting discussion.

When you allocate memory using the malloc function (part of the libraries), a void pointer is returned. This is a pointer to a piece of memory that has no type. This would not be very useful in itself, as you need to create a variable with a type to reference the data.

So that the compiler knows what kind of data you intend to put in there, and to help it manage the data for you, you need to cast the void pointer into a pointer of the type of data that you want to access. In this way, the compiler knows how to address and manipulate the memory.

The generic definition for the memory allocation function can be represented as:

```
void * malloc ( [size] );
```

In this definition (declaration), the [size] is the size of memory block, in bytes, that you want to allocate. The function returns a void pointer to that memory block to allow the programmer to begin to store data in it. At the time that the memory allocation function was implemented, the programmer had no idea what others would want to use it for. For example, you might know that you will have 100 pieces of numerical data but want to be able to deal with percentages as well as population figures. If you want the code to be all purpose and not try to force the users (or programmers) to declare a collection of integers (or floating-point numbers), you would simply use a void pointer and cast it to a type later on, when you knew what the users wanted the numbers for.

So it's implemented to work with memory in absence of that information, only creating a useable block of size bytes.

In other words, because the memory-allocation function does not know what the programmer intends to do with that memory—it is written with multiple uses in mind—the function makes no preconceptions as to how the memory should be referenced. The programmer is then free to cast the void pointer to something else.

This cast is always explicit, and the compiler will complain and throw an error if the programmer tries to make it perform an implicit cast into that memory block. An example of an explicit cast into a pointer of a basic type is as follows:

```
int * pInteger = (int *) malloc ( sizeof(int) );
```

You will meet this code again, but here is a brief summary of what it means. A pointer to an integer is created (pInteger) and set to point at a piece of memory that's the size of one integer. The cast is provided by the (int *) expression, and the sizeof function has been used to determine the correct size of an integer, which may change from platform to platform.

If all this seems a little abstract, you might want to refer again to this section after you've read further. It is important to be aware of the cast mechanism, but it will become clearer with some more concrete examples later on.

Arrays

An *array* is a dimensional information store. A variable contains one piece of information, whereas an array contains more than one piece of information of the same type. Types (numbers, letters, and user-defined types) cannot be mixed within an array.

However, user-defined complex types can be contained in an array, allowing you to store multiple objects with a variety of data, side by side. Arrays can be one dimensional or multidimensional. A one-dimensional array is rather like a row of boxes in memory, into which you can place values.

You can define a one-dimensional array thus:

```
int nIntegerArray[10];
```

This example declares a variable of type integer that can contain 10 individual numbers, one after the other.

A two-dimensional array, on the other hand, is like a grid of boxes, like postal sorting pigeonholes. Again, each slot in the array can contain a single value, but you can store values across and down, rather than just along or up. If it helps, think of it like a chessboard in which each square can contain a piece of the set.

So you could define it as follows:

```
int nChessBoard[8][8];
```

In fact, there is no real limit beyond the capacity of the computer to the dimensions of the array. You could, for example, have a three-dimensional array representing a cube of values as:

```
int nCube[8][8][8];
```

Even though you have declared these arrays as having the same dimension on each side, this is not necessary. You could define an array with a different number of slots in one dimension to the other. A rectangular grid of memory locations could be declared as follows:

```
int nRectangle[8][4];
```

If you need to reference a location, it can be treated as if it were a single variable slot by indicating the index into the array using an integer in the square brackets after the variable name. So if you wanted to put the value 3 in the location referenced by the [row, column] reference [4,1], use code such as:

```
nRectangle[4][1] = 3;
```

Note from this that you are treating the array location [4][1] as if it were a single integer variable. These indexes into arrays are zero based—in other words, the element at the end of the array is indexed as the dimension of the array minus one. The first location is referenced with index zero.

As with most programming examples, this is best understood in a few simple lines of code used as illustration:

```
int nArray[10]; // 10 elements
```

```
nArray[0] = 1; // The first element
nArray[9] = 10; // The last element
```

Notice that you do not actually know how the computer chooses to access or arrange the array in memory. It is simply a piece of memory in which you can store information—you can declare it and access it without knowing how the underlying array is being manipulated.

There are also some special properties that you can make use of when using arrays in your applications. Typically arrays will be one or two dimensional. A one-dimensional array of characters, for example, is otherwise known as a *string*. Two-dimensional arrays are often used to store representations of graphical screens.

The one drawback with arrays is that they are static. That is, you cannot resize them once the program has been written. An array can be sized at compile time, perhaps conditionally, but once the program is built, the array is fixed.

This is because the space that is required is in the program's *stack*, or local memory. Some compilers will place an artificial limit of 64KB on the stack, which is the only real limit on the size of array that can be declared.

The mechanism to get around this is called a *dynamic array*, which can be resized during the program's execution. This is not part of the C language and would need to be implemented by the programmer, but it is a reasonably simple data structure to implement and manipulate.

You'll learn about some kinds of dynamic array and other mechanisms later on, but it is important to remember that arrays declared as part of the program are static, and some extra work is required to manipulate memory to provide dynamic storage.

Enumerated Types

Another kind of type, known as the *enumerated* type, allows you to create sets of values that are referenced by name, but that enumerate to an indexed position within that set. For example, you might like to create a user-defined type to store days of the week:

```
enum week_days {
Mon = 0, Tue, Wed, Thu, Fri, Sat, Sun
};
```

In this example, the compiler will assign the integer values 0 through 6 to the days of the week, in the order that they are listed. The convenience in programming terms is that the user-friendly word Mon can be used in the program, rather than the value 0.

So, you might write code such as:

```
week_days DayOfWeek;
```

This declares a variable DayOfWeek as being of the appropriate type. You can assign a value to the variable as follows:

```
DayOfWeek = Wed;
```

Because you have enumerated these days to integers, you can also use the standard operators to manipulate them. These are the same operators as you have seen in the previous chapter on the C language structure. If you add 1 to Wed, you arrive at the value Thu, or Thursday.

If you wanted to test for a value between Mon and Fri (a working day, for example), the expression might contain:

```
((DayOfWeek >= Mon) && (DayOfWeek <= Fri)
```

The attentive reader will note several things. The first is that this example uses standard built-in type operators, made possible by the fact that it enumerated the type to be the same as integers. The second thing to note is that the example contains the individual conditions in brackets.

The last thing that you should note is the curious && symbol, which you have not yet come across in your exploration of programming in this book. I will deal with logic statements later on, but for now you should be content with knowing that it means *and*.

The example reads as follows: "the day of the week is greater than or equal to Monday" and "less than or equal to Friday." In plain English, this is the equivalent of Monday to Friday, inclusive.

If ever the values change, all you need to do is adjust the enumerated type—the rest of the code will still work. You also do not need to remember that Friday has been assigned week day number 4. In addition, you can write code that compares two values of the same type without worrying about the underlying representation.

Data Types and Variables

I covered the basic concept of variables in the previous chapter when you looked at how they can be named and declared. Recall that we imagined them as named slots (imagine pigeonholes) in memory, with space reserved for each piece of data that you would like to store.

In addition, that chapter looked at how a variable is defined by specifying a name and a type:

```
int nMyNumber;           // A simple variable
char szMyString[255];    // A 255 slot array
char * szString;         // Pointer to char's
```

This is called the variable *declaration*. Once a variable has been *declared*, it can only contain data of the type that was included in the declaration. Operations upon the data in that variable will be limited to those that are supported by the data type.

Recall also that, to assign a value to a variable, you use the assignment operator =. So to assign a numeric value to the nMyNumber value declared previously, you would use code such as:

```
nMyNumber = 3;
```

The exception to using the assignment operator is that it does not work with arrays. The following, for example, will not even compile:

```
szMyString = "Hello"; // Error
szString = "Hello";   // Error
```

You can, of course, assign values to individual elements to achieve this result:

```
szMyString[0] = 'H';
szMyString[1] = 'e';
szMyString[2] = 'l';
szMyString[3] = 'l';
szMyString[4] = 'o';
```

Notice that these examples use single quotes around the character value in order to differentiate it from a string constant. Luckily, as you'll see later on, the C libraries provide better string manipulation than you can achieve in single statements operating on an array.

However, when they were implemented, it is likely that, at the core, they operated on arrays of characters in memory. This is another example of a complex type—one that you refer to using a single named slot, but which contains more than one piece of data. Other languages, however, provide a built-in type for strings, but in C it is a user-defined type, luckily based around an ANSI specification for processing it.

Recap

You learned in the first chapters of the book how a variable is used in C, and in this chapter you extended your knowledge by adding a clear definition of the available built-in types. You can extend this range with complex types containing items of a specific type (which may also be a complex type).

You can also create collections of data referred to as *arrays,* which provide a series of numbered variable slots into which data of a single specific type can be placed. Memory can also be set aside to hold such collections.

The C language has built-in operators for assigning, manipulating, and comparing numerical values. For other data types, special functions must be built to enable comparison of complex data types or arrays. For string manipulation, the string.h library is provided by the standard C libraries.

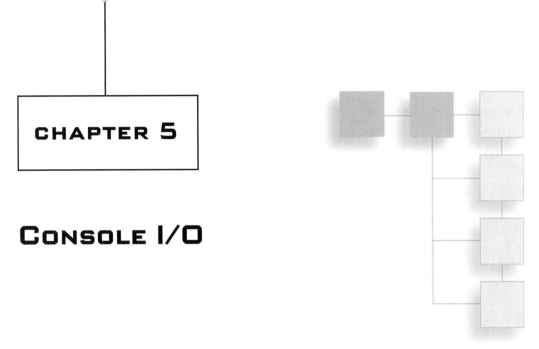

CHAPTER 5

CONSOLE I/O

The aim of this chapter is to introduce the libraries provided by the standard C implementations that provide interactivity between the users and program.

After you read this chapter, you will have covered the necessary function calls required to provide genuinely useful input and output operations within a program. It also provides a good introduction to the use of libraries in C programming.

Formatted Output

In the standard collection of libraries, output is directed to a function of the operating system often called *standard output*. This is a term that Linux users will be very familiar with and that DOS and Windows users will know as the command-line interface. It is plain text, with some additional, optional features to provide colors and other features on some interfaces.

Unlike other programming languages, the C language itself provides no way to deal with text output inherently; this functionality has been added through some standardized libraries. Each library is created for the platform supported by the compiler in question and adheres to ANSI standards.

When the program is built, the appropriate object code for the library for the target platform is linked in with the program code in order to provide the facility to place text on the screen. There are two aspects to this—a file that tells the compiler what the different functions in the library look like and the library file itself.

There are quite a number of libraries available, providing various output features. These vary in complexity and sophistication, allowing the programmer to write out simple text or position the cursor on the screen, and so on.

One such library is known as *stdio* and provides functions to (among other things) display lines of text in a formatted fashion. This formatting includes carriage returns, tabs, translation of variable values (such as integers), and plain text.

Although it allows a level of sophistication with respect to formatting text for output, it does not offer any control of the output screen itself. It is a console, line-by-line, column-by-column output library. When the text arrives at the end of the screen, the screen scrolls up—just like it would do if the user were typing in commands and pressing the Enter key.

In fact, the stdio library is only providing an interface to the existing operating system features that control the screen. For now, this is more than enough for your purposes. There are many functions for screen output in this library, of which the most commonly used is called printf.

Using printf

The printf function provides a way to direct output to the screen. The function performs several useful tasks in order to achieve this. Among those tasks is creating a string to be output using a set format given by the programmer, combining it with variables that the programmer wants to display the value of, and finally formatting it for correct output on the screen.

It takes at least one parameter (the format string) and as many more as needed to fill out any variables that are referenced to be replaced within that format string. First take a look at the ability of printf to display a constant string value.

There is a long-standing programming tradition that the very first piece of output code that a budding programmer is introduced to is called Hello World. Not wanting to break this tradition, I now present the traditional Hello World printf statement.

In its simplest form, printf allows you to write code such as:

```
printf ( "Hello World\n" );
```

This would display Hello World plus a carriage return (newline or linefeed) on the screen. Of course, in order to actually use it, you need to place it within the context of the skeleton program code from Chapter 3, compile it, and then execute the application.

For brevity, I have adjusted the skeleton slightly to leave out the return code management and present only a simple main function displaying the Hello World text string. Again, the HelloWorld.c program source code can be downloaded from the companion Web site (go to www.courseptr.com and click on the Downloads button), and you are welcome to save it to your hard drive and compile the program.

```c
#include <stdio.h>
int main ( )
{
  printf ( "Hello World\n" );
  return 0;
}
```

Code Sample 5.1: The Hello World Application

Before you go much further, you need to take a look at the very first line. It has a statement called the include statement, which is a directive to the compiler. It informs the compiler that you'll be using library code from a specific library file. The library file (in this case stdio.h) contains a collection of function declarations, some of which you might want to use in your program.

The stdio.h file contains all the declarations for the functions that you'll use, and you'll enable the compiler to check that you have used them correctly. Then, when the linker creates the application from the object files and the stdio library, it can combine your code with the standard code.

Now, the compiler knows where to find this file, because you placed it in chevrons, indicating that it should look in the usual place for include files. Take a look at where you installed your compiler kit, and you'll see a folder called *Include*, containing all the .h files that provide interfaces to the installed libraries.

There's also a folder called *Lib* that contains the actual object code. The linker knows that it should look through the Lib folder to find a library file that contains the function implementations required to actually do the work.

Usually, one library file covers many include files (.h, or header files), so the librarian does not have to spend much time looking for a specific function implementation.

You can also contain the filename in quotes—such as `"stdio.h"`—indicating that you have provided an exact path to the file. In my system, using the Borland C compiler, that would be `c:\Borland\Include\stdio.h`.

This is all well and good, but the reason that you use the chevron notation for standard libraries is so that if the program has to be compiled on another system, it can be done without changing all the paths to standard libraries.

If you provide non-standard libraries, you need to tell the compiler where to find the header file and the linker where to find the library; but more on that later.

The result of running the program is unremarkable, but there are a few points worth noting:

- The application does not clear the screen.

- The \n sequence causes a single carriage return.

- Output begins immediately.

In other words, nothing happens that you have not explicitly put in the program. The actual output looks like Figure 5.1.

However, with this one function, you can do remarkable things. If you wanted to clear the screen, you could use `printf` to output 25 or so carriage returns:

```
printf ( "\n\n\n\n\n\n\n\n\n\n\n\n\n\n\n\n\n\n\n\n\n\n\n\n\n" );
```

If, on the other hand, you wanted to center some text, you could work out how many space characters you would need to put in front of the text and write a couple of `printf` statements to do that:

```
printf ( "                              " );
printf ( "Hello World\n" );
```

Note that unless you include the \n character, no carriage return is printed. Hence, just because you have two `printf` statements on separate source lines, this does not equate to the output being on two different lines unless you use the \n sequence.

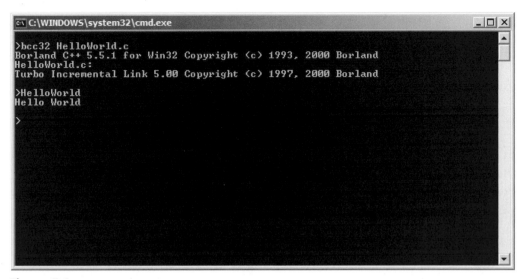

Figure 5.1
The Output of the HelloWorld Program

This \n sequence is known as an escape sequence, and there are several frequently used escape sequences:

\n   Carriage return

\t   Tab

\"   Quote

Escaping the quote character is necessary because the compiler would have trouble tokenizing the string. This is more clearly illustrated by the following examples:

```
printf ( ""Quoted Text"" );
printf ( ""Quoted " );
printf ( "Text"" );
```

None of these examples will compile. In the first case, the compiler would become confused after the first set of double quotes; the next token would be the string "Quoted", which would mean nothing in this context.

The third example would be fine right up until the last quote, which would be out of place and confuse the compiler. The corrected versions of these three examples are as follows:

```
printf ( "\"Quoted Text\"" );
```

```
printf ( "\"Quoted " );
printf ( "Text\"" );
```

Besides processing plain text and escape sequences, printf can also format variables for output. In the generic declaration of printf, note that it can take more than one parameter, with the first parameter always being present and always being the formatting string.

Within the formatting string, you can refer to values that you later pass through the additional parameters supplied to printf, for example, the %s *format specifier.*

A format specifier is a special value that the C compiler will substitute for a value taken from the printf parameter list following the format string. There must be an equal number of parameters as format specifiers, but most C compilers cannot flag this at compile time.

The result of not having the same number of specifiers as parameters ranges from system crashes (too few) to missing printed information (too many) and a range of strange output in between when the parameters are in a different order than the format specifiers.

The %s format specifier allows you to substitute a string from the parameter list. Thus, the following two examples produce identical results:

```
printf ( "Hello World" );
printf ( "%s", "Hello World" );
```

As an aside, if you want to print a % sign, you need to use a special format specifier %%. Otherwise, the compiler will translate the character following the % as some kind of format specifier, and this can create problems in the output.

The previous example used a constant string, but you can also put variables in the parameter list. Supposing you had also captured the user's name in a variable szUserName; you could write a piece of C code such as:

```
printf ( "Hello, %s\n", szUserName );
```

The printf function will substitute %s for the value stored in szUserName, allowing you to print out that value. If you had captured the user's first and last names, you could extend this to:

```
printf ( "Hello, %s %s\n", szFirstName, szLastName );
```

So each parameter after the first one is a value to substitute into the string in the first parameter, at the position denoted by the format specifier %s. You can also place escape characters in the string variable, and they will be correctly interpreted.

There is also a variety of format specifiers for handling the built-in numerical data types:

%d   Integer (int)

%f   Floating point (float or double)

%ld   Long integer (long int)

Using these will cause the compiler to substitute the value stored in the numerical variable into the string. This can also be performed with constant values or even the result of an expression:

```
printf ( "%d * %d = %d", 5, 25, 5*25 );
```

The previous example will produce the same output as the following code fragment:

```
int nMultiplier1, nMultiplier2;

nMultiplier1 = 5;
nMultipler2 = 25;

printf ( "%d * %d = %d",
        nMultiplier1, nMultiplier2, nMultiplier1*nMultiplier2 );
```

So far, you have looked only at basic substitution, but printf provides more formatting options to allow you to lay out your output more precisely. Between the % and the *format specifier*, you can add a number of flags. Each flag has a different meaning, dealing with the desired field width, leading characters, number of decimal places, and so on.

If you insert a number, it is interpreted as the minimum field width. In other words, if you tell printf that you want to output an integer on a field that is five characters wide, printf will pad appropriately for numbers that result in a piece of text that is less than five characters wide.

In the case of an unsigned integer, varying between 0 and 65565, that will be the case. If you know that it represents a percentage between 0 and 100, you can specify a field width of 3. However, if the resulting string is longer than three characters, printf will simply make the field wider—with possible disastrous effects on the remainder of the layout.

Values that are within the field width will be right justified within that field. In other words, printf will pad to the left. This is easier to see with a short example:

```
printf ( "Percentage : %3d\n", nPercent );
```

If you have a value in nPercent that is less than three characters wide (say, 10), the correct number of spaces will be inserted before the number to bring it up to a width of three characters. Using the previous code, with values 1, 10, 100, and 1000, the output would be:

```
Percentage :    1
Percentage :   10
Percentage :  100
Percentage : 1000
```

Note that the last example causes the field to overflow, with a knock-on effect along the rest of the line. The printf function is not smart enough to try and realign by balancing other under-used fields to retain the general layout, but there are some tricks you can use, as you'll see later in the book.

This is the default behavior, but it can be modified by adding a dash (–) before the number, indicating that you want the field to be left justified. In other words, rather than adding spaces to the left, you can have printf add spaces to the right. The code looks like this:

```
printf ( "Percentage : %-3d %%\n", nPercent );
```

I added a %% sequence after the field to illustrate where the field boundary is; it is not part of the format specifier string. The output, again for values of 1, 10, 100, and 1000, now looks like this:

```
Percentage :    1 %
Percentage :   10 %
Percentage :  100 %
Percentage : 1000 %
```

Again, note the final line and the fact that the field boundary has now been moved one character to the right. So, the – modifier changes the padding location. You can also change the padding character from a space to a 0 by adding a . (period) character in front of the field width specifier, as follows:

```
printf ( "Percentage : %.3d %%\n", nPercent );
```

If you are using zeros to pad, the addition of the – modifier to change the side on which the padding is added makes no difference. In other words, numbers are always padded to the left when zeros are used for padding. If this were not the case, the meaning of the number would be misinterpreted.

When used in conjunction with floating-point numbers, the . modifier takes on a slightly different role—it changes the precision with which the number is displayed. So if you have a floating-point number with 10 digits after the decimal place, you can use the . modifier to reduce that to 2.

By way of an example, an approximation of pi can be calculated as 22 divided by 7, which can be written into a printf statement for display as:

```
printf ( "PI : %f \n", 22.0/7.0 );
```

This will produce output similar to this:

```
PI : 3.142857
```

This might be too wide a field for your program—if you were displaying currency or something else that only needed two decimal places, for example—so you can change the precision by using a . character. Some examples are as follows:

%.1f for 3.14287, 3.1 will be output

%.2f for 3.14287, 3.14 will be output

%.3f for 3.14287, 3.143 will be output

Look at the last example and note an additional feature—the value has been rounded correctly so that the resulting display is a correct representation of the value, even given the change in precision.

If you specify a number preceding the . modifier, you can also dictate the *minimum* field width that you expect. By adding a zero in front of that number, you can change the left side padding. If the number is too great to fit inside the minimum width, the field will be expanded; if it is less, it will be padded to the left.

So for a floating-point percentage to two decimal places, you need to reserve five characters. The decimal point counts towards the field contents, as does the – sign, indicating a negative number.

There is a final use for the . character in modifying the output of character strings. It can be used to set a maximum field width, which has the side effect of cropping the string if it is too long to fit in the field. So for example, the two lines of code will produce the same output:

```
printf ( "%.10s \n", "1234567890" );
```

```
printf ( "%.10s \n", "12345678901234567890012345" );
```

In the second case, the string will be cropped to 1234567890. However, if the string is smaller than the field width, no padding is introduced. Luckily, you can also specify the minimum field with as well. This code specifies a character field between 10 and 15 characters wide:

```
%10.15s
```

If you specify a range of widths, the result will be that a string shorter than the minimum will be padded (and you can change the padding from right to left with the – modifier), and strings longer will be cropped. So if you want to restrict output to a field of an exact width, you can use code such as:

```
printf ( "%10.10s \n", "12345678901234567890012345" );
```

With this, the output will always be 10 characters wide on the screen. However, the same trick cannot be pulled with numbers, because the change in actual displayed value would not be acceptable.

You'll revisit this useful function time and time again. The secret in using it is in practicing—practically any kind of formatted output can be realized using printf, but some uses are more intuitive than others.

Using sprintf

The printf function directs the result of any formatted input string combined with parameters to the screen. There is a companion function (sprintf) that performs the same formatting, but that directs the result to a string (character array). This enables the programmer to perform a variety of pre-formatting tasks.

Possible uses for this include creating record data in memory to be formatted for screen printing and file output within certain parameters at a later stage. It can also be useful in building up a line (or page) for output in one call rather than using multiple calls to printf, which can be quite slow.

The generic form for the `sprintf` function is as follows:

```
sprintf ( <output>, <format>, <variables . . .> )
```

In this definition, the `<output>` is a string, as is the `<format>` parameter. The remainder of the parameters have to match the format specifiers from the `<format>` parameter. So aside from the initial `<output>` parameter, the rest of the parameters are identical to the `printf` function.

The two functions process the format string in exactly the same way, sharing the same format specifiers. The way that you can use this in practice is presented in Code Sample 5.2.

```
#include <stdio.h>
int main ( )
{
  char szOutputString[255];
  sprintf ( szOutputString, "Hello %s", "World" );
  printf( "%s !\n", szOutputString );
  return 0;
}
```

Code Sample 5.2: The HelloWorld2 Application

The output, once again, is fairly predictable, but the example in Code Sample 5.2 does illustrate what `sprintf` and `printf` can be used together to achieve. There are a few caveats for using `sprintf` that are worth noting.

First, `sprintf` cannot be used to concatenate strings unless a distinct target string is used. In other words, if you want to put two strings together using only `sprintf` and some variables, you need one for the target and two for the source. Furthermore, you cannot, at some later time, concatenate the target string with another string without first making a copy elsewhere.

This might all sound a bit abstract, so take a look at an example. Assume that you want to do the following:

1. `"Hello"` + `"World"` = `"Hello World"`

2. `"Hello"` + `"World"` + `"!"` = `"Hello World!"`

The first is just a slight revision of the `sprintf` call used in Code Sample 5.2:

```
char szWorldString[255];
sprintf ( szWorldString, "World" );
sprintf ( szOutputString, "Hello %s", szWorldString );
```

You take the string "Hello" and concatenate it with the string "World"—stored in szWorldString rather than a constant string as in Code Sample 5.2. This appending of one string to the other should be reasonably easy to understand.

It would be tempting to assume that you could just adapt this to add the exclamation mark by calling sprintf again:

```
sprintf ( szOutputString, "%s!", szOutputString ); // Will NOT work
```

As noted, this does not work. Instead, it places the exclamation mark into the output string held in szOutputString. If this is what you want to achieve using sprintf, you would have to copy the string into a third string and then concatenate the result together:

```
char szWorldString[255];
char szTempString[255];
sprintf ( szWorldString, "World" );
sprintf ( szOutputString, "Hello %s", szWorldString );
sprintf ( szTempString, "%s", szOutputString );
sprintf ( szOutputString, "%s!", szTempString );
```

Now this code is convoluted, and there is an easier answer using the string processing library covered in Chapter 8, "Standard Libraries." For now, take a look at the companion set of functions from the string library, dealing with console (or keyboard) input.

Formatted Input

In command-line programming, input comes from the keyboard, and the standard input and output library, stdio, gives the programmer an interface to that method of input in a formatted way.

The principle is similar to the printf function in that the input stream (be it the keyboard or a variable) is matched against the format string, and variables assign values according to the format specifiers encountered.

The two functions covered here—scanf and sscanf—mirror the printf and sprintf functions in that they work directly with the hardware and also with variables. In other words, the source data can come from the keyboard (via the operating system) or from a string that has to be broken into fields.

Using scanf

The basic syntax of the scanf function is almost identical to the printf equivalent:

```
scanf (<format>, <target variables . . .> )
```

In this definition, <format> is again a format string containing the same format specifiers, except that only the basic % plus a character actually make any sense in this context. In other words, the scanf function is not really appropriate for use in cases where fields have to be laid out in a specific way on the screen.

If you were to use the scanf function to specify a field width, the input library is not sophisticated enough to stop allowing data entry once the field with has been reached. However, only the data that fits inside the field is used in the variable that the field maps to.

If the data is too long, it will start to overwrite the next field, and any data that extends past the end of the input format will be discarded. This might be confusing at first, but consider the following code:

```
scanf ( "%5s %s %d", szFirst, szLast, &nShoeSize );
```

This small fragment assigns one field of width 5, another of variable width, and a number. As long as you stay within these confines, the result is as you might expect. So you could enter the following string via the keyboard:

```
12345 89 42
```

Entering this string would assign 12345 to szFirst, 89 to szLast, and the number 42 to nShoeSize. However, the moment you overstep the first field, the results become more unpredictable. For example, you might have a user who enters a string such as:

```
123456 89 42
```

At this point, you might expect that the result be the same as before, but what actually happens is that the first parameter is truncated as you might expect, but the next available parameter becomes the trailing 6. This means that the final state is:

szFirst contains 12345

szLast contains 6

nShoeSize contains 89

The last piece of the string (42) is then discarded. Clearly, while sized fields are powerful, you have to trust the users to enter the correct data when using sized fields. Consequently, unless you plan on doing a lot of testing and checking of values that are input, it is better not to use sized data entry areas using this method.

Conversely, the parsing and assignment of information when not using sized fields is predictable and useful. Any whitespace is discarded, and this includes space characters and return characters. This means that if you specify that three fields must be read, until each field contains meaningful data, the scanf function will not return.

Note that a new way of specifying parameters in the function call has crept in. Let's isolate this new functionality in a small example call to scanf so we can examine it more closely:

```
scanf ( "%d", &nNumber );
```

The & sign before the nNumber variable indicates that you would like to pass the variable *by reference*. This is an important concept in C programming, because you usually pass scalar variables to functions using a copy of the value. The function can alter the data in the variable, but as soon as the function returns, because a copy local to the function was used, those changes are lost.

However, when you pass by reference, you do not pass a copy of the data, but a reference to the data—the variable itself. Thus, any changes made to the contents of that variable are permanent.

So if the scanf function was called with a variable passed by value, it would not be able to return the value that the user entered, so you explicitly pass the variable by reference, using the & operator. This is true for all scalar variables.

The exception is when using arrays (including strings), because these are passed by reference as default. In essence, an array name is already a reference to a piece of memory. If this seems a little confusing, refer back to the discussion of arrays in Chapter 4.

Aside from these few caveats, using scanf is just the reverse of printf and is quite flexible when it comes to processing basic keyboard input. If you have data that is already contained in a variable, such as might have come from a file or external source, you can also parse it, using the noninteractive equivalent to scanf, sscanf.

Using sscanf

The companion to scanf, sscanf is used to read data from a string (perhaps acquired from a file) into the variables, rather than from the keyboard. As with sprintf, the first parameter is a variable, but it provides the source of the formatted string, rather than the target.

```
sscanf (<source string>, <format>, <target variables. . .> )
```

So the sscanf function will break up the source string according to the format specifiers included in the format string and place the results in the target variables. The same conversion rules apply with sscanf; in other words, although it can be used in conjunction with field width specifiers, they will not discard data in the way you might expect.

A simple usage of the sscanf function might be as follows:

```
sprintf( szDetails, "Guy Thompson 42" );
sscanf ( szDetails, "%s %*s %d", szFirstName, &nShoeSize );
```

This example first places the string "Guy Thompson 42" into the szDetails variable with a call to sprintf. It then extracts only the first name and shoe size into appropriate variables.

This is done using the last of the format specifiers that I'll introduce, the asterisk (*). When used in conjunction with a format specifier, the asterisk allows you to ignore the data, rather than assigning it to a variable. The skipped data does not need to be matched to a variable in the parameter list, either.

So once the previous code has executed, you are left with "Guy" in the szFirstName variable and 42 in nShoeSize. The "Thompson" part of the input string is ignored completely—it is parsed but ignored.

Note that this skipping functionality skips over items only that are bound by whitespace. If you wanted to skip over five words, you would need to put five %*s character sequences in order to do so. Whitespace includes any space characters, carriage returns, and tabs that might be in the string.

This concludes the discussion of formatted console-based input and output for the time being. You are now well on your way to being able to create programs that can perform simple functions.

Code Sample 5.3: The PercentageCalculator Program

As a way of covering everything you have learned thus far, including console input and output, Code Sample 5.3 contains a simple program that calculates the percentage based on a maximum and partial value. So if you were to enter 100 and 10, the result would be 10%.

Before reading the code, you might like to think about which features of the C language are used to create the program. You need a way to:

- Read in values

- Store the values

- Perform the calculation

- Display the result

You might not like to restrict the users to small values, so you should use the largest integers possible to store data. The percentage is likely to be between 0 and 100, but it could also be a floating-point value, so that needs to be taken into account.

The code, PercentageCalculator.c, is included on the companion Web site and is reproduced here:

```c
// A Simple Percentage Calculator

#include <stdio.h>

int main ()
{
  long int lMaximumValue;
  long int lPartialValue;
  float fPercentage;

  printf("\nPercentage Calculator\n=====================");
  printf("\n\nPlease enter the Maximum value : ");
  scanf( "%ld", &lMaximumValue );

  printf("\nPlease enter the Partial value : ");
  scanf( "%ld", &lPartialValue );

  fPercentage = 100.0 * (double) lPartialValue;
  fPercentage /= (double) lMaximumValue;
```

```
printf("\n%ld is %.2f%% of %ld\n\n",

  lPartialValue, fPercentage, lMaximumValue);

return 0;
}
```

There are a few points to note in the calculation part of the program:

- The cast to a double data type.

- The use of the constant 100.0 rather than 100.

- The combination division operator /=.

If you play around with and understand the Percentage Calculator program, you will be well on your way to understanding some of the fundamental building blocks of C programming.

Some customizations to try might include:

- Taking the maximum and a percentage and calculating the partial value.

- Taking the percentage and partial value and calculating the maximum.

These customizations require you to rearrange the formulae slightly, based on the standard mathematical process for calculating percentages. Once you have the three programs working, you will have made strides towards becoming a C programmer!

Non-Formatted I/O

The first part of this chapter dealt with formatted input and output. The term *formatted* means that you are giving the computer some kind of representation, and it is putting it on the screen after having done some additional processing, such as:

- Padding

- Floating-point transformation

- Cropping

On the input side, you expect the formatted input functions to be able to format the input stream or input string to break it into pieces that are then assigned to variables.

Non-formatted input and output deal with the keyboard and screen as a character stream—they process each character one at a time, leaving the programmer to decide how the stream is to be interpreted. You can read one character at a time or a whole line at a time.

Character Processing

The character stream interface takes some explaining. One might assume that each character is processed at a time, but that is a common misconception. *The stream is not processed until the Enter key is pressed.*

Understanding this is key—the character input interface is constructed in such a way that the input functions that I present here will access a stream that has been closed. If the user chooses to press 10 keys before pressing the Enter key, there will be 10 key presses in the queue.

If you then call the function to retrieve a character only once, you'll retrieve only the first character from the input stream. If you call it twice, you'll retrieve two. If you call it and it returns a special value EOF, you know that there is nothing in the stream to retrieve.

You need to provide all the logic to process the stream; hence the term *unformatted.* Single characters are manipulated using the following functions:

```
char getchar();
char putchar();
```

The getchar function will return a character value or EOF. The special EOF value is defined in the stdio library and can be tested for as part of a conditional statement (covered in the next chapter).

To write a character to the output stream, you use the putchar function. This also returns a value, the only one of any real use being EOF, to indicate some kind of error. Usually, however, you do not test the return character from putchar if you are using the console interface.

Code Sample 5.4: The GetChar Program

The GetChar.c program is reproduced in Code Sample 5.4 (you can also get it from the companion Web site). This program uses getchar and printf to illustrate the properties of the character stream.

```
// Simple GetChar Illustration

#include <stdio.h>

int main ()
{
  char cCharIn;

  printf("TeleType - Enter a Character Below: \n\n");

  cCharIn = getchar();
  printf("You entered : %c \n", cCharIn);

  cCharIn = getchar();
  printf("You entered : %c \n", cCharIn);

  return 0;
}
```

You might try compiling the program and seeing what happens when an entire line of text is entered before pressing the Enter key. You'll notice from the second call that the stream still contains data, even after the user might assume that the stream has been emptied when he or she pressed the Enter key.

However, this is not the case. The incoming data will remain in the stream until the fflush function is called. This useful function is quite complex, but for now, let's just look at the generic call:

```
fflush ( stdin );
```

The stdin parameter simply instructs the operating system to flush the standard input buffer. Now, if the user inserts this call between the two getchar calls in the program, the user will notice that it pauses for input at the second call, because the buffer has been emptied, or *flushed,* by the call to fflush.

Code Sample 5.4 makes a call to printf with a character format specifier, but you could have used the companion function to getchar, putchar. The pair of calls would then become three lines:

```
cCharIn = getchar();
printf("You entered : ");
putchar( cCharIn );
```

There is no more complexity to putchar than that. Whichever single character is used as a parameter is placed in the output stream, standard out, or stdout. This value can be used in the call to fflush also, to tell the operating system to flush the output stream:

```
fflush ( stdout );
```

It can be useful to do this, just to be sure that the stream is empty before proceeding to process some other data, but it is less important than flushing the input queue. Processing lines of data in this way can be quite tedious, however, so it can sometimes be more convenient to use the string-handling equivalents.

String Processing

Because the input stream is usually terminated by pressing the Enter key—telling the operating system that you have finished typing for the time being—it makes sense to collect all the characters that might be in that stream in one go if at all possible. The gets function allows you to do this.

The generic definition for gets is as follows:

```
char * gets ( char * <string variable> );
```

You have not yet read about pointers, and it is quite an advanced topic that bears some explanation once you've gained more experience with C in general. In the case of the char * pointer, however, it does actually refer to something that you have seen before—an array of characters, otherwise known as a string.

String input and output are performed using the following functions from the stdio library:

```
char * gets ( char * <string variable> )
puts ( char * <string variable> )
```

In the call to gets, you pass the reference to the string, and the function returns a pointer to it. You can test that pointer to be sure that the function call has worked and that the user has entered some data—if it is NULL, either there was no data entered by the user or the call failed in some other way.

When the user enters the string, he or she will type some words, possibly with spaces between, and then press Enter. The string that is returned will have a null terminator and the return character removed. A null terminator is a special kind of character that has the value \0, or zero, and ends a string.

By testing for it, you can tell where the string ends, which allows you to place strings in memory as arrays and process them without knowing the length beforehand. Strings are covered in detail when you look at the string-processing library in Chapter 8.

By way of an example, here is a simple piece of code to read and display a string:

```
char szInputString[255];

gets( szInputString );
printf ( "You typed : ");
puts( szInputString );
```

There are many advantages of using the gets function over repeated calls to getchar or using scanf to achieve the same result. The reason is that you can read a whole line (at least until the user presses the Enter key) at once. If you use scanf, you can read the line only one word at a time, and if you use getchar, you need to empty the buffer.

There will be times when the other input and output functions are more appropriate, such as when the program needs to read in numbers; however, for strings, gets will be more convenient. For output, unless you need a character-by-character interface, printf is usually going to be the best choice.

Recap

This chapter covered the most useful functions available for the input and output of any basic built-in data type. By extension, this means that anything that can be displayed using a text interface or read from the keyboard can be processed using one of the functions presented here.

Often you'll need to decide between using formatted I/O, unformatted I/O, or a mixture. Formatted input is good for reading in numerical data or single words. It allows a direct translation from the input into a variable, quickly and easily.

Formatted input is not very good for processing lines of text when the user might make a mistake, because the amount of error checking that needs to be done makes it rather hard work. If you assume that your users are reasonably error prone or that you need to read in a whole line, including whitespace, a string-based stream-oriented approach is best: the gets function.

The other side of this is formatted output. Formatted output is usually the best option for writing data to the screen or anywhere else because it gives programmers the best chance of displaying the output as they want. The stream-based interfaces are harder work when precise control of mixed data needs to be output because it requires multiple calls and advanced calculation based on the number of characters output and the screen location.

Unformatted input at the character level means you need to manage the buffer, whereas the string-based unformatted input will simply grab the entire string. You need to be sure that the array (string) is big enough to take all the data, however.

Any time that you need mixed data input (numbers and strings), multiple calls to string-based unformatted input will usually be more helpful than formatted input in a single call, unless, of course, you are prepared to trust your users and do a lot of error checking.

The unformatted output at the character level is rarely useful unless you are creating a binary file or some other interface. At the string level, it can be faster than the formatted output, but when you need to mix data, you have to call a function like sprintf to prepare the string beforehand.

Armed with the functions and some guidelines as to which one to choose for the various programming tasks, you're now ready to tackle the more advanced topics relating to flow control.

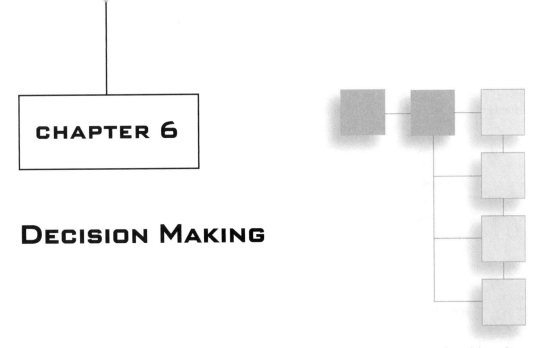

CHAPTER 6

DECISION MAKING

If you are making your way through the book sequentially, you should realize now that you know enough to write a program that has a beginning, middle, and end. It can take input from the users, do some processing, and return or display a result.

This in itself is an achievement. However, a computer is designed to make decisions, and I have not actually covered any decision-making facilities. You have read about the various operators available to test for the truth of a statement, but not how to combine that with C language keywords to actually evaluate a statement.

The aim of this chapter is to provide a thorough and complete discussion of the decision-making statements available to the C programmer.

After reading this chapter, you will understand all the decision-making processes that form an integral part of C programming. The statements covered here also provide a solid foundation for the discussion of looping mechanisms later on in the book.

Most of the decision-making statements used in C are applicable to both A-B type decisions as well as conditional testing for repetitive tasks. If you recall the egg-beating analogy, a recipe can tell you either to beat an egg 10 times or to beat it until it becomes fluffy.

In the latter case, you have a condition to test, and you should stop when you reach the condition (fluffy eggs). In the former case, you need to maintain some kind of counter and stop adding to it when it reaches 10, at which point the program can also stop what it's doing.

However, what happens if you are the chef in the kitchen, and you receive a bowl of half-beaten eggs from your kitchen helper? You need to decide whether the eggs are beaten enough to continue cooking or whether you have to stop and beat them some more.

This is an A-B decision, which is the kind of statement covered in this chapter.

The Basic if Statement

The premise behind decision making in programming is to allow conditional execution of a block of code. It is the equivalent of the programmer telling the computer "if <this> happens, I want you to do <that>."

This is an A-B type statement. It conveys a binary choice: There is no alternative. Once the condition is met, the code block will be executed. No matter how complex the condition that you are evaluating is, the final result is true or false. This kind of decision-making mechanism is called an if statement.

The if statement is the basic form of decision making in C. It allows the programmer to mark a set of statements for *conditional execution;* they will be evaluated only if a specific condition evaluates to true. The syntax is as follows:

```
if (<condition>)
{
    // Code statements
}
```

The <condition> clause can be a number of expressions ranging from simple value comparison to a *compound clause* comprising many statements. Compound clauses are the equivalent of adding multiple conditions to the if statement, rather like the equivalent of "If the eggs need beating AND I have time, I will beat them."

However, computers see the conditions in black and white, so they have no possibility to weigh the conditions so that an otherwise false evaluation might become true because one side of the condition outweighs the other. As a programmer, you have a number of comparison mechanisms that you have already seen, but the actual comparison steps can always be broken down into a set of A-B type clauses.

It is in the interest of beginning programmers to limit the use of compound clauses to promote coding clarity. On the other hand, they cannot be avoided completely because the programming process otherwise becomes a chore. Imagine a long program testing every possible combination of eventualities.

You'll read about compound if statements in detail later on. For now, let's continue with the basic mechanism. The code to be executed is enclosed in braces, as with all code blocks in C programming.

An example of a simple condition might be:

```
if ( nMyNumber == 42 )
{
  printf ( "Forty-two");
}
```

Remember the double equals == comparison operator tests for the equality of the arguments on the left and right sides. Of course, these arguments, or operands, can be comprised of variables, constants, function calls that return a value, and logical operations.

The other comparison operators that you read about in the previous chapter (==, !=, >=, <=, and so on) can also be used in if statements and are used extensively elsewhere in C programming. For example, as noted, they are also used in condition testing for exiting loops—another form of A-B condition test.

There is another acceptable syntax for the basic if statement that's worth noting here, because you'll likely encounter it when you look at existing code. If you do not have more than one statement that is to be executed, you can dispense with the braces. The statement becomes less of a code block and more a single statement to be executed:

```
if ( nMyNumber == 42 )
  printf ( "Forty-two");
```

This code block is identical to the previous example. Different programmers will have different viewpoints when it comes to this syntax. Some will embrace it, some will insist that the whole statement should be on the same line, and others will insist that programmers should always use braces for the sake of clarity.

You can decide for yourself which of the following variants you feel most comfortable with; functionally they are all the same:

```
// Variant #1a : With Braces
if ( nMyNumber == 42 )
{
  printf ( "Forty-two");
}

// Variant #1b : With Braces
if ( nMyNumber == 42 ) {
  printf ( "Forty-two");
}

// Variant #2 : No braces, indented
if ( nMyNumber == 42 )
  printf ( "Forty-two");

// Variant #3 : On a single line
if ( nMyNumber == 42 ) printf ( "Forty-two");
```

There are also many other variants, such as using braces, but with multiple code statements, all on one line; the C language *tokenizer* (which breaks the text into chunks that the compiler can understand) treats all whitespace as equal, and any layout options such as indenting and newlines are purely for the benefit of the programmers reading the code.

Subsequently, you have a lot of flexibility when it comes to building expressions— function return values can also be used in place of constants or variables, for example. This facility is very useful, especially when using the evaluation of non-scalar data types in an expression or those data types that have no built-in evaluation functions.

Scalars or other built-in data types from the limited list that C allows (integers, floating-point numbers, and characters) are all able to be evaluated directly. They have a discrete value that you can test against, whatever that test might be— equality, non-equality, greater than, less than, and so on.

However, the ability to use a user-defined or library function in a condition is vital in testing string values or complex data types that have no built-in evaluation functions. For example, to check whether a string contains a specific substring, you can use code such as this:

```
if ( strstr( szString, "elo" ) != NULL )
```

Even though you haven't read about string processing in detail, you can probably see that the new piece of code is the strstr function, along with a test against this curious value NULL. In plain English, the first part of the previous statement says "If the value in szString contains elo, then. . . ."

If you were to break apart the strstr function, you could refine this further, as "If you ask for the location of elo in szString and do not receive NULL, then. . . ."

The strstr function scans a string and returns the location in that string of the first occurrence of the string that you are searching for. If the string is not found, you obtain this curious NULL, or empty, value. You'll read about the string library in detail in later chapters, and look at NULL when you learn about pointers.

Compound Condition Statements

Recall that the operands on either side of the basic condition test can contain combinations of values to check. You combine these values to create a compound condition using something called *Boolean logic*. A Boolean value is either true or false, sometimes represented as a 1 or 0.

There is a set of operators in Boolean logic that can be used to combine two input values and return a single output value. If you've studied basic physics or electronics, you might find the following refreshingly familiar—these ideas are based around things called *logic gates*, which take two inputs that can be either high or low (1 or 0, true or false) and set the output to a value that is either high or low.

Don't worry, though, if you've never met logic gates before, because you're about to embark on a crash course in logic that will fill in the gaps.

When you study logic gates, you create tables, called *truth tables*, to help you ascertain, for a given collection of logic gates, what the various inputs and outputs will be. Certain outputs will provide the input to other gates, and a complex web of interdependencies can be built up.

In programming, you can do exactly the same thing, using operators to combine values together. Two operands, when combined with a logical operator, will yield a single value that you can then test for veracity like any other scalar value. Although there are many logical operators, the two most frequently used are AND and OR.

The truth table for the AND operator is shown in Table 6.1.

You can see from Table 6.1 that the output is true only if both inputs are true—the condition is satisfied only if both of the operands evaluate to true. In C programming, the AND logic operation is represented by the && symbol. It takes two operands, both of which must evaluate to 1 or 0, usually the result of a comparison.

If you have two integer inputs, you can construct a compound if statement to produce the same results as in Table 6.1.

```
if ( nInputOne == 1 && nInputTwo == 1 )
```

You can substitute the == for any of the comparison operators and the variables for anything that can be evaluated to a single value that you can test using those operators. The result will only be true when both the conditions are met.

In plain English, it is the equivalent of a decision statement like "If my car is dirty, and I have time, I will wash it."

The OR logical operation has a truth table shown in Table 6.2.

Table 6.1 The AND Truth Table

AND		
Inputs		Output
0	0	0
0	1	0
1	0	0
1	1	1

Table 6.2 The OR Truth Table

OR		
Inputs		Output
0	0	0
0	1	1
1	0	1
1	1	1

Again it is read in the same way, only this time the output is 1 when one or the other *or both* of the inputs is 1. Following the same process as before, you can construct a compound if statement to evaluate it as follows:

```
if ( nInputOne == 1 || nInputTwo == 1 )
```

The C language operator for the OR operation is the symbol ||. A plain language example of the OR operator is "If it is raining or windy, I will wear a coat."

We can also combine multiple OR and AND statements within a condition to build up a complex web of binary decisions. Imagine being confronted by the following:

```
if ( strstr ( szUserName, "admin" ) != NULL && nMail >= 1 || nMessage >= 1 )
```

Without even starting to determine what it might mean in practice, you might already deduce that there are three conditions. But what sequence are they to be evaluated in? Given the code statement, you would have to know or look up the precedence rules for the && and || operators. That way, you can decide if you were trying to say:

"If the user is the administrator and he or she has mail or a message"

or

"If the user is the administrator and he or she has mail, or if the user has a message"

The difference is subtle, but important: Perhaps you want to do something only if the user is an administrator *and* has either mail or a message. On the other hand, you might want to do something if the user is an administrator with mail or any other kind of user with at least one message.

For this reason, it is good practice to build up a compound statement as a collection of individual statements, enclosed in brackets. If you also put the individual conditions on different lines, you can easily see the true intention of the statement. In fact, what you meant to say was:

```
if ( ( strstr ( szUserName, "admin" ) != NULL && nMail >= 1)
    || nMessage >= 1 )
```

This is entirely different from:

```
if ( strstr ( szUserName, "admin" ) != NULL &&
    ( nMail >=1 || nMessage >= 1 ) )
```

It is much easier to see what the intentions are, however, when they are broken down and contained in brackets. The last Boolean operator covered in this section is the negation operation, or NOT. The NOT truth table is shown in Table 6.3.

Table 6.3 The NOT Truth Table

NOT	
Input	**Output**
0	1
1	0

Note that the NOT operator (the ! sign) takes only one operand and that it inverts the input. So a statement that evaluates to true will become false, and a statement that evaluates to false, true. You have come across the NOT operator before, combined with the = sign to create the "is not equal to" operator, !=.

Another important facet of the NOT operator is that in C programming it can be combined with integers and pointers. In other words, if you look back to the strstr function, you'll note that the empty value returned is, in fact, an empty pointer to a character string. Had the computer been able to find a string, the pointer would be a pointer to a character string. More explicitly, it's a pointer to the start of the substring that you're looking for.

In other words, to test for a value *not* being in a string, you can use:

```
if ( !strstr ( szUserName, "admin" ) )
```

Again, in plain English, this is equivalent to "If szUserName does not contain admin."

In this example, if the strstr function were to return a pointer not equal to NULL, the NOT operator would invert that, and the statement would evaluate to false, which means the if statement would not be true. On the other hand, a NULL pointer normally evaluating to a value other than false would be inverted to true, and the if statement would therefore be true.

At this point, if this seems a little confusing, don't worry too much, because you will have plenty of practice with Boolean logic, NOT operators, and if statements as you progress through the rest of the book. It quickly becomes second nature because it is one of the fundamental building blocks of C programming that you cannot escape.

The else **Keyword**

You could construct all your condition testing in programs with a series of compound if statements—after all, if you can test for one condition to be true, you can also test for it to be false and do something else. The if statement provides a *binary* condition test: The result is either true (1) or false (0). Based upon the result of the evaluation, the code that follows the condition is executed or not.

It is helpful, however, to have the possibility to selectively execute code as an alternative without having to create a specific condition for it. In other words, you would like to have the equivalent of the plain English:

"If it is raining then I will take an umbrella; otherwise, I will take sunglasses."

You can state this condition in two parts—if it is raining, then do this and if it is not raining, then do another thing. This method is quite cumbersome, however. If you need to provide alternative code to be executed if the condition test fails (returns false, or 0), you can use an else statement.

The else keyword is the equivalent of the English *otherwise*. It does not need any condition to test because it equates implicitly to the opposite of the if statement that precedes it. Hence, for each else statement, you need a partner if statement. This becomes obvious when you look at the following code:

```
if ( nMyNumber == 42 )
{
     // Condition TRUE code
}
else
{
     // Condition FALSE code
}
```

Again, as with other constructs, the code block to be executed is enclosed in braces. There is, as before, a variety of ways that you can lay out the code. If there is only one code statement to execute, you can dispense with the braces. A common variation on the previous code is the functionally equivalent:

```
if ( nMyNumber == 42 ) {
```

```
      // Condition TRUE code
}
else {
      // Condition FALSE code
}
```

It is also possible to place the entire set of statements on the same line:

```
if ( nMyNumber == 42 ) printf( "Forty Two" ); else printf( "Not Forty Two" );
```

This can be rendered unreadable if multiple conditions are used, along with lengthy code statements, and is probably best avoided. I mention it here to illustrate once again how the code tokenizing process offered by the C compiler works, and because you're likely to come across it when reusing other people's code.

The else syntax can be read as "either do this or do this" and still allows only a binary condition test, however complex that might be. You can only test for a value not being true; you cannot test for something else as an alternative without some additional code.

The else statement also provides a final catch-all condition for other decision constructs, as you'll see in due course. Before you move on, you need to look at another variant of else, called else if, which allows you to add a further refinement to the binary decision-making process.

Using else if

For cases when the simple binary condition test is not quite enough, an if statement can be refined with one or more else if clauses. These are similar to the else statement, except that they can also test for additional conditions. So, rather than having an A-B either-or type of test, you can add an additional dimension by testing a second condition.

Take a moment to consider the design implications of this mechanism; the two conditions do not need to be related in the same way that the if and else conditions are. In fact, the if condition in the else if statement can stand alone and test something entirely different.

The compiler and C language both allow this, but it can lead to quite convoluted coding if not used carefully. On the other hand, it will sometimes be necessary to construct a decision-making process that tests one variable or condition and, if that fails, go on to test for something entirely different.

It is a design decision to know whether this will be necessary. So wherever possible, you should restrict the different clauses to test variables that are at least on the same subject even if they are not testing the same variable or combination of variables. Of course, good commenting will help to clarify exactly what the logic is when it's not immediately apparent.

The else if statement is simply a combination of the else and if keywords, as the following snippet of code illustrates:

```
if ( nMyNumber == 42 )
{
    // Condition TRUE code
}
else if ( nMyNumber == 41 )
{
    // Alternative condition TRUE code
}
else
{
    // Condition FALSE catch-all code
}
```

In this example, there are three code blocks that could be executed, depending on the outcome of the conditions. The first condition tests for a specific value. Should that test fail, control passes to the next clause in the compound if statement. The next condition tests for another, different value, and if it succeeds, the middle block of code is executed.

Should the second test fail, control inevitably passes to the third, and final, code block. There could have been more else if statements, testing for various values of the variable, but only one of the associated code blocks will be executed. It is not possible, for example, to use this technique to selectively execute more than one code block.

You can, however, have as many else if conditions as you like, but only one else condition, and it must be the last part of the compound if statement. One word of caution—it is easy to lose track of the various conditions that the if statement contains if it extends down the page too far.

You'll see later on how you can mitigate this effect, but for now, it's time to take a look at another facet of C programming—nesting.

Nesting

A *nested* if statement forms part of a code block that is executed after the evaluation of another if, else, or else if clause. In other words, you can use an if statement inside another. Like a nest of tables, or Russian dolls contained one inside the other, nesting is a way to narrow down the result until you get to a point where you can execute some code.

It is always easier to show, rather than just describe, C programming, so here is a possible nested if statement:

```
if ( nValue < 10 )
{
    // Execute code

    if ( nValue < 5 )
    {
        // This will also execute
        // if the condition is satisfied.
    }
    // Code here would also be executed
}
```

There are two very important points to note. First, the nested if statement is treated as if it is in isolation. The code in the block that is executed after the first condition evaluates to true (if it does) and is treated as a block on its own. This means that you can include any kind of C statements that you have at your disposal, including another if statement.

The second point to note is that all the code in the block will be executed. So if you have tested a condition and executed a nested code block, once that block has been executed, the compiler continues to execute the code in the outer block.

One point to be very careful of when nesting to several levels: It can be easy to make a mistake in the logic, which will lead to unexpected behavior. Consider the following and try some hand execution to see what various values of nValue yield in terms of behavior:

```
if ( nValue < 5 )
{
```

```
    // Execute code

    if ( nValue > 5 )
    {
        // This code is unreachable
    }
    // Code here would be executed
}
```

Hopefully you realize that the inner nested code block will never be executed because the outer condition precludes the inner condition ever being satisfied. How can a value greater than five occur inside a code block that's executed only if the outer condition evaluates to true for values less than five?

The answer is never. With these simple values and conditions—a single variable, tested against constants—this conundrum is easy to spot. However, if you combine the nesting with compound statements that never test against constants and are full of variables, it can be very hard to see exactly what will happen for a given set of values.

To wrap up the discussion of nesting, note also that statements can be nested as many times as you like. However, the scope of any variables declared inside these code blocks (some compilers will not allow this) is restricted to that code block. So, for example, the following will not compile even if the compiler allows this:

```
if ( nOuterValue < 5 )
{
    // Execute code
    int nInnerValue = nOuterValue * 10;
    if ( nOuterValue > 20 )
    {
        int nInnerInnerValue = nOuterValue * 10;
        // Do something with nInnerInnerValue
    }
    printf ( "%d", nInnerInnerValue ); // ERROR : Out of scope
}
```

The nInnerInnerValue variable is in scope only when the second if statement has evaluated to true, which makes sense. The same is true outside the outer nest, where the nInnerValue variable is also not accessible. Again, this makes sense, because neither is initialized unless the code block that they are held inside is executed.

Finally, by the same token that you can nest as deeply as you like (within reason), you can also contain as many same-level nested if statements as you like, given that it is evaluated as a code block on its own. Again, the danger of deep nesting and long if statements is obvious, and trying to keep the code within one screen page is sound advice.

The switch statement is a good, clean alternative to all this deep nesting. It allows you to test multiple values against a single scalar variable and is the next topic in your exploration of C programming.

The switch **Statement**

The switch statement is a mechanism by which you can test a given scalar variable against a set of discrete values. If you have an integer variable that you want to test against a limited set of constant values, you have two choices:

- A series of if statements.

- A multipart switch statement.

The key points to note are that the switch statement is available only when you're testing for integer values, and you can only test for equality against a constant value. You cannot test for a variance (between one value and another), nor can you test floating-point values. The final restriction is that you cannot use a variable as a value to test against.

The generic syntax for the switch statement emulates multiple if/else if statements with a closing final else statement. The layout, however, is slightly easier to follow when a large number of conditions are involved. It is generally accepted to be both cleaner and more efficient and looks like this:

```
switch ( <condition> )
{
    // Case statements

    case <value_1>:
        // If <condition> is equal to <value_1>
      break;

    case <value_2>:
        // If <condition> is equal to <value_2>
      break;

    default:
        // If <condition> has not been matched
}
```

For the sake of comparison, the equivalent if/else if/else statement would look like this:

```
if ( <condition> == <value_1> )
{
    // Do something
}
else if ( <condition> == <value_2> )
{
    // Do something else
}
else
{
    // Default processing
}
```

Comparing the two approaches, you can see that the switch statement produces code that is easier to manage. If you needed to change the condition for some reason, you would need to change only a single case statement, but you would need to alter multiple if conditions.

Looking at the switch statement line by line, you can see that the first line, the switch keyword itself, contains the condition that you want to test. It must be included in brackets and must evaluate to a single value, but it can contain any expression, including mathematical operators, constants, variables, and function calls.

Each case keyword must be followed by a constant value that you are to test the condition for, followed by a colon :. If the case evaluates to true, with the value clause being exactly equal to the value you are testing for, all the code following it is executed. Execution continues until a break keyword is encountered.

The default keyword is used to indicate that, if all else fails, you have some default processing that must be executed instead. It does not need to be followed by a break statement, as it is normally the last part of the switch statement. However, that is not mandated, but if for some reason you want to put the default clause at the top of the condition block, the associated code block must end with a break statement.

This last point is very important. The break keyword serves two purposes—to stop execution after all the statements have been processed as a result of an evaluation of the condition and to allow you to selectively execute code in a cumulative fashion. This is shown in the following:

```
switch ( nValueToTest )
```

```
{
    // Case statements

    case 1 :
        // If <condition> is equal to <value_1>
        printf ( "1" );
    break;
     case 2 :
        // If <condition> is equal to <value_2>
        printf ( "2" );
    break;
    case 3 :
    case 4 :
        printf ( "3 or 4" );
     break;

    default:
        // If <condition> has not been matched
        printf ( "0" );
}
```

In this snippet, you can simulate what will happen based on a variety of input values for nValueToTest. Assuming that it varies between 1 and 5, Table 6.4 shows the result for various values of nValueToTest.

If you experiment with the SwitchTest.c code from the companion Web site and compile it with various values for nValueToTest, you can check that the code does indeed produce the results in Table 6.4. However, if you remove the break statements, something curious happens. For an input value of 1, the following is output:

    123 or 40

Table 6.4 Testing switch Statements

Input, nValueToTest ==	Output to Screen
1	"1"
2	"2"
3	"3 or 4"
4	"3 or 4"
5	"0"

Table 6.5 Testing switch Statements Without Breaks

Input, nValueToTest ==	Output to Screen
1	"123 or 40"
2	"23 or 40"
3	"3 or 40"
4	"3 or 40"
5	"0"

The execution sequence is as follows. If the first case statement evaluates to true, no further case statements are evaluated. They are all treated as evaluating to true until either:

- The end of the code block.

- A break statement is encountered.

You can see the result in Table 6.5.

So the break statement is very important. Some programmers will go a step further and also include the code blocks that are executed as a result of a case statement evaluating to true in braces. For the final code snippet of the chapter:

```
switch ( nValueToTest )
{
    // Case statements
    case 1 : {
        // If <condition> is equal to <value_1>
        printf ( "1" );
    }
    break;
     case 2 : {
        // If <condition> is equal to <value_2>
        printf ( "2" );
    }
    break;
    case 3 : {
    case 4 : {
        printf ( "3 or 4" );
    } }
```

```
        break;

    default:
        // If <condition> has not been matched
        printf ( "0" );
}
```

The multiple-choice nature of the last two `case` statements reveals the slight clumsiness of this approach, but it does have the advantage of making code blocks associated with other `case` statements a little clearer. It does not, however, change the way the code blocks are executed—you still need to include the `break` statements when you want the computer to abandon execution of the `switch` statement.

So the `switch` statement allows you to test for various values but also to group values together to execute code that is applicable to several cases. You can insert code between them, in the following manner:

```
case 3 :
    printf (" Processing 3..." );
case 4 :
    printf ( " Processing 3 and 4" );

  break;
```

If you test for a value of 4, the case 3 code will not be executed. However, if you test for a value of 3, the case 3 code will be executed, followed by the case 4. If you insert a `break` statement between the end of the case 3 code and the next `case` statement, the behavior will revert to the standard case-by-case processing.

This is a powerful mechanism when processing like values, but it needs to be used with care because the order of the statements becomes vitally important. However, as with multiple `if` statements and nested conditions, good design will help make the best use of this mechanism.

Recap

For simple condition testing, the `if`/`else` statements provide a way to selectively execute code based on one or more conditions. These conditions can be a test of a single value against a variable, two variables, or complex compound statements combined with Boolean logic. The code is executed only if the condition evaluates to true; the final outcome is binary in nature.

Nesting of if statements is allowed, allowing you to build up several depths of decision making rather than having too many complex compound conditions. You can also have multiple single-level if statements within another if statement code block, allowing you to select between values.

The else if mechanism allows for the possibility to test another value in case the original if fails (evaluates to false), with a final else statement allowing for execution of code when no other conditions match. Quite long multiple if... else if... else if... else code blocks are possible, which is why there is another, more elegant solution.

Where there are many possible but discrete possibilities, you can use a switch construct. This includes mechanisms such as message processing—keyboard handling, for example. However, the switch condition statement is limited to the scalar values of built-in types. This means that if you need to evaluate strings, floating-point numbers, or user-defined data types, you have no choice but to use multiple if statements.

The various decision-making constructs provide a way for you to selectively control the flow of execution through a program. The condition testing mechanism also provides the basis for many other useful programming constructs, such as loops. The possibility to test conditions and evaluate them with Boolean logic is a core building block of C programming.

Finally, you can combine any of these techniques, placing multiple switch statements inside each other, nesting if and switch statements, and using complex conditions to test against. The only restriction is that case labels have to be used with a constant value, determined at design time.

You need to be careful when you create decision flows based on combining case and if constructs within the same code block, because such flows can lead to unintended consequences. Testing is vital in order to ensure that the correct decision path through the code is being taken.

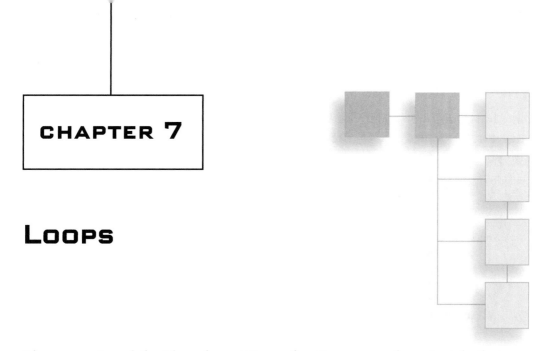

CHAPTER 7

LOOPS

I have mentioned the idea of repetition a few times now, the principle that you can ask the machine to perform the same task over and over for either a set number of times or until a condition is satisfied. Recall the analogy of beating eggs until they are fluffy; it is a loop in a cooking instruction.

In C programming, you have code blocks that can be executed a set number of times or until a given condition evaluates to true. This last mechanism uses the same kind of condition testing as the if statement that you saw in the previous chapter, so that should be familiar territory.

So the aim of this chapter is to discuss the various looping statements that C provides.

This chapter represents the built-in keywords and statements available to C programmers and used to control the flow of execution within a code block. The goal of this chapter is to give you an appreciation of the looping possibilities available and the ways that they can be applied, as well as an understanding of loops compared to other techniques for selectively executing code.

The for **Loop**

The classic loop construct is known as a *counted* loop, and the for loop is the only such construct provided by the C language. This is the equivalent of telling the computer that you want to execute the same block of code a set number of times. You can count up or down, in single steps or multiples of steps.

So you can loop from 1 to 10:

```
1   2   3   4   5   6   7   8   9   10
```

You can also loop from 10 to 1:

```
10   9   8   7   6   5   4   3   2   1
```

Or you can loop forwards or backwards, skipping every second number:

```
1   3   5   7   9
```

Note that even though the start and end points are the same (1 and 10, respectively), when you skip numbers, you loop fewer times. If you were to execute code on each of the numbers, you would only execute it five times, rather than 10. In the last example, because it's skipping one number each time, the loop reaches the number 9—the next number would have been 11, but that's too big for a loop that is only supposed to go up to 10.

You might be thinking that this is a bit abstract and doesn't relate to the programming tasks you might encounter. So here is a quick analogy. Let's assume you have an address book application, and you want to flick through it to find an entry.

You read about arrays in Chapter 4, and one method for storing an address book might be as an array. Don't worry what goes in each slot for now, just assume it is an array of names and phone numbers. An array of strings, if you like.

To look for an entry, knowing that you have 100 to go through, you might choose to start at the first one and use a counted loop to look at each one in turn. If you get to the end without finding the entry you need, it isn't there.

However, you have to look at each one. Instead of doing this, you might adjust the routine a little bit. Assuming that the array is sorted alphabetically, you could look at every second or third entry and then stop when the name you process appears *alphabetically* after the one you're looking for.

Having gone too far, you then work back through the array (a reverse-counted loop) until you either get to the start or find the name you want. This is one use for a counted loop—as a way to index, into arrays.

A variable is used to count the number of iterations (the index, for example). When you design a for loop, you need to decide three important characteristics:

- The starting value of the variable.

- The operation on the variable.

- A comparison test of the variable to end the loop.

The comparison test can be any of the standard comparison operators that you are now familiar with:

== Equal to

!= Not equal to

< Less than

> Greater than

<= Less than or equal to

>= Greater than or equal to

The operation part can be any of the mathematical operators, in combination (usually) with the variable that you are testing against. This can include any of the mathematical operators in the long or short form or other expressions that evaluate to a single value. This value must match the type of the variable being used to keep track of the number of iterations that you have performed.

The general form for a for loop is as follows:

```
for ( <variable> = <starting_value>;
     <condition test>;
     <operation> )
    {
        // Code statements
    }
```

In this snippet, ⟨variable⟩ refers to a variable of a built-in type (int, float, char, and so on), the ⟨condition test⟩ checks to see whether a value has been attained (or passed), and the ⟨operation⟩ defines the operation to be applied to the variable. This operation can be any operation supported by the data type used for the counting variable and is known as the *step*.

If, for example, you wanted to print each letter in the range a to z, you could use code such as the following:

```
char cLetter;
for ( cLetter = 'a'; cLetter <= 'z'; cLetter++)
{
    printf( "%c", cLetter );
}
```

Note that the compiler is quite happy to treat the character data type as a number (with the value equal to the ASCII code of the character) or as a character value. This implicit internal cast is used fairly frequently in programming but cannot be applied to entire strings because they are arrays of a data type, and as such are not scalar.

This example uses the <= operator because we wanted the program to print every letter. Had you used the < operator, the program would have stopped at y because the evaluation of the variable is performed at the top of the loop, with the variable value updated at the end of the loop.

If you wanted to print out every second letter starting at z and going back to a, you could use:

```
char cLetter;
for ( cLetter = 'z'; cLetter >= 'a'; cLetter -= 2)
{
    printf( "%c", cLetter );
}
```

Both of these examples use short forms of the + and – operators—in the first instance a post-increment, and in the second a combination (– and =, with a 2 as the second operand). Most for loops that you'll encounter are constructed in this way; many learning programmers are taught how to use the post-increment operator before they really know what it means.

So as an aside, you might need a slight recap on possible variable operation notation. You've met the various forms before, but it is worth refreshing your memory. The following are equivalent:

```
cLetter++
cLetter = cLetter + 1
cLetter += 1
```

The following are also equivalent:

```
cLetter = cLetter - 2
cLetter -= 2
```

All of these example use a variable in conjunction with a constant value. However, you can introduce a variable step by providing a for statement constructed as follows:

```
int nCounter, nStep;
// Code statements . . .
for ( nCounter = 0; nCounter < 10; nCounter += nStep )
```

This example adds the value of nStep to nCounter at the end of each iteration. If nStep is 1, the program will count from 0 to 9, which is a loop of 10 iterations. On the other hand, if you assign a value of 5 to nStep, you will have the following:

Iteration	1	2	3
nCounter	0	5	10

This is one aspect to be careful of when constructing for loops. Usually, you use a zero-based index (that is, you start at 0) and test against a value that is the actual number of steps that you require. For 10 steps, you start at 0 and add 1 while the counter is less than 10; this is almost a tradition in C programming, but there are reasons for it.

For example, if you had code similar to the following:

```
int cLetterIndex;
for ( cLetterIndex = 1; cLetterIndex <= 26; cLetterIndex++)
{
     printf( "%c", cLetterIndex + 'a' );
}
```

If you were to hand execute this code, you would find that it does not quite do what you might expect. The reason is that you have started by loading the cLetterIndex variable with 1. In natural language, when you count, you start with 1, so it is logical to do the same in a computer program.

However, in the previous example, the first letter to be displayed would be b, and the last one would be the character code equivalent to z + 26. Clearly not what was intended. In order to get back to the original definition, you would need to use a clumsy fix such as:

```
printf( "%c", (cLetterIndex - 1) + 'a' );
```

This is why programmers tend to use a zero-based index almost by habit. It makes any subsequent code that needs to use the counter easier to apply.

Finally, consider some variables in other areas. One such variation can be to provide variables for the starting and ending values:

```
int nCounter, nStep, nStart, nEnd;
// Code statements to set variables . . .
for ( nCounter = nStart;
        nCounter < nEnd;
        nCounter += nStep )
```

However, it should be noted that there is no equivalent mechanism to introduce a variable condition. In other words, if you specify that the variable should be incremented, it will always be incremented; you cannot specify a value that would cause it to be decremented instead.

You contain the code block to be executed during each for iteration in braces following the for statement itself. This follows the C language standard and should be very familiar to you.

There are two points to be wary of when using for loops. The first is that the counter variable is in scope during the loop, and so it could feasibly be changed during each loop cycle. This is a valid technique in some cases, but you need to be very aware of what it is you are trying to achieve, because the compiler will not pick up on this (legal) behavior.

This is especially important when checking for inequality against a value, as you could skip over the target value accidentally. This is illustrated in the following piece of code:

```
int nCounter;
for ( nCounter = 0; nCounter != 9; nCounter++ )
{
```

```
        nCounter += 1; // Don't do this!
}
```

This loop will never exit. It will enter something known as an *infinite loop*, which means that it will never stop. The code will start at 0 and add 1 to it in the execution of the code block. When that execution has finished, the for loop will then add 1 to nCounter *again*, meaning that the loop will add 2 to it during each cycle.

Hence, the counter will go from 0 to 2 to 4 to 6 to 8 to 10 and on and on. Because it is never equal to 9, the end condition will never evaluate to true, and the loop will go on forever.

There is a place for infinite loops in programming, but they are very rare and considered by some to be bad style. In fact, it is almost always possible (and indeed preferable) to find a non-infinite alternative solution.

A related issue is to always ensure that the correct operation is used in conjunction with the condition being tested. For example, another unintentional infinite loop might be:

```
int nCounter;
for ( nCounter = 0; nCounter != 10; nCounter- - )
{
        // Code statements
}
```

Because the start value is 0 and the end value is 10, if the counter counts down as opposed to up, the condition will never be satisfied. This is another area in which it is easy to make a mistake—a mistake the compiler isn't likely to identify.

One last point to note before you look at non-counted loops. The compiler will compile a for loop without complaining, even if all the parts of the for statement operate on entirely different variables. So if you were to use nCounter as the starting variable and test nOutput against a condition while incrementing nInput, the compiler will happily generate the code.

If you're having trouble conceptualizing this, consider the following code:

```
int nCounter, nInput, nOutput;
for ( nCounter = 0; nOutput != 10; nInput- - )
{
        // Code statements
}
```

This code is legal but probably not very useful to someone trying to maintain the code and is probably the result of a design error. Unless you go to great lengths to make sure that you correctly update nOutput, the chances of the loop doing what you intend are very slim.

This kind of code construction can sometimes be the result of evolving code that started out well designed but has run awry during the development process. In fact, it is no longer really a counted loop at all and would be better serviced with another kind of loop, called the while loop, discussed next.

The while Loop

The first of the uncounted loops that you'll read about is the while loop. In this context, an uncounted loop is simply one where you might not know in advance how many iterations you need to perform, but you can test for a condition that will enable you to determine that the loop is complete, in other words, that it has repeated enough times to perform a given task.

A while loop consists of a condition to be evaluated and a set of statements, contained in braces, that are executed until the condition evaluates to false (in other words, fails). So while the condition is true, you continue to execute the associated code block.

The condition that you test can be anything that could be used in an if statement. This might include variables, constants, or compound statements combined with Boolean logic, but must evaluate to true or false. Therefore, one of the comparison operators that you have seen will have to be used in the condition.

Here's the general form for the syntax of the while loop:

```
while (<condition test>)
    {
        // Code statements
    }
```

The <condition test> is evaluated at the start of the loop. This is the same as the for loop. Each time the loop iterates, the condition is re-evaluated before the program decides whether to execute the code in braces again. It is very important to remember that, if the condition never evaluates to false, the loop will never end.

Therefore, any variable that is in the condition statement should be altered within the code block. There are exceptions to this, usually relating to return values from functions, that you'll look at when you read about other aspects of programming, but in general you'll be testing for a value that is created *outside* the loop and altered *inside* the loop.

In order to illustrate the while loop, I constructed one that is designed to emulate the behavior of the a-to-z for loop that you saw in the previous section. The following code snippet will display the same letters as in the previous example.

Before jumping ahead to the code, you might want to go back and review the for loop presented in the early part of the chapter. The while equivalent is as follows:

```c
char cLetter = 'a';
while ( cLetter <= 'z' ) // Less than or equal to . . .
{
    // Code statements
    printf ( "%c", cLetter );
    cLetter++;
}
```

As noted, the important points are that:

- You initialize cLetter outside the loop.

- The condition evaluates to true or false.

- You modify cLetter inside the loop.

You must initialize cLetter outside the loop because otherwise it would not be in scope for the condition test, and even if it were, it would not be initialized before the first pass of that condition test. By way of another example, the reverse for loop illustrated in the previous section can also be written as a while loop:

```c
int nCounter = 0;
while ( nCounter != 10 )
{
    // Code statements
    nCounter--;
}
```

These examples always place the statement that modifies the variable used to test for completion of the loop after the other code lines. The decision as to where to put this variable will depend on whether it is to be used as part of the code block that performs a given task. This being the case, you should use the most relevant value—the one against which the condition was tested.

This is most often the case. It is rare to find that the variable that has just been tested to see if the loop can be exited is updated before being used to perform a specific task. For example, if you were to place the statement that prints the letters from a to z *before* the printing statement, you would get the following output:

```
bcdefghijklmnopqrstuvwxyzA
```

The reason for skipping the first a is that the cLetter variable has been incremented before the printf statement is executed. By the same token, the comparison of cLetter against z in the last iteration of the loop succeeds, but because the variable is then immediately incremented, it goes beyond the a-to-z range.

Every letter in between is displayed as one higher than you would expect, as a side-effect of incrementing the variable in the wrong place. You might think that (as in a for loop) because a post-increment operator is used, the increment would be performed after the code block has executed, but this is not the case.

In this example, the result is not disastrous; however, if you were using a numerical index into an array of a limited size, the result might easily lead to the application crashing, as it overstepped the bounds of the array.

Note that the for loop is just a convenient implementation of a while loop using a variable to count iterations. There are good reasons to use a for loop instead of a while loop, as long as you update and test the variable in the for statement and don't alter it in the main body of the code block.

If you respect this rule, there will be less chance of entering an infinite loop, and it will be far easier to debug (find errors). However, you do need to be able to express the constraints at design time (start, end, and increment/decrement/ other operation), even if the actual values are not known until runtime.

Generally, a for loop is more applicable for counted loops, and a while loop and its variants are more suited to applications whereby the value being tested is indirectly affected by the code within the braces, or where there's a test for a binary value (true/false).

Such indirect modification may be the result of a function call, for example, which can be used in a for loop condition, but which makes the implementation unnecessarily complex.

The while loop that you have examined here has one possible drawback. There is no guarantee that the code block will be executed at all. Think of it this way: Suppose you create a menu system and want to display the current menu. You wait for a key press; if that key press is X, for example, the user wants to exit the program.

The code might look something like the following:

```
char nChoice;
while ( nChoice != 'x' )
{
    // Code statements
    // Display menu
    nChoice = getchar();
    fflush(stdin); // Empty the buffer
}
```

Unless you initialize nChoice prior to entering the loop (which is easy to do), you have no way of knowing if the loop will execute. In this case, it is easy to fix, but more complex programs might prove more challenging. If you need to be sure that the loop will be executed *at least* once, you have to use a different kind of while loop.

More do and while

Whereas a while loop evaluates the termination condition before the code block is executed (at the top of the loop), it makes sense to evaluate that condition at the *end* of the code block when you need to be sure that the loop will execute *at least* once. In other words, you want the condition to be evaluated at the bottom of the loop.

A do . . . while loop consists of a set of statements contained within braces that are executed for as long as a given condition evaluates to true (that is, it succeeds). The do keyword starts the loop, and the while statement provides the condition testing mechanism and is identical to the while statement that might appear at the top of the loop in place of the do.

All that's been done here is that the termination condition evaluation has been moved to the end of the loop, and the computer has been instructed to execute the code block (via the do keyword). The general form for a do . . . while loop is as follows:

```
do
{
    // Code statements

} while (<condition test>);
```

The computer starts at the do keyword, processes the code block, and then tests the condition at the end. So you know that it will process the code block once, at the very least. The same caveats apply—you must be sure that you can test a value that is in scope at the time the do loop is entered and that the value being tested makes sense. For example, there is nothing stopping you from writing code such as:

```
do
{
    // Code statements

} while ( 1 == 1);
```

This snippet will loop forever, because the statement 1 == 1 will always evaluate to true. This is a valid technique, as you'll see later on, but with some specific usage restrictions. It is also easy to see in the previous example that the evaluation is a constant true value, but the more complex the condition is, the harder it becomes to see whether the intention matches the implementation.

Another point to note is that there is a trailing ; (semicolon) on the line containing the while statement. This is a syntactic requirement that is not applicable in a standard while loop, which is followed by a code block. Any keyword or definition that is followed by a code block does not need a trailing semicolon.

However, those statements that are not followed by an enclosed code block must be terminated with a semicolon. I mention it because a compiler will not flag an error if the semicolon is included by accident. The tokenizing of the code will still be correct, but the behavior could prove wildly incorrect.

Consider, for example, the following code:

```
while ( <condition test> );
```

```
{
    // Code statements
}
```

This code illustrates a fairly common error that beginning programmers make. If the condition evaluates to true, the trailing semicolon forces the execution to end and the condition to be re-evaluated. Because no code has been executed, the condition will again evaluate to true, and the program will become stuck in an endless loop.

Many compilers will generate a warning, which might not be reported if the programmer has turned off this mechanism.

By the same token that you can create a counter for a loop equivalent to a while loop, you can also create one for a do . . . while loop. It is a little more involved, and there are some subtle differences.

A counted loop using the do . . . while construct might look like this:

```
int nCount = 0;
do
{
    // Code statements

    nCount += 1;

} while ( nCount < 10 );
```

This code fragment will execute exactly 10 times (nCount has values from 0 to 9). The placement of the statement that modifies the variable to be tested is important if that variable is used by statements inside the braces.

This is a similar concern to the while loop, but with slightly different consequences. If you reconstruct the a-to-z loop using a do . . . while construct, you could arrive at code similar to the following snippet:

```
char cLetter = 'a';
do
{
    // Code statements
    printf ( "%c", cLetter );
    cLetter++;
} while ( cLetter <= 'z' );
```

This code will print out the characters a to y. The z will be dropped because the condition is tested immediately after the increment is applied. So rather than put the increment at the end of the loop, what happens if you put it at the start of the loop? You might try to work that out before looking at the following example code:

```
char cLetter = 'a';
do
{
    // Code statements
    cLetter++;
    printf ( "%c", cLetter );

} while ( cLetter <= 'z' );
```

Again, this does not quite do what you might intend. Instead the code will print out b through z. The a is being dropped because of the increment happening before the `printf` statement. The solution is to have the program exit the loop when it has printed out z, and not before.

The clue is in the test for the condition by which you terminate the loop. You want to test for a value that is greater than z. This brings its own problems but luckily works in this instance. One case where it would not work is if you arrived at the end of a range; in the case of the `char` data type, this is at the character with ASCII code 254.

Luckily, there's another mechanism at your disposal that lets you test explicitly and quit a loop that might overrun the boundary of an array, index, or range. The following two keywords, `break` and `continue`, work within any loop and provide a greater degree of control over the repetition mechanisms available to C programmers.

Using `break` **and** `continue`

Recall the `break` keyword from the discussion of the `switch . . . case` conditional execution construct that you saw in Chapter 6. In that context it was used to exit the construct and resume normal program execution with the statement immediately following the closing brace of the `switch` code block. It usually followed a `case` statement in such instances.

The address book example from the counted loop section would also benefit from the break keyword. Rather than just storing the index of the found entry, you could choose to jump out of the loop and save a few cycles of precious processing time.

The break keyword has the same functionality inside a while loop—it stops execution. You could use a break statement to halt a for loop, as follows:

```
for (n = 0; n < 100; n++)
{
        // Some code
        if ( <condition> )
        {
        // <condition> is true, so exit
        break;
        }
}
```

In this snippet, execution of the loop will halt at the break keyword. Program execution will then restart directly after the loop (after the closing brace }), leaving the values for the various variables used intact. A premature exit from the loop can then be tested for by evaluating for one of those variables, as long is it is in scope.

Typically, this usage is reserved for cases where some unintended behavior has been encountered, and continuing to process the loop will lead to an unrecoverable error. If you know the bounds of an array or the range of values allowed in a data type, you now have a mechanism to break out of the loop if you are about to test a value that might lead to that class of error.

The partner keyword to break is continue. The continue keyword also halts the current cycle of the loop. However, it does not cause the program to continue execution after the code block but returns control to the start of the loop in the next iteration. In a for loop, this would mean that control passes to the for statement, which would be evaluated as if the code inside the loop had come to a natural end.

By way of example, the following code prints alternate numbers in a counted sequence:

```
for ( n   = 0; n < 10; n++ )
{
        if ( n % 2 == 0 ) // Even number
        {
```

```
            // Stop this cycle, back to top
            continue;
        }
        printf ( "%d ", n );
    }
```

This snippet will print only the odd numbers from 0 to 9 and is the core of the ForTest.c program supplied on the companion Web site (www.courseptr.com; click on the Downloads button). The equivalent of this example using a `while` loop and the `continue` keyword is supplied on the Web site, too, in the While-Test.c source file. The core of that program is repeated here:

```
int n = 0;
while ( n < 10 )
{
    n++;
    if ( n % 2 == 0 ) // Even number
    {
        // Stop this cycle, back to top
        continue;
    }
    printf ( "%d ", n );
}
```

If you play around with the code and try different values for the variable and the constants involved, you'll soon realize that this implementation is inadequate. For example, if you change the starting value to 1, the first number in the expected sequence will not be printed. This is because the increment is before the condition test associated with the `continue` keyword.

On the other hand, if you put the increment statement after the `continue`, as long as the `n % 2 == 0` condition evaluates to true, the loop will run infinitely between the `while` statement and the `continue` keyword. In this case, a `for` loop is preferable because having to check all the various limits and possible problems results in a large amount of error-prone condition testing code.

Clearly, the `continue` statement has its uses, but great care needs to be taken when deploying it. To round off the set, the DoTest.c file has the same approach, but with a do . . . `while` loop. Again, the core is reproduced here:

```
int n = 0;
do
```

```
{
    n++;
    if ( n % 2 == 0 ) // Even number
    {
        // Stop this cycle, back to top
        continue;
    }
    printf ( "%d ", n );
} while ( n < 10 );
```

This works as intended, but you might want to play around with it to see whether the shortcomings are the same as in the while loop example. The trick is in determining whether the termination condition test is reachable. In these examples, that is quite easy, but the more complex the relationship between the variables, the more difficult it becomes.

Finally, a common use for these kinds of loops is in menu processing. More advanced programs will usually have a menu at the core. Such a program (containing only a menu loop) is included in the MenuTest.c source file:

```
int nChoice = 'x';
do
{
    // Print the menu
    printf ( "Menu\n\n1 : Do something\n2 : Save and Quit\n\n\nE(x)it\n" );
    nChoice = getchar();
    fflush ( stdin );
    // Test the value
    switch ( nChoice )
    {
        case '1':
                printf ( "User chose Option 1\n\n" );
        break;

        case '2':
                printf ( "User chose Save & Quit\n\n" );
                printf ( "\tSaving. . .\n");
                nChoice = 'x';
        break;

        case 'x':
                printf ( "User chose exit.\n\n" );
        break;
```

```
        default:

                printf ( "\n\nInvalid Option Selected\n\n" );
            break;
    }
} while ( nChoice != 'x' );
```

The execution sequence is very easy to follow. The default choice is set to x, just to be sure that it contains a valid selection at the outset. The menu is displayed; the users can press a key followed by the Enter key. The choice is evaluated, and depending on the option selected, a message is displayed.

Where the execution is interesting is when the users choose option 2; the nChoice variable is set to x. This causes the while loop to exit. As an exercise, you might like to determine what happens when a break keyword is replaced with continue. It does not behave quite as you might expect.

By placing some strategic printf statements in the code to display the changing value of the nChoice variable, you should be able to determine what the computer is doing when it encounters the continue statement and where it goes from there. This is a valuable exercise that shows:

- How to print debug values.

- How to follow execution through code.

- How to use break and continue.

As an aside, you could also have used the following statement at the top or bottom of the loop:

```
while ( 1 == 1 )
```

This would create an infinite loop—quite typical in menu system code that the reader might want to reuse—but would also need an explicit break statement to exit. However, that break statement would have to occur outside of the switch construct in an if statement.

Otherwise, it would be confused with the break statements designed to end case selections. For example, at the end of the loop, you might have the following

```
if ( nChoice == 'x' )
    break;
```

The decision to choose one or the other approach is left up to you, as are so many choices in a programming language with many different ways to achieve the same results. However, it is easier to debug a program with explicit tests on variable values as termination conditions, rather than use an infinite loop and break keywords.

Nesting Loops

In Chapter 6, you read about a technique called nesting, where you were able to put conditions within conditions as a substitute for using multiple conditions, logically combined together. Loops can also be nested, but you don't nest to avoid nested conditions. You nest loops because you need to do additional repetitive work within an outer loop.

So you have a nest of loops where the outermost loop will be executed first (one iteration), and then the inside loop will be executed until it reaches a conclusion. Control is then returned to the outer loop. In this way, the inner loop is executed *n* times for every pass of the outer loop.

Figure 7.1 depicts loop nesting in a diagram format.

If you execute the outer loop in Figure 7.1 10 times and the inner loop 5 times, a piece of code inside the inner rectangle will be executed $10 \times 5 = 50$ times. If you have an outer or inner loop that is uncounted—in other words, that exits on a condition that you cannot know the dimension of beforehand—the number of times that same piece of inner-inner code is executed becomes more difficult to predict.

A typical use of a nested loop is to move through an *n*-dimensional array of a known size (such as a screen buffer). Using the standard 80×25 screen grid, you can construct a screen buffer as follows:

```
char cScreenBuffer[25][80];
```

Recall the [][] notation for arrays from Chapter 4. The previous has an array of two dimensions, with 80 columns and 25 rows, each containing one char type of data. If you wanted to print out the array from top to bottom, recall that as long as the last character in each line (row) is a \0 null terminator, you can simply use printf.

To print the first line, you would use a call such as:

```
printf ( "%s", cScreenBuffer[0] );
```

Outer Loop

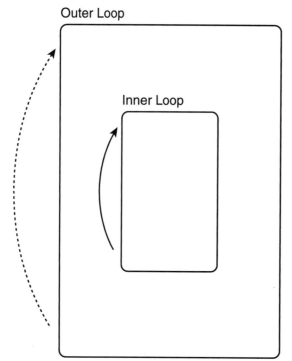

Inner Loop

Figure 7.1
Loop Nesting

If you wanted to print out the whole screen, you could duplicate this code and change the index to 1, 2, 3 . . . 24 and achieve the goal. However, if you needed to change the printf statement in any way, you would be presented with a lot of cut and paste operations.

Instead, with the possibility to use a loop to run through all the indexes, you can construct code such as the following snippet:

```
for ( nRow = 0; nRow < 25; nRow++)
{
    printf ( "%s", cScreenBuffer[nRow] );
}
```

This prints the screen update one line at a time. However, there may be times when you want more control—one character at a time—for example, if you need to check and/or translate each element in the array before displaying it. To do that, you need to construct a nested loop to move through each individual cell in the array.

The following illustrates moving through the two-dimensional screen buffer array:

```
char cScreenBuffer [ X_DIMENSION] [ Y_DIMENSION ];

for ( nRow = 0; nRow < Y_DIMENSION; nRow++ )
{
    for ( nCol = 0; nCol < X_DIMENSION; nCol++ )
    {
        printf ( "%c", cScreenBuffer [ nRow ][ nCol ] );
    }
}
```

Note at this point that the nesting order is usually very important, especially when dealing with a nested loop operating on strings. Assume that you accidentally swapped nRow and nColumn and arrived at the following statement:

```
printf ( "%c", cScreenBuffer [ nCol ][ nRow ] );
```

This statement would take letters first from the column and then the row, rather than the other way around. It might also run outside the bounds of the array because the dimensions are probably different.

The same is true of the order of nesting the loops, but without the array-overrun problem; the result is still not quite correct. Instead of evaluating the array from top to bottom and then left to right, if you change the nesting order, the program would evaluate the array from left to right, and then top to bottom. However, it would still print the characters from top to bottom, left to right.

So you can see from these snippets that the order of nesting and use of indexes within the array are of utmost importance. As a second example, consider plotting pixels on a screen. If you wanted to plot them left to right, top to bottom, you would need to be sure that the nesting is correct; otherwise you might find yourself plotting them top to bottom, left to right.

This might not matter, but if you are creating a graphical effect, it is the equivalent of plotting horizontal lines, when what you wanted were vertical ones!

Scoping Revisited

Think back to the sections on variable scoping, where you learned that a variable initialized within a code block is local to that code block. Within loops and nested loops, the scoping rules still apply. Consider, for example, the following code:

```
int x, y;

for (x = 0; x < 10; x++)
{
        for (y = 0; y < 10; y++)
        {
                int z = nArray[x][y];
        }
        if (z == 3) // Error, z out of scope
        {
                // .. do something
        }
}
```

Although in this snippet z has been declared within a nested loop, its scope is restricted to the nested loop, and so will not be accessible outside it. It is important to remember this when using nested loops, especially for programmers who insist on declaring variables upon use, rather than at the head of a code block.

Declaration on use allows you to declare the variable only at the time you need it, and this includes inside condition statements used to manage loops. You could, for example, decide to declare the counter variables for some nested loops inside the associated for statement.

This would lead to code such as:

```
for (int x = 0; x < 10; x++)
{
        for (int y = 0; y < 10; y++)
        {
            // .. do something
        }
        if (y < 10) // Error, y out of scope
        {
                // .. do something
        }
}
```

This code might not be allowed by some compilers and is not recommended by many programmers. It also illustrates how tight scoping rules can be and how easy it is to make errors. These errors will, however, be caught by the compiler.

Of course, a variable declared inside a code block will be available to any code blocks nested inside it. However, the scoping rules effectively mask variables. Masking a variable means that it has a different definition if redeclared inside a code block where it has been declared in an outer code block.

If you have a piece of code such as the following:

```
int x;
for (x = 0; x < 10; x++)
{
    int y;
    for (y = 0; y < 10; y++)
    {
        int y; // Compiles, but silly

        // .. do something
    }
    if (y < 10) // y now in scope
    {
        // .. do something
    }
}
```

The inner definition of y is likely not to be one that is intended. It has been redeclared inside a for statement, which is probably going to depend on the value to do some processing. However, the redeclaration will initialize it again to an undefined value.

Nesting and scoping are two mechanisms you should use with care. It is vital that you understand them before you move on to more complex programming exercises. The simpler the code is in terms of nesting depth, the easier it is to determine how the unintended behavior was caused.

Recap

Looping is a valuable part of programming. Generally speaking, a for loop is used when:

- You know the start value.

- You know the end value.

- You can get from start to end value by counting.

This is called a counted loop. You can count up or down or use any of the mathematical operators to manipulate the variable being used as a counter. You initialize the counter to the start value and then check it against an end value, which can be constant or derived.

A `while` loop is useful when you are testing for a given condition to arise where the number of iterations may vary, depending on the code executed within the loop itself. Thus, it is useful when you do not know how you will get from the start to the end value and need to do some complex processing at each iteration.

The principle is still the same:

- You have a starting condition.

- You perform some processing.

- You check against an end condition.

Of course, judicious use of the `break` and `continue` keywords can alter the behavior of the `for` or `while` loop so that it is possible to only learn and use a single loop type (probably a `while` loop). However, from the point of view of code efficiency, making full and correct use of the loops available to you generally leads to more optimized results.

As with any code block, you can:

- Nest loops

- Declare variables

However, scoping rules apply to the extent that deep nesting can cause problems when you're trying to establish the cause of an error that's been introduced by re-declaring a variable inside a code block. This is something to be wary of, because not all compilers will catch the ambiguity of such programming style.

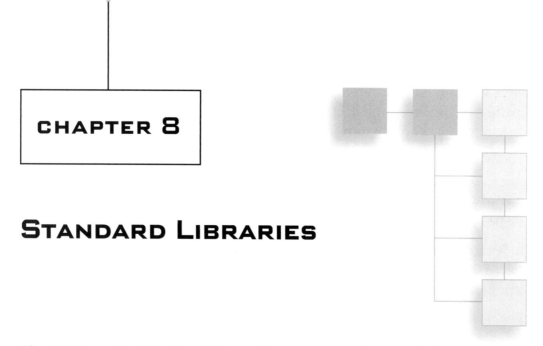

CHAPTER 8

STANDARD LIBRARIES

The ANSI standard for C and C++ offers some extensions to the basic language that allow you to access the underlying operating system (for input and output and time functions), handle strings, and perform calculations. You used some of the standard input and output functions in Chapter 5.

The aim of this chapter is to give you a good overview of the functions provided in the C standard libraries that come with all compliant C development environments.

The intention is that you'll glance through the functions available and absorb the general philosophy. You might find this chapter better utilized as a reference during future programming projects and when reading through the remainder of the book.

Standard I/O: stdio.h

The standard input and output library, *stdio*, defines the interface for input and output of data to and from streams. A stream can be the keyboard, display, or a file. You already saw a few of the console I/O functions, but there are many more presented here that cover functionality such as file handling and more advanced uses such as creating temporary files.

The implementation of the library delivered with the development environment for a target platform will handle differences in platforms. For example, a Linux box has a different base implementation than a Windows command-line processor (such as DOS). The net effect, however, should be exactly the same, so that the code, once recompiled, will perform in the same way regardless of the platform.

The syntax for the formatted I/O functions for data output is as follows:

```
printf ( <format string>, [variables] )
sprintf( <output>, <format string>, [variables] )
fprintf( <file handle>, <format string>, [variables])
```

In each case, the format string contains the format specifiers that provide the conversion from each variable to a value. The output parameter for sprintf is a string and will receive the output specified by the format string and variables.

The final variant, fprintf, takes a file handle (resulting from a call to fopen, as described shortly) and directs the output to there, rather than to stdout or to a variable. Other than these differences, all three printf variants work in the same way in regard to output specifiers and formatting of control characters.

The syntax for the formatted I/O functions for data input is as follows:

```
scanf ( <format string>, [output variables] )
sscanf( <input>, <format string>, [output variables] )
fscanf( <file>, <format string>, [output variables])
```

In each case, the format string provides the mapping from the input to a list of fields. The data from those fields is then used to populate the output variables. There must be as many variables as input specifiers in the format string.

The sscanf variant takes its input from the first parameter, rather than stdin, and the fscanf takes input from the file specified in the first parameter. The file handle should have been acquired with a call to fopen, as described shortly.

For sprintf and sscanf, the input and output specifiers are as follows:

%d   Integers

%f   Floating-point

%c   Character

%ld   Long integer

%lf   Long floating-point

%s   String

They can be combined with field width and precision information, as follows:

```
For strings : %[max width].[min width]s
For floating-point numbers : %[width].[precision]f
For integers : %[width]d
```

In addition, a leading 0 indicates that the field must be padded to the left with zeros, whereas a leading dash (–) will right-justify the field. These format specifiers are applicable to both input and output streams.

Basic file handling is provided by four functions in two pairs. The first pair opens and closes files, whereas the second pair gets and sets the location of the file pointer.

The fopen function takes two parameters and returns a file handle upon success. The first parameter is the filename (path), and the second parameter indicates the kinds of operations that will be performed on that file. For example:

```
FILE * hFile; // File handle, defined in stdio.h
hFile = fopen ( "test.txt", "r" ); // Read from file
```

In this code extract, hFile will contain NULL (a null pointer) if the file cannot be found. However, if you specify write access to the file, it will be created, regardless of whether the file already exists; the existing file, if any, will be overwritten. If you specify read-write or append, the function will fail should the file not exist. The most common possibilities are as follows:

"r"   Read only

"r+"   Read-write

"w"   Write only

"a"   Append

These can be used to test for file existence and creation.

Code Sample 8.1: File Open or Create

```
FILE * FileOpenOrCreate( char * szFileName,
                         char * szAccess,
                         int nCreate )
{
```

```
    FILE * hReturnValue;

    hReturnValue = fopen ( szFileName, szAccess );

    if ( (nCreate == 1) && (hReturnValue == NULL) )
    {
      hReturnValue = fopen ( szFileName, "w" );
    }

    return hReturnValue;
}
```

An improvement to this code sample might be to allow the users to intervene—perhaps locating the file if it has not been found. Variations "w+" and "a+" are also allowed; both will create a file if it does not exist. If "a+" is used, then writing will always take place at the end of the file, whereas reading can take place anywhere, using the positioning functions (described shortly).

When the program has finished with the file, a call to fclose should be made to close it. The function takes a single parameter—the file handle returned by a call to fopen.

There are two file-positioning functions: fseek changes the file position, and ftell reports the current file position. The ftell function takes the file handle as a parameter and returns a long integer, giving the offset, in bytes, from the start to the end of the file—in essence, the file size.

The fseek function takes the file handle, a value indicating the number of bytes offset to apply, and the final parameter that indicates the position from which the offset will apply. Some common fseek calls are:

```
fseek( hfile, 0, 0 );        // Beginning of file
fseek( hfile, 0, 2 );        // End of file
fseek( hfile, lBytes, 1 );   // lBytes from this pos
```

If you put these two functions together, you can derive a function to find the file size in a way that retains the current position.

Code Sample 8.2: File Size

```
long int GetFileSize( FILE * hFile )
{
  long int lFileSize, lFilePos;
```

```
if (hFile == NULL)
{
    return -1;
}

lFilePos = ftell(hFile); // Store current filepos
fseek(hFile, 0, 2);       // Go to the end of the file
lFileSize = ftell(hFile);// Get final position

fseek(hFile, lFilePos, 0); // Restore filepos

return lFileSize;
}
```

In order to process character-level I/O, there are two groups of functions for processing individual characters and strings terminated by a carriage return. The most commonly used character-by-character functions are:

fgetc (<handle>)	Gets the next character in the file
fputc (<handle>, <character>)	Puts a character to the file
getchar()	Gets a character from stdin
putchar(<character>)	Writes a character to stdin

These are accompanied by string-handling equivalents:

fgets (<handle>, <variable>)	Gets a line from the file
fputs (<handle>, <string>)	Puts a string to the file
gets()	Gets a string from stdout
puts(<string>)	Writes a string to stdout

In the case of fgets, the line of text terminated by a carriage return (as represented by the special character \n) will be read from the file into the variable, which must be a string (character array). It will return EOF if no data was available. However useful these might seem, it is generally a better idea to use the low-level binary file-handling routines, even where strings are concerned.

These are laid out a little differently and are much more rigid:

```
fread  ( <buffer>, <size>, <count>, <handle> )
fwrite ( <buffer>, <size>, <count>, <handle> )
```

In both cases, the buffer is a void pointer to the data that will be read to or written from. The <size> parameter indicates the size of each item in the buffer, and the <count> parameter indicates the number of items in the buffer. The handle contains a file handle returned by a call to fopen.

The following code sample implements a possible function for writing a string as a length-value pair. As an exercise, you might try reading the string back in—one point to remember is that, when reading the length back in, the buffer should be a pointer to an integer.

Code Sample 8.3: Write String to File

```
long int WriteString( FILE * hFile, char * szString )
{
  long int lNumChars, lItemsWritten;

  // Check the file pointer is valid
  if (hFile == NULL )
  {
    return -1;
  }

  // Count the number of characters in szString
  lNumChars = strlen( szString );

  // Write the two data blocks
  fwrite( &lNumChars, sizeof(lNumChars), 1, hFile);
  lItemsWritten =
      fwrite( szString, sizeof(char), lNumChars, hFile);

  return lItemsWritten;
}
```

Notice that this example uses the sizeof function to return the size of the variable to be written. The reason for this is that different systems will have different sizes of the basic types (a two-byte character, for example). The caveat is that a file created with the previous function on a one-byte character system will not be correctly read on a system that uses a two-byte character data type.

There are also two other functions that are not part of the ANSI recommended C supporting libraries, but that are supported on most compilers:

```
getw ( <handle> )                Returns an integer read from file

putw ( <variable>, <handle>)     Writes integer to file
```

These are more convenient for implementing string-reading and writing functions as in the previous code sample. However, they only handle integers, so they cannot be used to write large strings that are longer than 32KB in size.

String Handling: string.h

The C language has no built-in string data type and as such no built-in operators for string handling. The string library provides many functions for manipulating character arrays as memory blocks, known as null-terminated strings.

This last point is important—all strings that are to be processed with the string library must be *null terminated*. In essence, this just means that the last character in the array must be a \0 character. Assuming you have a character array with the characters Hello in it, you could do this as follows:

```
szMyString[5] = '\0';
```

The only slight issues are remembering that arrays are zero indexed, meaning that the first element is 0, and the last element is size - 1, and that each array will have one less usable element because the final character needs to be reserved for the null terminator.

One of the most useful functions in the library returns the length of any null-terminated string:

```
strlen ( <string> )     returns a long integer, length of string
```

Note that this does not return the size of the array, but the actual number of characters before the null terminator. If you had a 15-character array, placed the characters Hello into it, and set the last character to a null character, everything between the o and the end of the array would be filled with undefined data.

The best way to create a null-terminated string, given a string constant and character array, is to use the strcpy function:

```
strcpy ( <string>, "constant" ) // copy the constant into string
```

For the hello text example, you would write:

```
strcpy ( szMyString, "Hello" );
```

This will result in a null-terminated string in szMyString containing the word Hello, assuming that there is enough space. To create a blank string (for initialization purposes) you would write:

```
strcpy ( szMyString, "" );
```

To add two null-terminated strings together (or a string variable and a constant), use the strcat function:

```
strcat ( <target>, <source> )        // append source to target
```

Both arguments are defined as character arrays (pointers to characters), and the source is appended to the target, with the result being a concatenation of the two:

```
strcpy ( szMyString, "Hel");
strcpy ( szMyString, "lo"); // Result is 'Hello'
```

Of course, you can also append two null-terminated strings together. On the other hand, you cannot attempt to specify a constant in the first parameter, because it cannot be modified. The compiler will complain if the first parameter is a constant.

The library also provides functions for searching and comparing strings. To search a string for a character, you have two options. One option is as follows:

```
strchr ( <string>, <character> )
```

This function returns a pointer to the first occurrence of the character in the string supplied in the first parameter. Because it is a pointer, you can also use pointer arithmetic to look for subsequent occurrences of the character by making multiple calls to strchr with the updated pointer in the first parameter:

```
char * pChr;
pChr = strchr ( szString, 'l' ); // Initial call
while (pChr != NULL)
```

```
{
    // Do some processing
    pChr = pChr + 1; // Start at next character
    pChr = strchr ( pChr, 'l' );
}
```

You can also find the zero-based index of the place in the character array that the character was found in using pointer arithmetic:

```
nIndex = pChr - szString;
```

Also note that there is a companion function, `strrchr`, that returns the last character in the string:

```
strrchr ( <string>, <character> )   // returns last character in string
```

To find a substring within a string and to return a pointer where that substring starts, use the `strstr` function:

```
strstr ( <src>, <tar> )      // returns pointer to tar in src
```

The function takes two null-terminated strings. A pointer to NULL is returned if the string is not found. Either parameter could feasibly be a constant value, but this might not make sense, depending on the application.

To compare strings for equality, character by character, you can use one of two functions:

```
strcmp ( <string 1>, <string 2> )
      // compares string 1 with string 2
strcmpi( <string 1>, <string 2> )
      // compares string 1 with string 2
```

These functions return 0 if the two strings are the same. If the first string is lower than (that is, would appear alphabetically before) the second, −1 is returned, if it is "higher," 1 is returned. The comparison is strictly character value based, so certain alphabetization principles might not be respected.

The `strcmpi` function is simply a case-insensitive version of `strcmp`. This means that `strcmp` treats A and a as having different values, whereas `strcmpi` treats them both as being equal to the character a. This would also have an effect in sorting strings using these functions.

You can also insert a substring into a string using the `strncpy` function. This function takes a pointer to a place within a string to insert the second string and a third parameter that indicates how many characters will be inserted. This will likely make more sense with an example:

```
pChr = strstr ( szMyString, "llo" );
strncpy ( pChr, "lp!", 3);
```

Assuming that szMyString contains "Hello", this code will turn the string into "Help!". This is useful for substituting parts of strings with other values, as in a search-and-replace function.

Finally, I present a useful but dangerous function. It is dangerous because it actually modifies the source argument, so it should only be used on a copy of the string. The function, strtok, tokenizes a source string, using a user-defined character as delimiter.

So if you wanted to break a line down into tokens, and you knew that the input was comma separated, you might use code such as:

```
char * szToken;
szToken = strtok ( szMyString, "," ); // Initial call

while ( szToken != NULL ) // NULL when no more found
{
  // Do something with szToken

  szToken = strtok ( NULL, "," ); // Next token
}
```

You could change the token delimiter between calls to strtok if you wanted to. Each call after the initial call should specify a NULL pointer in the first parameter, or else the program will use the original szMyString value, which is usually reset once the function has successfully completed, but because it is modified between calls, don't count on this.

Math Functions: math.h

The math library contains extensions to the built-in data type handling for integer and floating-point numbers, as well as some useful trigonometric functions. There are also some complex math functions, but nothing concentrating on formulae processing or statistics.

There are two rounding functions that return an integer from a floating-point number, rounded up or down accordingly, expressed as a floating point. These functions are as follows:

`ceil ( <value> )`   Returns value, rounded up

`floor (<value> )`   Returns value, rounded down

Note that rounding is to the next whole number (up or down) and that the resulting value is represented as a floating point (double), and not as an integer. It can, however, be cast back to an integer. The advantage of this approach is that it avoids the usual truncation that happens when using a pure cast from floating point to integer.

There are also three functions that return the absolute of the input parameter—which is the number stripped of any sign, positive or negative. The three functions are as follows:

```
abs ( <integer> )              abs(-1) returns 1
fabs ( <floating-point> )      fabs(-3.2) returns 3.2
labs ( <long integer> )        labs(-759471) returns 759471
```

Of course, should the input value not be negative, the result is unchanged. The actual result is the mathematical equivalent of a multiplication by −1 or −1.0 (depending on the data type).

Trigonometric functions are also supported. The exact description of these functions and how they are used is beyond the scope of this discussion. The functions are defined as:

`sin ( <angle> )`   Calculates the sine of angle

`cos ( <angle> )`   Calculates the cosine of angle

`tan ( <angle> )`   Calculates the tangent of angle

`axxx ( <angle> )`   Calculates arc sine, cosine, and tangent

`xxxh ( <angle> )`   Calculates hyperbolic sin, cos, and tan

It should be noted that these functions assume that the angle supplied is expressed in radians and not degrees. Because the constant `PI` is also not included in the standard libraries, conversion to and from radians is rendered unnecessarily complicated. The functions in the following code sample might be of help.

Code Sample 8.4: Degrees to Radians to Degrees

```
#define PI 3.14159265 // Since is not supplied...

double DegreesToRadians ( double dDegrees )
{
  return dDegrees*(PI/180.0); // Deg->Rad
}

double RadiansToDegrees ( double dRadians )
{
  return dRadians/(PI/180.0); // Rad->Deg
}
```

Other complex math functions that are included in the library are:

```
p;sqrt ( <number> )              // calculate the square root
pow ( <number>, <exponent> )     // raises to exponent
log10 ( <number> )               // base 10 log of number
```

All of the arguments in the previous functions are double-precision floating-point (double) values. They also return double-precision floating-point values, which can be cast to integers if appropriate.

Memory Handling: malloc.h

Memory blocks are very useful in C programming, especially when creating dynamic arrays or when working in memory-restricted environments. If you create large user-defined complex data types, reserving array space ahead of processing time might also not be possible.

Being able to allocate, free, and reallocate memory is therefore vital in many applications. The two basic functions are malloc and free. The malloc function is defined as:

```
malloc ( <block size> )    // allocate a piece of memory
```

The function returns a void pointer, which can be cast to any type, including user-defined and complex data types. The <block size> parameter is usually a long integer, which may place a maximum block size on the memory that can be allocated. Should there not be enough memory available, the function will return NULL.

Once the memory block has been allocated, it has to be freed with the free function:

```
free ( <pointer> ) // free memory pointed to by pointer
```

The pointer can be of the type that the void pointer was cast into when the memory block was created. All memory that has been allocated using malloc must be freed in this way. This includes a block that is the result of a call to realloc, used to resize the memory block:

```
realloc ( <pointer>, <new size> )
    // returns resized memory block
```

The realloc function can accept the cast pointer that was returned from malloc and will resize the memory (growing or shrinking) to the value specified as the new size. The return value can be cast to any data type and may be the same variable as the original pointer.

```
int * pIntegerBlock;

pIntegerBlock =
  (int *) malloc (sizeof (int) * nNumberOfItems);

// Processing...
pIntegerBlock =
 (int *) realloc ( sizeof (int) * nNumberOfItems + 1);

// Processing
free ( pIntegerBlock );
```

The only drawback to using malloc and realloc is that it's necessary to explicitly calculate the size of the memory block required by multiplying it by the data type size. The calloc function provides a more user-friendly interface to achieve the same result:

```
calloc ( <number>, <size> )
```

The function will allocate a block of memory that is large enough to accommodate the number items of a given size each. The return value can then be cast into an appropriate data type for use in the program.

The memory must be returned to the system once it is no longer of use by using the free function. Reallocating memory must be done using the realloc function or creating a parallel data block and copying each element from one block to the other.

The Standard Library: stdlib.h

Often seen as a collection point for all the miscellaneous functionality that seems to fit nowhere else, the stdlib contains many interesting features for a variety of applications.

You previously used the return keyword in the main function to leave the program itself; however, stdlib also offers some additional exit handling that extends this behavior. The first, atexit, is defined as:

```
atexit ( <function> )         execute function on exit
```

This function allows you to specify up to 32 functions (in separate calls to atexit) to execute when the program terminates normally. These functions cannot accept any parameters and will be executed in the reverse order to which they were set up by repeated calls to the atexit function.

To stop the program immediately due to an unrecoverable error being encountered, you use the abort function. It is defined, quite simply, as:

```
abort     ( )              stop the program
```

When the program exits, the message Abnormal Program Termination is printed and exit code 3 set. To forcefully end the program without causing the effects of a call to abort, you use the exit function. This function is defined as:

```
exit ( <0 or 1> )     exit the program, returning 0 or 1
```

Generally speaking, 0 is used to signal normal program termination (to the operating system), whereas 1 is used to signify an abnormal program termination. The key difference between exit and abort is that exit will call any functions set up with calls to atexit, whereas abort will not.

In order to return a specific code to the operating system, it is necessary to use the return keyword. The drawback is that the operating system must check the return value against a list to determine whether the program has completed successfully. The two termination functions allow you to indicate this, but without a specific return code.

One piece of functionality that might have been left in the math library but has instead been included in stdlib is used to generate a stream of pseudorandom numbers. A pseudorandom number sequence is one that has no immediately discernable pattern, but that will eventually repeat over time since it is created using a static algorithm.

To prepare the algorithm, a *seed* is required, which is a number used in the first iteration of the algorithm. As a consequence, if the same seed value is used every time the algorithm is used, the same sequence of pseudorandom numbers will ensue. The seed function is defined as:

```
srand ( <seed value> )      // seed the random number generator
```

The seed value is a long integer. Commonly used values include the current system time (in clock ticks). For a full discussion of the time functions available in the Time library, see the next section. Seeding with the time function can be done as follows:

```
srand ( time ( NULL ) );
```

The function does not return a value. To obtain the next pseudorandom number in the sequence, the rand function is used, and defined as:

```
rand ( )      // returns a random value
```

The compiler environment will probably have set a constant RAND_MAX, which is usually set to 32,767. This means that the function will return a number between 0 and 32,767. You can obtain a number with an arbitrary maximum by using the modulo % operator:

```
int nMyRandomNumber;
nMyRandomNumber = rand ( ) % nMyMax;
```

This code will return a value between 0 and whatever nMyMax is set to. Repeated calls to rand will result in a sequence of different numbers, but the sequence will repeat after a large number of calls.

Two other functions might have been included elsewhere but are usually also defined in stdlib handle string-to-number conversions. You can convert from strings to floating-point or integer values using the following two functions:

```
atof ( <string> )      returns floating-point from string
atoll ( <string> )     returns integer from string
```

These functions take a string and return either a floating-point or integer conversion. Various options are supported, including correct translation of signed values.

A very useful but slightly advanced function called qsort is provided to help sort arrays of information. Before reading the following, please note that it may benefit you if you're new to programming to read Chapter 10, "User-Defined Functions," first and come back to this discussion afterwards. I provide it here for completeness and ease of reference.

Before using qsort, a comparison function needs to be set up, which receives two elements and returns −1 if the first element goes before the second one, 0 if they are both equal, and 1 if the first element goes after the second element.

The function must be user defined, with parameters that have data types that match the expected input data types. These can, however, be built-in or user-defined data types, including complex data types such as structures.

In addition, you need a pointer to the first element in the array (or memory block), the number of items in the array, and the width (size) of each element. The function cannot therefore be used to sort variable-width items. The definition of qsort looks like:

```
qsort ( <pointer>, <items>, <size>,
    <compare function> )
```

<pointer> is the pointer to memory block or array, <items> is the number of items to be sorted, and <compare function> takes two elements of the same data type. If you want to sort a memory block of 100 integers, you should first set up a comparison function.

Code Sample 8.5: Integer Comparison Function

```
int IntegerCompare ( int nA, int nB )
{
  // Should nA be before nB?
  if ( nA < nB )
  {
    return -1;
  }

  // Should nA be after nB?
  if ( nA > nB )
```

```
  {
    return 1;
  }

  // They must be equal
  return 0;
}
```

You could have reduced this to a single statement:

```
return nA - nB;
```

However, this would return a number less than 0, equal to 0, or greater than 0, which might not follow the same behavior as, for example, strcmp. It is preferable, therefore, to perform an explicit comparison.

With this function defined, you can set up a memory block of 100 integers:

```
int * pIntegerArray;
pIntegerArray = (int * ) malloc (sizeof (int) * 100);
```

Once you have populated it with values, you can sort them:

```
qsort ( pIntegerArray, 100, sizeof (int),
          IntegerCompare);
```

The qsort function does not return a value to indicate the outcome of the sorting process.

The Time Library: time.h

The Time library provides the data structures and functions required to retrieve the system time, perform time calculations, and output formatted strings that allow the time to be displayed in a variety of common formats. Time is stored as ticks since 1 Jan 1970, midnight, known as UTC. This value must be converted to be of use, either into a structure or formatted output.

The structure in question, tm, contains the following members:

```
tm_hour     the current hour, from 0 to 23
tm_min      the current minute, from 0 to 59
tm_sec      the current second, from 0 to 59
tm_mday     day of the month, 1 to 31
tm_mon      month of the year, 0 (January) to 11
tm_wday     day of the week, 0 (Sunday) to 6
tm_yday     day of the year, 0 to 365
tm_year     year less 1900, i.e. 2006 will be 106
```

So to get the correct year from the `tm` structure, you need to use the following:

```
struct tm * myTime; // Pointer to tm structure
myTime = localtime ( time (NULL) ); // Get the time
printf ( "The year is %d", myTime.tm_year + 1900 );
```

Notice that this code snippet introduces another function, `localtime`. This function takes the current time expressed in clock ticks and returns a pointer to a tm structure:

```
localtime ( <time> )
            // returns pointer to tm structure, from time
```

The return value is the time, adjusted for local parameters (such as Daylight Savings Time). The value placed into the function was the return value from another function, `time`, which simply returns the current number of clock ticks, as discussed previously.

```
time ( )               returns current UTC
```

There is a companion function, `gmtime`, which returns a pointer to the same structure as before, so it is overwritten but expressed in GMT. The definition is the same as for `localtime`:

```
gmtime ( <time> )
      // returns a pointer to tm structure, from time, in GMT
```

If you want to calculate the difference between two times, you can do so using the `difftime` function, which takes two UTC values:

```
difftime ( <time 1>, <time 2> )
         // returns difference between two times
```

The return value can then be supplied to a call to `gmtime` (for example) to populate a tm structure. For completeness, note also that you can convert a tm structure into a UTC value using:

```
mktime ( <pointer to tm> )
         // returns UTC from tm structure
```

If you would rather report the number of clock ticks since the process started, you can use the `clock` function:

```
clock ( )
         // returns clock ticks since process start
```

Because the value of a *clock tick* is platform dependent, a constant `CLK_TCK` gives the relation between clock ticks and seconds. To calculate the number of seconds that a clock tick value represents, you can use code such as:

```
nNumSeconds = lClockTicks / CLK_TCK;
```

Finally, there are some useful functions that return pointers to a statically maintained string containing formatted time values. You need to remember to copy this string if you want to preserve the value between calls to the conversion functions, of which there are two:

```
ctime ( <UTC time> )
      // returns string from UTC
asctime (<tm struct>)
      // returns string from pointer to a tm structure
```

The `ctime` function returns a string that is formatted as follows:

```
Www Mmm dd hh:mm:ss yyyy
```

Where `Www` is the abbreviated week day, `Mmm` is the abbreviated month name, and `dd` is the day of the month. The other values should be self-explanatory. The `ctime` function returns the local time.

The companion function takes a pointer to a `tm` structure and returns a string of the same format as `ctime` from it. The `asctime` function is defined as:

```
asctime ( <tm struct> )
   // returns string from pointer to tm
```

These functions represent the only possibilities for time handling and formatting in the C libraries. However, various implementations extend the ANSI definitions to provide even more formatting possibilities.

Recap

This chapter has just enough standard reference information for a working programmer to use on a daily basis. I have left out a lot of the baggage that a full C reference manual would contain; after all, it is largely unnecessary and complex. You should have a thorough understanding of input and output, string handling, memory management, and math and time manipulation as a result.

This is the place to come in the future when you need to look up a part of the code samples that you do not understand fully. The remainder of the book will frequently use, in examples, many of the functions referred to here, and you will find yourself consulting these pages frequently in the future.

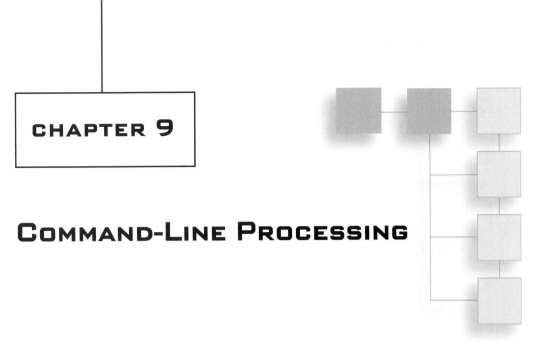

CHAPTER 9

COMMAND-LINE PROCESSING

This is the first of the book's forays into practical applications of everything you have learned to date. You know how to structure a program. You know about data types, variables, and compiling and building applications and accessing them from the command line. In addition, you can control the flow of control around the program, and you have looked at the standard libraries.

Now you need to apply this knowledge. The first place to do that is in processing data that the users might offer on the command line.

Once you master it, you'll find that command-line processing is vital to creating all kinds of software, especially programs used in a Web server environment. This chapter ends with an example that adds a debug flag to a program to allow it to display debugging information.

Any reader who has used software with a command-line interface will be familiar with the practice, and luckily, there are some standard interfaces to take the data from the operating system and process it.

The `argv` and `argc` Variables

When creating a program that's controlled by parameters passed to it from the command line, two variables are of utmost importance. The first of these is called `argc`, which provides a count of all parameters passed by the command line. The executable name is considered to be a parameter, so `argc` will always contain a value greater than or equal to 1.

The `argv` variable contains a two-dimensional array of strings, each one containing a parameter as received from the command line. A parameter is considered to be a value that is flanked by whitespace, although the command-line processor will also allow spaces inside a parameter if the parameter is placed inside quotes.

Because `argc` is zero-based, you will always find the name of the executable in:

```
argv [ 0 ]
```

The complete path will be returned in the string, no matter how the executable was called, so to retrieve the actual executable filename, some string manipulation is necessary. Access to the `argv` and `argc` variables is provided through the call to the entry point of the program, the `main` function. The following example prints the name of the executable and the number of parameters passed to it:

```
int g_nReturnValue; // An integer variable

void SetDefaultReturnValue()
{
    g_nReturnValue = 0; // Set to a non-error value
}

int main ( int argc, char argv [][]) // Entry point
{
    SetDefaultReturnValue(); // Set default return value

    printf ("Executable %s was passed %d parameter(s)\n",
        argv[0], argc);

    return g_nReturnValue;
}
```

The pertinent lines in this code sample are shown in bold for clarification. The code itself is contained in the ArgTest.c source file. Figure 9.1 shows the effect of various commands from the Windows XP command line on the output of the program.

You can see in Figure 9.1 that when you pass no parameters, `argc` contains 1, which is displayed in the output from the program. If you place the "Arg 2" (with space) in quotes, it is counted as a single parameter. Otherwise, it is broken into two separate parameters—the `Arg` and the `2`—hence the program outputs 4 rather than 3.

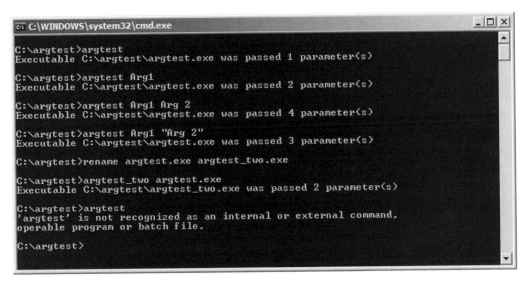

Figure 9.1
Using the ArgTest Program

Having renamed the program executable, when you run it, the command line contains the new name of the executable. This allows you to perform some quite useful decisions based on the name of the executable. For example, the Linux zip/ unzip commands are essentially the same executable.

If it is called as zip, it will act as a compression program, if unzip is supplied, it will act as a decompression program. This is a useful technique.

You can also, of course, print all the parameters passed (known as the *parameter list*) using a simple `for` loop:

```
for (nParameter = 1; nParameter < argc; nParameter++)
{
printf ( "%d : %s\n",
            nParameter, argv[nParameter] );
}
```

This loop is encoded in the ArgList.c program, which shows the executable path and then lists any arguments supplied on the command line. Figure 9.2 shows the output of this program for several different calls similar to those made for the ArgTest program.

In Figure 9.2, you can clearly see the effect of putting quotes around a single argument in the Windows XP command-line environment.

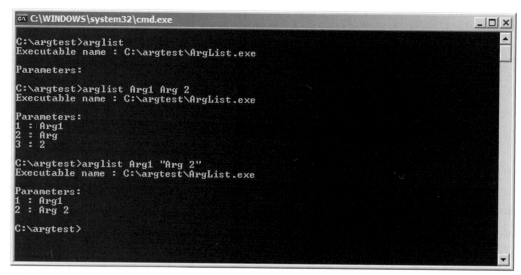

Figure 9.2
Using the ArgList Program

It is a useful technique to know if you need to supply arguments that can contain spaces and for which you have no choice.

Pathnames fall into this category—you have no control over them, and so in order to be able to process a pathname from the command line, you need to ask the users to put it in quotes.

Because the `argv` variable is an array containing strings, all the usual string.h functions from the Standard Libraries can be used on individual entries in the array. In addition, there are also multiple ways that the array can be introduced in the main function parameter list. The following are all equivalent for an array of unknown size (at compile time):

```
char * argv []     // a simple array of pointers
char ** argv       // an array of pointers to pointers
```

This code shows you what is passed to the program and how you can access it. However, what exactly can you use it for? Generally speaking, you want to be able to pass parameters that are of three types:

- Data (information, filenames, and so on)

- Options (`-compress`, `-decompress`, and so on)

- Flags (`-debug`, `-verbose`, `-silent`, and so on)

The first of these allows you to pass information that the program needs in order to perform the various tasks that are required of it. This category does not contain anything that would form part of the decision-making process but contains information that might be processed in a different way when combined with the other two categories.

One of these is the various options that you could supply to the program in order to tell it exactly what to do. It is common for options to be preceded by a hyphen, to distinguish them from actual parameters. You might use options to change the nature of the program slightly, such as to compress or decompress, to include subfolders, to use a specific compression level, and so on.

The other category to consider is the various flags that might change the behavior of the program within the different combinations of options that you supply. So you can tell the program to take some data, do something with it, and in addition specify some flags that tell the program what you might expect from it while it is performing the processing.

This can allow you to specify different levels of output for debugging purposes, for example, or tell the program not to give any output at all. This is helpful for writing and testing command-line packages designed to be called as Web server applications. In such cases, you might want to be able to change the output based on whether you are testing or actually using the program.

In the latter case, you might not even want the program to display anything, if it is designed to be used as a daemon process that runs in the background. To have access to all these pieces of information, it is useful to know how to process the command line in a standard way and use the same code over and over.

Processing the Command Line

As you've seen, the command line is retrieved as a set of individual parameters—a list of strings contained by whitespace or in quotes. You need a mechanism to go from that to a list of parameters that you can access from within the program in order to determine the behavior of the program.

Users expect you to adhere to certain standards that they have become accustomed to. For example, they are used to starting a program with the following style of command line:

```
dir /o:n *.txt
```

This code calls the directory listing function from the Windows command line. Non-Windows users will find their own version of this: All operating systems that have a command-line interface will allow a similar level of control. The point is that the users expect to be able to provide flags and arguments to the program in a similar manner.

Therefore, in order to process the command line, you need to be able to split it into chunks or construct a list of command-line parameters that you can check against. Depending on the program and its requirements, you can be relaxed or strict in interpreting the parameter list in terms of order and format of individual parameters.

The most flexible way to process a command line is to do so in pairs of values:

```
-<type> value
```

or

```
-<type> "value with spaces"
```

The alternative is to require that the users list parameters in a specific order, which is less flexible for the users and programmers alike, because each argument needs to be in a specific place, probably a list of values that are hard to remember.

It is much easier to type a command such as the following:

```
make -file myfile.txt -output myfile_out.exe
```

A quick side note—many application programmers use terminology such as *flags* and *switches* interchangeably, mixed with the parameters. For the sake of clarity, I usually just call these parameters. The most common variants of such arguments when used as flags or switches are as follows:

```
/<p>:<value>
-<p> <value>
-<p><value>
```

In these examples, `<p>` is the parameter, and `<value>` is a value used to determine the parameter. For example, the Borland `make` command uses the last of these:

```
make -fmakefile.mak
```

In the interest of promoting easy-to-read and easy-to-deploy command lines, I stick with the second option, specifying the flag or switch, followed by a value in quotes or whitespace. This way, anything starting with a - gives you the action, with the (optional) parameter following afterwards.

One of the simplest ways to actually retrieve a parameter from the list of possible values on the command line is to parse the list in search of such a value. The function described in the following code sample extracts a value from the command line, based on a supplied parameter.

Code Sample 9.1: Searching Command-Line Supplied Parameters

This function extracts a value from the command line, based on a supplied parameter:

```
// Purpose : to return the value associated with a
// specific parameter from an array of strings.
// The assumption is :
//    that each <parameter> starts with '-'. The string
//    TRUE is returned if a parameter is found, with no
//    value associated with it.

char * GetParameterValue ( char ** szCommandLine,
                           char * szParameter,
                           int nParameters )
{
  int nParameter = 1;

 // Check that we had some parameters supplied
  if ( nParameters-1 < nParameter )
    return NULL;

  do
  {
    // Check to see if nParameter starts with '-'
    if ( szCommandLine[nParameter][0] == '-' )
    {
      // Does it match?
      if ( strcmp( szCommandLine[nParameter],
            szParameter ) == 0 )
      {
        // Test to see if nParameter + 1 is a value
        if ( nParameter + 1 < nParameters )
```

```
    {
      if ( szCommandLine[nParameter+1][0] != '-' )
      {
        // Return a pointer to the string
        return szCommandLine[nParameter+1];
      }
    }
    // It's not a value, it's a parameter, or not
    //   present, so just return TRUE
    return "TRUE";
  }
}
nParameter++;
} while (nParameter < nParameters);

// We didn't find the szParameter,
// so return error value

return NULL;
}
```

You have not yet read about user-defined functions in detail, which is the next practical application topic in the book. However, you should be familiar with calling library functions, and so this concept is not entirely new.

The GetParameterValue works by scanning the command line, looking for the parameter that has been specified as a string in the szParameter variable, which is defined in the function declaration. It is one of the parameters in brackets.

It then loops through the szCommandLine parameter, which is just the argv variable passed through to the function through the first parameter. Because it's an array of strings, you can test the first character in each parameter with the code:

```
if ( szCommandLine[nParameter][0] == '-' )
```

Assuming that it evaluates to true, you then look at the next parameter (should it exist) and do the test again. This lets you determine whether it's a parameter or a value. Finally, you decide what the return value for the function should be:

- NULL—You did not find the parameter.

- "TRUE"—You found the parameter, with no value.

- <parameter string>—You found the parameter, and it has a value.

The drawback to this approach is that the entire argument list needs to be parsed each time the program looks for a value. However, it does allow you to write code such as:

```
char * szValue =
      GetParameterValue ( argv, "-Filename", argc);

if ( szValue != NULL )
{
     // Do something with szValue
}
```

Note that you need to test for failure by evaluating szValue, and that because it is a pointer you can test for NULL. I'll cover pointers in more detail later, but recall for now the concept behind the string pointer:

```
char * szString;
```

This is the same type of array definition for a string that is used in calls to and from the library functions in the string.h standard library. When you pass the value "TRUE" back to the calling program through the return statement, you do not have to cast the constant value to a pointer to a string, as it is implicit.

When you read about user-defined functions in the next chapter, this will become much clearer. For now, concentrate on the algorithm that searches the command-line parameters. This is important because it allows you to conditionally execute pieces of code within the program, depending on the wishes of the users, or during testing.

Conditional Execution

You've seen the phrase *conditional execution* before—it just means that you can execute code within a program based on testing for a given condition. Using the command-line options to selectively control a program allows you to offer flexibility and user friendliness both to the end users and to anyone testing the application.

Besides to affect the way in which the program behaves, you use conditional execution to display various messages:

- Missing parameters required to run the application.

- Missing conditional parameters (in conjunction with other parameters).

- Missing values for parameters supplied.

- Invalid parameters (including file not found).

- Debug statements when something goes wrong.

- General error messages.

Depending on what the users are doing with the application and what actions it is designed to perform, you might want to change the number of error messages reported. For example, if the user is testing the program with different inputs, you might require one level of output, whereas if the program is running in an unattended mode, the user might want it to fail silently so as not to disturb any other output performed during its execution.

These error messages fall into four categories of verbosity:

- Debug—Print all messages: error, progress, and debug information.

- Verbose—Print all messages.

- Normal—Report errors.

- Silent—Report nothing.

In the Silent mode, no messages are printed, either success or failure, but return values must be set to indicate the final status. The Normal and Verbose categories differ only in the fact that Verbose prints progress messages as well.

The Debug mode generally prints all information building up to the outcome so that you can effectively trace the output to find errors. This category might include output to a file as well as to the screen to help the debugging process.

Users will generally work in the Normal or Verbose category. These are unofficial classifications that make sense for a wide number of applications, and I present them here in the interest of allowing you to create applications that offer the right level of information to the right kind of user.

Reporting Parameter Errors

One of the purposes for checking the supplied argument list is that you can identify potential errors in the parameters supplied before you begin execution of the program itself. This helps you identify the true source of the errors and helps the users when they are deploying the program for the first time.

There are two kinds of command-line arguments—those with and without values. Normally, a program should run without optional parameters or switches; any required parameters should indicate a value. Flags, or switches without parameters, should always be optional.

Certain parameters will be listed as mandatory; in other words, they are required for the program to be able to do its job correctly. These parameters have to be identified and rectified at the start of the program. You can rectify them in one of two ways:

- Print an error message.

- Prompt for a value.

If you use the first option, you need to terminate the program and set an appropriate return code to indicate the error. The second option is more helpful to the users, as long as you prompt with an appropriate question string (such as the parameter name) and give the users the option to enter an empty value to stop the program.

Because you will need to assign values to in-program variables as part of the command-line parsing process, you can just substitute the user's response for the variable, without making too many changes to the way that the program works.

Some of the values or options chosen in the mandatory parameters will cause conditional parameters to become required. If this is the case, you need to go through a second scan of the command-line parameter list in order to determine whether these have been supplied.

The procedure for dealing with any missing parameters is the same as before— report an error or request the missing parameter. Depending on the level of verbosity indicated by the users, you might also give a reason for why you are asking for this parameter.

One point to remember is that if the users are running in non-interactive mode, they cannot be prompted for input data. In such cases, the program should take account of this and fail silently. You need to be aware of the order in which you process input arguments to be sure that you know the level of verbosity in advance of parsing parameter values.

What you are trying to avoid is the case when the users specify a high level of verbosity in one of the parameters, but that this is never taken into account, due to an error in a previous parameter. If the default verbosity is set to Silent, the users will never know why the program does not run.

So verbosity flags need to be processed as a priority, no matter where they occur. Either that or you should set the default verbosity to high and informative, an approach that might not be acceptable in certain circumstances.

Finally, you need to be able to deal with invalid values in an appropriate manner. These can fall into many categories, from missing files to values that are just wrong (for example, numbers instead of words).

Again, these need to be identified and discarded at the start of the program to avoid inappropriate error messages being printed later on in the execution. The level of information provided will depend on the verbosity asked for by the users, and you can even prompt for a replacement value as necessary.

In command-line programming, this can often be more difficult than in a GUI-based environment such as Windows. If you'll be programming for Windows after having mastered the C language, you'll find that it is reasonably common to provide much more information to the users.

The reason is that a GUI by default requires user interaction. It is much more difficult to run a GUI quietly, although some system utilities do manage it. Consider, for example, the program that requires a file to be supplied in order to perform a task.

If the user supplies the filename on the command line, and it is correct, the program will open it. However, if the user supplies an incorrect value, and the programmer decides that the users should be prompted for the actual filename, the standard Windows File Open dialog box is prompted.

In the command-line environment, unless the programmer wants to provide one, there is no equivalent, and entering a full pathname and filename might prove to be cumbersome for the users. Subsequently, the choice of how invalid parameters are processed is one that needs some thought; do not take this issue lightly.

The most verbose setting is usually Debug. Here, you have a little more freedom to report every problem that you find and give actual readings of the parameters that were supplied, as well as what the program has made of them. To do this, however, you need to use a *debug flag*, an option that tells the program that it should report as much detail as possible.

Adding a Debug Flag

Debug information can be displayed on the screen, in a file, in a separate window, or through other reporting means. A computer that is starting up, for example, uses something called POST (power on self-test) and makes a series of beeps that tell the user which POST tests have been successfully executed.

Let's assume that you want to supply a flag in the following format:

```
My_Program -debug
```

From here, you need to perform some actions to identify and process the flag:

1. Introduce a global runtime variable to contain the debug status.

2. Ensure that debug behavior statements are executed selectively.

3. Process the command line for the -debug flag.

These are very straightforward steps, with a few caveats that I'll cover in Chapters 10 and 14. For now, the knowledge you have now allows you only to put the code in the main.c file.

Code Sample 9.2: Example Program Using the Debug Flag

```
// We assume that the GetParameterValue function is
// in this file too

int g_nReturnValue; // An integer variable
int g_nDebug; // The debug on/off flag

void SetDefaultReturnValue()
{
  g_nReturnValue = 0; // Set to a non-error value
}

int main ( int argc, char argv [][]) // Entry point
```

```
{
  SetDefaultReturnValue(); // Set default return value

  if ( GetParameterValue( argv, DEBUG_FLAG, argc ) != NULL )
  {
    g_nDebug = 1; // Debug is ON
  }
  else
  {
    g_nDebug = 0; // Debug is OFF
  }

  return g_nReturnValue;
}
```

The program uses the global g_nDebug variable to indicate to all parts of the program that debugging is switched on. This is a simple case of checking the value returned from GetParameterValue against NULL. Note that the != NULL clause from the if statement is optional because it will always treat an expression with no test for equality as being evaluated for truth.

A NULL pointer equates to false for the purposes of this kind of implicit test, and so you could leave the explicit comparison out. However, I chose to leave it in for clarity.

Rather than test for a parameter, you could have tested the first parameter in the argument list (which is the application name) against a debug value. The users are not likely to guess that it can be run in this way. The actual application call might look something like the following:

```
My_Program_debug_version -file InputFile.txt
```

I changed the name of the program to My_Program_debug_version in order to indicate that it is to be run in Debug mode. This requires actually renaming the file that is delivered to the users, by the users, so is unlikely to be something they will be able to do unless so instructed.

The test for the debug flag setting then needs to use the string.h library function strstr to check that the argument contains the correct text. Because the entire path will be in that first parameter, you cannot use strcmp without first stripping the path. The strstr function is more convenient:

```
if ( strstr ( agrv[0], "_debug_version.exe" ) != NULL )
```

Figure 9.3
Running the DebugFlagTest Program

By not including the program name in the comparison, you make the call applicable across all future applications that the reader might want to use this technique with. The actual code for all of this is in the DebugFlagTest.c source code. Figure 9.3 shows it in action.

You might well find that there are refinements that can be made to this code, but this chapter has provided the basic mechanism—a starting point—for a reasonably robust approach to the problem.

Displaying Help

The final topic that falls under the general heading of command-line processing is what to do when the users run the program but supply nothing. The answer is that you must display some kind of usage instructions. Those from the UNIX world will recall that almost every command that is typed on the command line needs parameters, and often typing it without any parameters will cause the standard usage information to be displayed.

You can also add a level of user choice by including a help flag:

```
/h      -h      -?
```

In addition, you might be able to offer the users help on a specific option:

```
My_Program -h File
```

This code is probably robust enough to let the programmers test for all of these. After all, if it returns `false`, no help is required; if it returns `true`, general help is required, and if it returns a string other than `true`, specific help is required.

However, the test for help needs to be done before anything else is evaluated; otherwise, the program might just start processing after showing the help that was asked for and overwrite the information. In fact, the help option needs to be invoked even if it is used with other parameters, and the others need to be ignored.

Therefore, the test for help is the first thing that should be done, and the program should exit after having displayed the required help page.

Recap

Command-line processing is an easy way to provide a program with the possibility to perform tasks non-interactively or for an interactive program to be started in a given mode. It is also very helpful for use with daemons and programs for use in the back office part of a Web solution.

The Debug flag example can be used with many other flags, and the sample code for the `GetParameterValue` function is flexible enough to allow quite rich command-line parameter-list processing. In cases where certain parameters are mandatory, or in the event that the users place a `-?` on the command line, it is customary to display a usage screen, complete with all the various flags and options that can be supplied.

This can be enriched by treating the `-?` option as a parameter in its own right, followed by a keyword indicating where the users need help. This keyword could be a parameter name, a concept, or just the simple word `all`.

Any of these option must be documented so that the users can determine what combinations are valid. At the very least, execution on the command line with no other parameters should display a full list of parameters. If the program does not require any, then of course, no action needs to be taken.

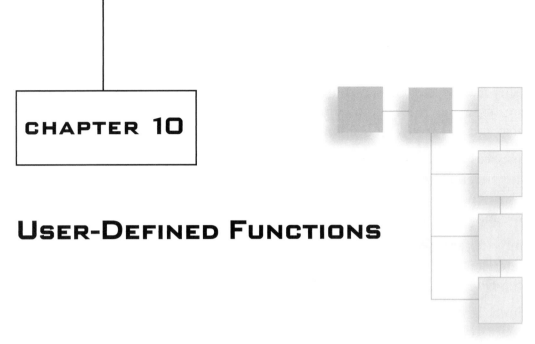

CHAPTER 10

USER-DEFINED FUNCTIONS

You've been using many functions in this book that are defined outside of the C and C++ languages. When using the Standard Libraries, for example, you always #include a library header file containing the definitions of the functions you want to use. Until now, the text has glossed over the actual mechanism that allows you to reuse this code.

In fact, despite these functions being part of the ANSI standard C definition, someone has to write functions to provide the functionality, and the exact implementations will differ from platform to platform. All that the ANSI stubs give you is the input and output; it is up to a developer to write code that satisfies the design.

You can also deploy your own functions using the same mechanism. When you write your own programs, you have access to the source; you must write everything. There is no source code provided for many of the standard compilers. Only Open Source development environments will let programmers look at, for example, string.c, which implements the string handling.

The aim of this chapter is to provide an in-depth look at how user-defined functions are declared and used in C programming.

The chapter discusses functions that are defined within the same source file as the main function, as well as functions that are imported from separate source files, or even separate projects. A separate discussion of recursion looks at this advanced technique, which can be useful in data processing.

After reading this chapter, you'll be equipped with enough information to begin creating larger, more complex programs. It is a necessary stepping stone to being able to create larger applications.

The reason that programmers typically create functions is to break the code up into manageable chunks and create reusable solutions. For example, I have some file-handling routines that you'll look at in the next chapter that were created specifically to provide ready-made solutions for a variety of projects.

Although functions may evolve with time, it is important not to change the functionality so that the interface has to change. Otherwise, any possible reuse will be negated by the fact that the parameters supplied to the function have changed.

So the key is in designing and creating the function. If new functionality must be added, it must be done in a way that makes the result usable in any projects that it might already have been included in. The best way to achieve this is through documenting any code that is to be reused, either through inline comments or using separate documents.

Declaring Functions

Every function has a declaration that is designed to tell the compiler and linker how other code is allowed to interface with it. The declaration gives no information to the compiler as to what the function does or how it does it, just how it can be called.

The usual way to declare a function is to give a return type (or void if no value is to be returned), a valid function name, and a list of parameters, with their types, in parentheses. As always, when naming user-defined objects in C, the names should be:

- Meaningful (real language, szUserName, for example).

- Case-appropriate (not szusername).

- Not C keywords, or similar to them, without good reason.

The main function is a good example of a function declaration:

```
void main () // No return value, not good practice

int main ( int argc, char argv[][] ) // Usual usage
```

The code to be executed follows the declaration in a block contained by braces, as is the standard in C programming. Any variables declared inside the code block are local to the function, and the parameters supplied are treated as:

- Input: Not changed by the function

- Output: Initialized and/or changed by the function

When the closing brace is reached, the function will end, and control passes back to the line of code in the calling process immediately following the function call. The exception to this is with functions that return a value, in other words, a function that has a type identifier rather than the void keyword preceding the name. It is good practice for functions, as much as possible, to return an indication of success or failure if they do not express that through the functions or via a returned value.

If you do not do this, you have little way of knowing, directly, whether the function has managed to do what you asked. The return keyword can be used to exit the function, whether it has succeeded or not, rather like the break keyword that is used to exit a loop.

All functions, including ones that return void (no value), can be exited in this way. There are two forms of the return keyword—with and without a value:

```
return;   // to return from a void function
```

```
return <value>;   // to return a value from a function
```

This technique also works for exiting a program, by returning a value (or no value) from the main function.

The <value> can be any variable used inside the function whose type matches the type specified in the function declaration, or a constant of that type. A compiler error will occur (or a warning, if more relaxed rules are applied) should the return keyword be used with no value, where the function has been declared as returning a value.

For example, the following function returns the uppercase version of the letter supplied as a parameter or the space character if it is not within the a-to-z limit.

```
char LowerToUpper ( char nLower )
{
  char nUpper; // The return variable
```

```
if ( nLower >= 'A' && nLower <= 'Z' )
{
  // It is already uppercase
  nUpper = nLower;
}
else if ( nLower < 'a' || nLower > 'z' )
{
  // It is invalid
  nUpper = ' ';
}
else
{
  // Do the conversion
  nUpper = 'A' + ( ( 'Z' - nLower ) - 1 );
}
return nUpper;
}
```

If you had a string that you wanted to convert to uppercase, you could use a `for` loop as follows:

```
for ( nIndex = 0; nIndex < nLength; nIndex++)
{
  szLowerCase[nIndex] = LowerToUpper ( szLowerCase[nIndex] );
}
```

Note that if you do this, you lose the original string, so it is probably best to run the function over a copy of szLowerCase, rather than the string itself. The chances are that this code is calling the function from another part of the program, possibly even in another file. You need some way to tell the compiler how to deal with this eventuality.

So a function must be declared before it is called, either in its entirety, complete with code, or just a stub (known as a *prototype*), showing how the function is to be called. The prototype contains information such as what it returns, what parameters it accepts, and its name. The prototype can be present in the same file as the code that implements the function or in a different file altogether and can take one of two acceptable forms:

```
int AFunction ( int nOne, char * szTwo );
int AFunction ( int, char * );
```

Note that some compilers will issue a warning when the first prototype is used, and that others will happily accept both. You'll find out reasonably quickly which form you should be using. Let's look in more detail now at how prototyping is used in C programming.

Prototyping

A function prototype can be in one of two places: in a header file (like stdio.h) or in the main source code file. Generally speaking, you should break the program into as many source code files as makes sense for the scope (size) of the project, possibility to reuse functions created for it (or reusing other functions).

For a small program that performs a single task, you might contain all the code in a single source file. For a medium-size project that uses functions that have already been defined alongside some original code, you might also be able to put all the new code in a single source file. However, you might also break the code up if the application covers different functional areas.

If a program contains two source code files, one of which contains a function that is required by the other, the prototype must be placed in a shared header file for the complete application to compile correctly.

This might feel a little abstract, so Figure 10.1 shows the relationship between three files: a header and two source code files. Notice how the header file is shared between the two source code files, because they are compiled independently.

If you look at Figure 10.1, you'll realize that you could probably also have taken a different approach and put the prototype for MyFunction in each of the source code files rather than use a header file. On the other hand, if you want to then include the same prototype in other files or change it, you would have more work to do. It is easier to keep all the prototypes for a given set of functions in a .c file in a related .h file and include it as necessary.

The compiler will compile the main.c and functions.c source files separately, using the functions.h file to provide the prototype for MyFunction. Therefore, the compiler knows what the interface to MyFunction looks like without needing to know exactly what it does.

When the linker comes to create the executable from the resulting object code generated by the compiler, it will make sure that the prototype has been

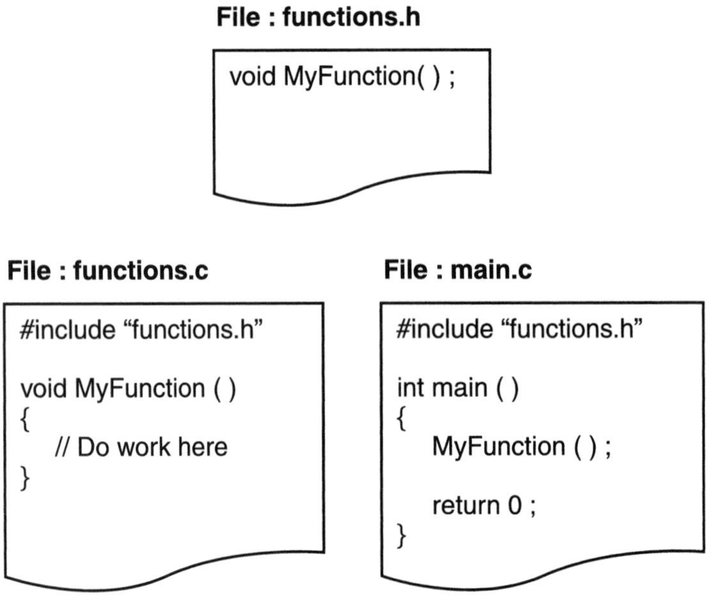

File : functions.h

```
void MyFunction( ) ;
```

File : functions.c

```
#include "functions.h"

void MyFunction ( )
{
    // Do work here
}
```

File : main.c

```
#include "functions.h"

int main ( )
{
    MyFunction ( ) ;

    return 0 ;
}
```

Figure 10.1
Prototypes in Multiple File Compilation

expanded to an implementation in the functions.obj code. If not, a link error will be generated.

If it is in a standard header file (stdio.h, string.h, and so on), the standard object code libraries specified in the makefile will be searched for the function. Typically, flags are introduced in the makefile to point the linker to a standard location for the library files containing the implementation of the functions prototyped in the header files.

In the Borland C environment, the line is as follows:

```
LFLAGS  = -aa -V4.0 -c -x -Gn -L"C:\borland\bcc55\lib"
```

If the function is not part of the Standard Libraries, and the object code should be built from existing source, a separate line showing all the object code files to be built is used:

```
OBJFILES = main.obj functions.obj
```

In this code line, functions.obj is just used as an example. The compiler will expect the source code files to have the same main filename. For example, main.obj can only be compiled from a file named main.c. This is the way that the make program builds an application, and the behavior is governed by convention and standards.

You can also place library and object files in other places within the Borland C environment:

```
LIBFILES =

STDOBJS =
STDLIBS =
```

The prototypes for these needs to be in a separate header file. This header file needs to be included by the main file, and the source file used to compile the object code should be present unless a library is to be used. In the latter case, where the compiled library is available but the source code is not, the compiled library will be linked at compile time.

For this to work, the library must have been compiled by the original author as a static library. Commercially available library files, as well as Open Source offerings, are usually supplied in compiled binaries as static or dynamic libraries, depending on the target platform and expected use.

Libraries and Linking

For readers who will be going on to more complex environments, including all kinds of specialized libraries and platforms, I'll just take a few moments to look at the background of libraries and the linking process. The examples you've seen thus far all assume that you'll be linking with the libraries that provide the functions you need at build time.

In other words, these libraries will be statically linked. We cannot change the functionality included in the application without recompiling the libraries (into object code) and the application before linking the object code for the libraries and the application.

Build tools typically provide a way to create a special kind of object code, called a *lib file*, which contains the source code packaged as a library that can be distributed. Object code formats change from platform to platform and from compiler to compiler within platforms. There are some standards, as there are for library code files, and these are generally widely supported.

In order to allow programmers who might have used the library file to update their code, it is necessary to:

- Distribute the new library files.

- Rebuild all applications.

- Redistribute the applications.

To minimize this, the concept of dynamic linking has evolved. A dynamically linked library can be linked to by an application, through the operating system, at runtime, rather than at build time. These are sometimes called *dynalink libraries* or DLLs.

A dynamic link library has to be connected to through the operating system. Some will come with header files that allow the compiler to access the functions directly, and some offer a feature to connect to the DLL by loading it temporarily, in which case you must make sure that they do so in the correct manner.

This includes making sure that the function parameters are passed correctly, something that the compiler can do only if a suitable prototype declaration for the function has been provided. If not, you need to make sure that they have the correct usage.

The key advantage with using a dynamic link library is that new versions of the library can be released directly to the users, and the third-party applications do not need to be rebuilt. Even when new functionality is added to the library, as long as it remains backward compatible, all applications that use it will continue to work.

Function Parameter Lists

As noted in the function declaration and prototyping sections, a function can have zero or more parameters contained in a list in parentheses. As you've seen, these are declared in the usual fashion of a data type, followed by a variable name. If a calling process wants to use the function, it must do so using the same form.

The act of calling the function with parameters is known as *passing values* (or variables) to the function. The calling code can pass constant values that match the type of the parameters or a variable. The variable must match the type of the parameter, either by casting into the target type or using a variable of the correct type from the outset.

The types are fairly strict and will be caught at compile time by the compiler. Should there not be an explicit match, the compiler will issue an error or a warning. Errors are issued when there is a type conflict or invalid cast; warnings occur when the types match but are of different sizes (for example, a signed integer being passed instead of an unsigned integer).

Variables can be passed to functions in one of two ways: by *reference* or by *value*. Constants, however, should be treated as if they are always passed by *value*. Bearing this in mind, passing by reference or value will have implications on how the variable is treated before, during, and after the function exits.

Passing by Value

Passing by value simply means that the actual value is passed as if it were a constant. The variable is treated as a constant inside the function. If any changes are made, they will not be persistent, and it is bad programming practice to alter a variable that has been passed by value.

Bear in mind that the code inside the function is executing in isolation. Hence, you might not know whether the calling code specified a variable or constant in the call itself, and so this logic affects the way that the variable is treated inside the function body.

Consider the following function:

```
int AddTwoValues ( int nOne, int nTwo )
{
   return nOne + nTwo;
}
```

nOne and nTwo are local to the AddTwoValues function. You can call the function in a variety of ways:

```
nAdded = AddTwoValues ( 2, 2); // nAdded contains 4
```

```
nAdded = AddTwoValues ( 2, nAnotherValue ); // nAdded contains 2 + nAnotherValue
```

If you were to alter either of the local variables in the function, you would not be able to pass back the value in the first call because 2 is constant. In the second call, even though you used a variable, the function is not aware of this once it has been called.

Remember that constants cannot be changed, so treat parameters as such. Therefore, variables passed by value should be treated as constants, and no attempt should be made to change them. Of course, you can always make a copy of a variable if changes are required in order to implement the function.

Passing by Reference

Sometimes you'll need to pass an updated value of a variable back to the calling function and update the variable at the same time. A good example of this is in reading a number from the keyboard with the familiar scanf library function:

```
scanf ( "%d", &nNumber );
```

In this function call to scanf, the nNumber variable is passed by reference, (denoted by <type> and <name>). The reference in question is an actual pointer to the memory that contains the variable, and subsequently, the value can be modified.

This modification will hold outside the function, because you've allowed the function to access the place where it is stored. Of course, a constant value should not be passed by reference.

You can declare a function as containing a variable to be passed by reference using code such as:

```
int MyFunction ( int & nPassedByReference );
```

If you then write a piece of code to pass an integer variable in a function call to MyFunction and subsequently modify it inside MyFunction, the value will remain updated once the function exits. Another way to pass by reference is to specify that a pointer to the data should be provided.

A declaration of such a function would look like the following:

```
int MyFunction ( int * pnPassedByReference );
```

If you wanted to pass a variable that was not declared as a pointer to an integer to MyFunction, you would have to use the & operator to create a reference to it. This is preferable to creating an explicit cast to the new variable. The following, for example, is not considered portable C code by some compilers:

```
int nNumber, nReturn;

nReturn = MyFunction ( (int *) nNumber );
```

The more acceptable version of the previous snippet is:

```
int nNumber, nReturn;

nReturn = MyFunction ( &nNumber );
```

Some data types (strings, arrays, and so on) are passed by reference by default, because they are effectively pointers to areas of memory containing data. By inference, pointers are also always passed by reference, as you've seen previously.

Equally, user-defined complex types (see Chapter 12) such as structs can be passed by value or reference, but it is more common to pass a pointer to the struct or to create a reference to the variable. If the struct is passed by value, again, it may not be changed.

The only slightly confusing point to watch out for is that if you have an array, you pass it without explicitly putting a reference operator in the code. This is the way that the compiler works, and you have no choice over that. This means that it is possible to change the data in the array and have that change reflected directly in memory.

However, there's a useful keyword that you can use to avoid this having unintended effects. Consider the following function definition:

```
char * strcat(char *__dest, const char *__src);
```

The destination string (__dest) is altered by adding the unalterable source string (__src) to it. The pointer to the destination string (with the newly added source string) is returned. The strcat function can change the __dest variable but not the __src variable, even though they are both declared as pointers.

The const keyword essentially means that the object following it may not be changed. Although the most common usage for const is as shown here, it is also perfectly legal C programming to define any variable as const. The program just cannot change it once it has been initialized, which might not make sense in the application code.

Recursion

Recursion is a programming technique that can be described simply as a function calling itself. This is accomplished by a line calling the function being present inside the function body. This call must be conditionally executed; otherwise the function will continue to call itself forever.

You must define a condition under which the recursion will end and make sure that at some point you reach that point. The implementation will mean either prematurely exiting the function or simply calling the function again, based on the evaluation of a conditional statement.

The technique is tricky to use well but very powerful. It's effective for traversing arrays or lists of items. One issue with recursion is that it builds a *stack* of intermediate values during the recursive evaluation of the function, so that the values of variables are retained as the evaluation continues.

Creating such a stack is reasonably memory intensive—more so for deep recursion having long parameter lists—so use recursion with care.

As a simple example of recursion with a single execution path, you could create a function to evaluate the mathematical n!. This function should be started with a non-zero parameter, n, and return the result of multiplying by successively decreasing values until 1 is reached. In other words:

1	5
2	× 4
3	× 3
4	× 2
5	× 1 = 120

A recursive function to achieve this has to do two things:

■ Stop at 1.

■ Return the result of a multiplication by successive values of n−1.

Before you look at the following code, try to imagine how this will look as a recursive function. When you're ready, a possible solution awaits:

```
long int Function_n ( int nMul )
{
    if ( nMul == 1 )
    {
        return 1;
    }
```

```
    else
    {
        return nMul * Function_n ( nMul - 1 );
    }
}
```

This snippet might not be the best implementation, but it satisfies all the criteria. You can call it from a program by using a line such as:

```
printf ( "%ld", Function_n ( 5 ) );
```

This should print 120, and you can check the result with a calculator. This is an example of a single execution path function. You can also introduce a selection process by which you can execute the recursive function with different values, depending upon the values passed in the call to the function.

This can be useful for performing binary searches, where a tree can be traversed by evaluating the nodes at specific branches, which eventually leads to a leaf node (that has no children) and returns that value. The same rules apply—the recursion must end at some point, and a calling stack will be created containing intermediate values for the parameters passed.

So, you need to:

- Stop when there are no more children.

- Stop and return this node if the values match.

- Search the left tree if the value is higher.

- Search the right tree if the value is lower.

This is a fairly advanced concept, but you should again think about how it could be achieved. Because you've not read about trees, pointers, structures, and so forth, the following code will contain some unfamiliar notation. The intention should be clear, based on the preceding description.

```
node * SearchTree ( node * head, int nValue )
{
    if ( head == NULL )
    {
        return NULL;
    }
    if ( head->nValue == nValue )
```

```
    {
      return head;
    }
    else
    {
      // Assuming binary sorted tree
      if ( head->nValue > nValue )
      {
          return SearchTree ( head->left, nValue );
      }
        else
        {
        return SearchTree ( head->right, nValue );
      }
    }
  }
```

Again, this code snippet might not be the most efficient solution, but it is easy to follow. If you don't immediately understand the notation and use of pointers, you're invited to come back to this topic once you've read Chapters 12 and 13, covering complex data types and pointers.

Recap

User-defined functions are a good way to break up a programming project to allow functionality to be spread across modules. In software-engineering terms, this permits the programmer to reuse modules that might have functionality that can be shared across application projects and makes each source code module easier to maintain.

Each function should be prototyped before use and can take a number of parameters while also returning a value (or none at all—void). Be careful when altering the value of parameters that have been passed, as it will depend on whether the value (or variable) has been passed by value or reference.

Finally, you can use recursion as a special technique to solve otherwise complex programming problems that cannot be easily addressed via a simple looping structure. However, be wary when applying recursive techniques, because they can lead to bugs that are difficult to track down.

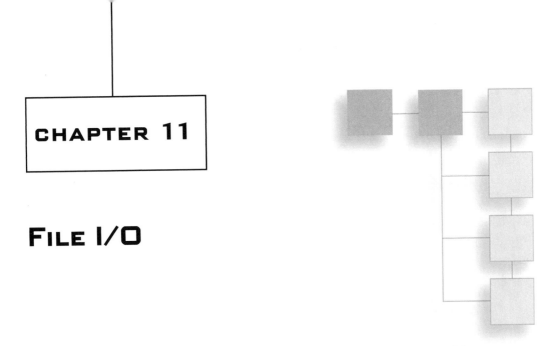

CHAPTER 11

FILE I/O

Handling files is a very important part of being able to write useful programs. Whether you're using back-end daemons for delivering content on the World Wide Web, using database files, editing text, or processing data in other ways, you'll need files in order to accomplish these tasks.

When you store data in files, it's persistently stored, whereas any of the other functions for data manipulation only do so while maintaining data in memory. Once the computer is turned off or the application has been terminated, the data is lost.

The aim of this chapter is to show you how to use standard input and output manipulation functions to process information in files.

Using these functions, you can use files to store data permanently. These functions server as a cornerstone of other file processing functions such as reading files from the Internet and importing files generated by other programs.

Before reading this chapter, you might want to review the standard input and output functions discussed in the appropriate chapters. Bear in mind that Chapter 8 on the Standard Libraries can help you understand some of the code samples if need be.

Formatted I/O Revisited

You first read about formatted I/O in Chapter 5, "Console I/O," where you learned to direct output to the screen and retrieve input from the keyboard. These interfaces with the outside world are called *streams*. A stream is a sequential source of data and can be read-only or read-write. The operating system is responsible for connecting the streams to the actual hardware (screen, printer, hard disk drive, keyboard, and so on).

In most C language implementations, the operating system-specific code is written in such a way as to treat files and streams in roughly the same manner. For example, you have already seen that the console can be referred to as:

stdin   Standard input stream

stdout   Standard output stream

These are essentially file handles, predetermined by the compiler toolkit to represent the appropriate streams—in essence, you are treating the screen and keyboard as character stream interfaces. These can then be referenced like files that are stored externally and can be read from and written to.

So the screen and keyboard can be treated as if they are streams and are handled as if they are files, at a low level. Consider, for example, the following function call:

```
fflush ( stdin );
```

The starting f in the function name indicates that this is likely to be a function that is to be used with files. Thus, stdin is a file handle. There are other standard input and output functions from stdio.h that also have an f at the start of the function name; again, these are file-handling functions.

Before you can tackle how to use these with files, you first need to look at how to open a file. The act of opening a file usually returns a file handle, which gives you a reference to that file. The stdin and stdout constants are examples of file handles.

Although stdin and stdout are, in a sense, always open, other files need to be opened and closed by using function calls designed to work with persistent storage, such as files. The stdio.h library includes functions for doing this as well as manipulating the data to be stored and retrieved.

You can read and write data to files using the standard formatted input and output functions, which are mirror images of the printf and scanf functions you saw earlier, but tailored for use with files. Data is mostly stored as text in these cases, even if the variable is something else, because they print to the file as if printing to the screen.

The only syntactical difference between, for example, printf and fprintf is an additional parameter (the first one) that points to a stream that has been opened using the fopen function. The fopen function returns the file handle, which gives the application access to the stream.

The fopen function has been covered in Chapter 8, which you can use as reference in the future. As a reminder, here is the prototype:

```
FILE * fopen (const char * filename,
              const char * mode);
```

The mode parameter is a string that's formed from one of the following characters and an optional + sign:

r   Read from file

w   Write to file

a   Append to file

The + sign indicates that you want access to the file in both directions. So if you only want to read from the file, you can specify the flag r. Reading starts at the beginning of the file, and the file pointer can move anywhere within it.

If you also want to write to the file, you need to specify r+, which tells the compiler that you need to be able to read *and* write to the file (bidirectional access). Writing occurs wherever the current file pointer is positioned. The file pointer is just a byte offset into the file (a numerical value), which you can retrieve with a call to ftell:

```
ftell ( FILE * hFile )
```

If you try to open a file for reading or reading/writing, the file must exist. If it does not, the function call to open it will fail. The handle returned in this case is equal to NULL. If you want to test whether a file exists, you could form an if statement as follows:

```
if ( (hFile = fopen ( szFileName, "r" ) = = NULL)
```

This statement will execute if the call to fopen returns NULL, indicating that the file does not exist. It is a legitimate test, because the only way that the function can return NULL is if the filename is incorrect or the file really does not exist. fopen will create a file that does not exist only if you specify a write or write/read mode.

If all you need to do is write to the file, you must use the w mode. In this mode, the file will be created if it does not exist. However, should the file already exist, it will be truncated as a result of creating a new file over the top of the old one. Of course, to prevent this, you can perform the previous test first to check if the file exists.

If the file does exist and you still need to write to it, you can simply open it with the r+ mode set. Recall, however, that in this case, writing occurs at the current file position. In order to write at the end of the file (append), you can reposition the file pointer at the end of the file or use the append mode.

The append modes are indicated by specifying the a or a+ mode value. In the first case, the file is opened and the pointer is positioned for writing at the end. In the latter case, the file is opened for both reading and writing. Reading may occur anywhere in the file, but writing will always occur at the end.

To use append modes, the file needs to be present, or any subsequent calls will fail because the handle returned by fopen will be NULL. The only indication you can get to determine that anything is amiss is either by testing the file handle or testing the result of each call to the formatted I/O functions. This is good practice in any case as it helps to write a more robust application, provided that any errors returned are correctly handled.

Once you have finished with the file, you must close it with a call to the fclose function. The prototype for fclose is as follows:

```
fclose ( FILE * hFile )
```

This will close the file indiscriminately and independently of any items in the buffer that might need to be read from or written to the file. In other words, there might still be some data that's not been accessed that has been prepared by the operating system in order to help process the file efficiently.

This is not usually a problem when reading from files, but can be a problem when writing data because a call to fclose might not flush the buffer to the file. So it is advisable to call fflush to make sure that the read/write operations are complete *before* closing the file with fclose.

Any standard file handle can be closed, but you're advised against trying to close stdin or stdout, because these are standard handles provided for access to the screen and keyboard, so their behavior could be undefined. However, these streams should be explicitly flushed with fflush because data could remain in the buffer between the hardware and the application.

One final note on flushing is that, once flushed, the buffer will be cleared of data. Any data that might have remained in an input buffer is therefore lost. In other words, if you are reading from a file, you have to rewind in order to retrieve the data again. Clearly, though, this is not possible when using stdin because that stream is linked to the user via the keyboard.

Fully Qualified Pathnames

I've been vague about the value of the filename parameter to date in the discussion of files. No matter the operating system being written for, there are always two kinds of filenames that can be used to open a file. The first kind is just a simple name, as in:

```
FILE * hFile = fopen ( "Myfile.txt", "r" );
```

Here, the file Myfile.txt is assumed to be located in the same directory folder as the application that tries to access it. If not, the operating system *may* try to search for the file along the standard paths associated with the user's application; if the file is to be created, it will be created in the same directory folder as the application.

You can also access other locations by specifying a fully qualified filename—one that includes the path as well as the file. So if you know that a directory exists in the root directory of a Windows-based PC called MyFiles, you can access a file in it by specifying the whole path, as follows:

```
FILE * hFile = fopen ( "c:\MyFiles\Myfile.txt", "r" );
```

So far, so good. However, the best advice for programmers using files and paths is to use fully qualified pathnames only from the root if it is specified by the users. In other words, if you have prompted for a path and filename, only then can you be sure that the path exists and is probably correct.

On the other hand, you access most applications' files from the applications' own folders. This includes creating sub-folders for use during the session. In these cases, you can specify a filename that begins with the . (period) character. This essentially makes a fully qualified path starting from the application's folder.

Using the previous example, you could indicate a filename value as follows:

```
FILE * hFile = fopen ( ".\Myfile.txt", "r" );
```

This code line would access a file in the application folder. However, if you use two period characters, you can access the folder *above* the application folder. For example:

```
FILE * hFile = fopen ( "..\Myfile.txt", "r" );
```

These paths are always relative to the current application folder and can also include folder names:

```
FILE * hFile = fopen ( ".\Files\Myfile.txt", "r" );
```

This example would access a file called Myfile.txt in the application folder's subfolder, called Files, should it exist. If either the path or the file does not exist, hFile will be set to NULL.

Finally, note that the parameter passed to the main function through the argv variable in the first position contains the fully qualified pathname for the application's executable file. You can strip this back to get the fully qualified pathname to the application's folder, should you need it.

Using fprintf

The first of the formatted I/O functions covered here is parallel to the printf function you learned about in Chapter 5. It is called fprintf and allows you to output text to a file that has been opened for writing (or reading and writing).

The fprintf function allows you to output data to the file exactly as if it were outputting to the screen. The definition of fprintf is as follows:

```
int fprintf (FILE * stream,
        const char * format [, argument list]);
```

The [argument list] will depend on the contents of the format parameter; it may be that there are zero parameters or many, depending on how many translatable data fields exist in format. In this respect, the function is identical to the standard printf. The file handle is provided in the first parameter.

By way of a slight aside, you can also perform console output by specifying stdout as the stream instead of a file handle:

```
fprintf ( stdout, "%s", "A String" );
```

If the function succeeds, the number of characters written to the file is returned; otherwise, a negative number is returned. Failure can indicate that the file doesn't exist or is only open for reading and not writing, or that some other error occurred.

Because you're treating the file as a text-based interface, the parameters should usually be passed by value. In other words, you cannot (should not) pass an array directly, but rather you should pass each element to the `fprintf` function individually. The following, for example, would not work:

```
fprintf ( stdout, "%s", "A String" );
```

However, you can pass an array of characters directly, because the compiler understands that this is supported by the `%s` format specifier. In the previous example, `%d` can refer only to a single integer. This means that if you want to write an array of integers to a file, you need to use a loop to move through each element and write them individually.

Code Sample 11.1: Writing Multiple Integers to a File

The code to do this might look akin to the following code snippet, which assumes you know how many integers there are in the array:

```
void WriteIntegers( int * nIntegerArray, int nNumberOfIntegers )
{
  for ( int n = 0; n < nNumberOfIntegers; n++ )
      fprintf ( hFile, "%d ", nIntegerArray[n] );
}
```

These lines will print a line of integers, each separated by a space character, for as many as are indicated by the `nNumberOfIntegers` variable. You could also calculate the number of elements in the array by using a formula such as `sizeof ( nIntegerArray ) / sizeof ( int )`, which is usually portable to most platforms.

The first parameter is also new yet should be familiar. I've used a pointer to an array of integers, rather than a static array. You can still refer to the variable as you would an array, but the `sizeof` calculation will not work. This is because it will return the size of the pointer rather than the memory allocated.

You'll look at this again in Chapter 13, when you learn about pointers and their relationship to variables and arrays.

Using fscanf

In the same way that printf has a companion function scanf for handling keyboard input, fprintf has a companion function fscanf for handling formatted file input based on the conversion of input fields. The fscanf function reads and translates fields according to a specific format and assigns them to the parameter list from left to right.

The function definition is as follows:

```
int fscanf (FILE * stream,
    const char * format [, argument list]);
```

The return value from fscanf is slightly different from fprintf, in that it contains the number of specific items read and converted, without counting any fields that have been ignored. Recall that fprintf returns the number of actual characters output to the file.

Also, if an error occurs, this is indicated by the return value only when it occurs before the first assignment of a field value to a variable could be done. Otherwise, if the number of assignments made is less than the number of parameters supplied, this is a good indication that an error occurred.

The only possible errors are end of file or some other hardware problem. The function will interpret the input stream to the best of its ability, converting fields as best it can. Sometimes this might cause an application crash if the types are incompatible; there is no real way in C programming to trap this kind of event. You have the responsibility to make sure that it cannot happen.

In addition, when calling fscanf, you should be careful to always pass the parameters by reference, as they will be modified by the function. If, for example, you want to read in an integer, you might attempt to do so using code such as the following:

```
int nInt;
fscanf ( hFile, " %d ", &nInt ); // Correct
fscanf (hFile, " %d ", nInt); // Error
int * pInt; // Pointer to int
pInt = (int *) malloc ( sizeof ( int ) );
fscanf (hFile, " %d ", pInt); // Correct
```

The first fscanf call is correct, as it uses the indirection operator & to pass a reference to the nInt variable. The second is incorrect, as it passes the variable by value, and any changes made to it will not be correctly interpreted.

The final call to fscanf explicitly creates a reference to an integer by making a pointer to memory, which you then allocate with a call to malloc. You supply the size of an integer to the malloc call so that the program can correctly allocate the memory block.

The pointer is then valid and can be used as a reference to the place where you want to store the integer value. When you have finished with the pInt variable, be sure to call free to release the memory.

Following the previous example, if you want to read in an array of integers, you might assume that the fscanf function would be capable of reading them all in at once. After all, an array is, by default, a collection that is passed by reference. So, the code you might *attempt* would look something like:

```
int sInt[10];
fscanf ( hFile, " %d ", sInt); // Error
```

Code Sample 11.2: Reading Multiple Integers from a File

Although this code might compile, it will not do exactly what you expect. Part of the problem is that, as you saw with fprintf, the function works on fields and not on chains of numbers. Therefore, you need to loop through the array and read in each item by passing by reference:

```
int nItem, sInt[10];
for ( nItem = 0; nItem < 10; nItem++ )
{
     fscanf ( hFile, " %d ", &sInt[nItem] );
}
```

When used together, the two functions fprintf and fscanf can provide some powerful formatted data file-manipulation possibilities. If, for example, you need to create an address book application, you can write out, in a formatted fashion, the address details and read them back in relatively easily.

Using `fprintf` and `scanf` Together

The benefit of using formatted data processing in text mode is that the resulting file can be edited by a text editor, and error checking is much easier to enforce. It is also easier to verify that the correct processing has been performed.

However, the ease of editing and ability to view the file directly is its downfall, because files tend to be slightly bloated (an integer in binary format takes much less space for larger numbers) and can be changed by anyone, which is not always desirable. Consider, for example, a game where the data file contains information relating to the challenges that the players might encounter.

The ability to easily edit the file might lead players to cheat—either by looking ahead in the file to seek out the solution to a problem or by changing the file so that they can win the game more easily. These are perhaps trivial examples, and you might find more serious possible downfalls by looking at your own problem domain.

Bearing this in mind, one of the best uses for formatted input is in reading and writing strings efficiently. Coupled with memory-management functions, you can create a sophisticated mechanism for variable-length string reading and writing that makes the most of the formatted file input and output functions.

This is also a good exercise for putting many of the memory, stream, and C language constructs together in a practical example. It touches on many useful general programming techniques, and it is worth it to you to take some time to understand how to achieve the final solution.

First, to write a variable length null-terminated (last character is \0) string to a file, you need to write out the length of the string and then the string itself. This can be completed in a single function call:

```
fprintf ( hFile, "%d %s ",
    strlen ( szString) , szString );
```

Note that the strlen function from string.h is used to obtain the length (excluding the null terminator) of the string. An alternative to consider is to use the sizeof function to determine the length of the string pointed to by the szString variable. In this case, it's easier to use strlen, because you don't know, platform to platform, the size of the character type being used.

Code Sample 11.3: Reading Variable-Length Strings from a File

Writing the string is therefore an easy proposition. Reading the string back in is a little more delicate and requires several steps.

These steps are as follows:

- Read the required length.

- Allocate the memory.

- Read the string.

- Add a null terminator.

The following is a possible implementation of the outlined approach:

```
fscanf ( hFile, "%d ", &nLength );

// Allocate enough space for string and
//   a null terminator

szString = (char *) malloc
        ( sizeof (char) * (nLength+1));

fscanf ( hFile, "%s ", szString );

// Assign the null terminator.
szString[nLength] = '\0';
```

This implementation will cope with any length of string and will read in any string. The limitation, as you might have noticed, is that the `fscanf` function will stop reading the string when it reaches the first whitespace character, as it is reading a field bound by whitespace.

Code Sample 11.4: Reading Multiple Characters from a File

To make the string reading work properly with strings that contain whitespace, you need to substitute the single `fscanf` call with a loop:

```
for ( n = 0; n < nLength,; n++ )
{
    fscanf ( hFile, "%c", &szString[n] );
}
```

Remember also to terminate the string by adding a null character to the end of the array. Although this implementation is perfectly valid, there is an alternative that's slightly more efficient, using binary file input and output. Before you look at this, let's review a few other functions for reading and writing streams—using unformatted I/O.

Unformatted I/O Revisited

Whereas formatted I/O deals with the translation of variables into text fields and vice versa, unformatted I/O can handle single or multiple characters. Recall that you saw the functions `getchar`, `putchar`, `gets`, and `puts` to process character data on `stdin` and `stdout`.

It is no surprise to learn that there are file equivalents to these that work in exactly the same way, except that the character data is output to and input from a file stream. This approach does have some uses, but it is not as flexible as other methods since it can cope only with character data.

Using Single Character I/O

To read a single character from a file that has been opened with a call to `fopen` and from which reading may occur, use the `fgetc` function, whose definition is as follows:

```
int fgetc ( FILE * stream )
```

This function will read the next character from the input stream, should one exist. If there is no character available, it will return an error value. Because 0 is an appropriate value for a character (if maybe a little unusual), the return value is likely to be –1. However, this might change, depending on the compiler, so you're advised to check beforehand.

The companion function to `fgetc` is `fputc`, which has the following definition:

```
int fputc ( char character, FILE * stream )
```

Not surprisingly, this function will write the character variable to the file opened with `fopen`, with the possibility to write to it. Should an error occur during the writing process, an error value will be returned by the function. Again, you might want to check which values are considered errors by your compiler.

Using Line-Based Multicharacter I/O

If you want to write out a whole line of characters (a string), you can do so with a single call to `fputs`. The definition of `fputs` is as follows:

```
int fputs ( const char * string, FILE * stream )
```

This function ignores whitespace and could have equally well been used in the variable-length string-reading and -writing example. This being the case, you might also have replaced the reading facility with a single call to the companion function fgets instead of multiple calls to fscanf. The definition of fgets is as follows:

```
int fgets ( char * string, int max_length, FILE * stream )
```

This would seem to be an elegant solution; fgets can read in a number of characters (limited by the max_length parameter) from an open stream. Because you have written out the length, you can then read it back in and know how many characters you need to read. This, however, is the crux of the problem in using these functions: You still have to use fprintf and fscanf to deal with integers.

If you want to use only fgets and fputs, you need to have some way of reading and writing character representations of the integers. Conversion between them is possible, as you learned in Chapter 8, but that's a longwinded solution to what should be an easy-to-solve problem.

The most elegant solution to these problems is often to use binary I/O. This does not have an equivalent in the stdin or stdout stream-handling world and is strictly for use with files.

Binary Input and Output

You can also write variables to files as binary values—an integer (for example) will remain an integer. Some advantages of space and processing time are apparent: For example, an integer takes two bytes to store in memory, but this could expand to up to five bytes of characters when written to a file.

Using binary representation keeps the size of the stored integer down to two bytes, a clear advantage if there are many numbers in a file. The same analysis can be performed on floating-point numbers of large accuracy. Storing them as binary data will be much more space efficient than storing them as text. The gain is in the size of file and a boost in speed and efficiency when reading or writing the file.

A binary file can also not be easily read by a text editor, which might be an advantage. Such a file (like a Word document) is often called a closed binary format data file because the structure is often not widely publicized or easily divulged from the file itself.

It is not impossible, given enough patience, to determine the layout of a file from its binary representation, but it does make it more difficult. Add to this the fact that you can use binary input and output to read and write encrypted data, and the advantages become obvious.

Binary files can be used to ensure that data is not tampered with—this is especially useful for game data (you don't want players to cheat) and sensitive banking details. Encryption is part of the standard approach to keeping data safe from prying eyes and requires binary-level manipulation to work correctly.

Even if security is not the primary concern, a binary structure file makes for a more efficient data exchange method. For a start, you are no longer limited to printable characters and can use the full 0–255 range allowed in the short integer data type.

Binary files include audio, video, and static images, all of which use a special format for the file and encode data using a standard algorithm. Although it might be possible to encode an image using printable characters only, it is not as efficient or practical as using binary manipulation.

Using `fread` and `fwrite`

The two binary file-processing functions are `fread` and `fwrite`. They are similar in definition:

```
int fread ( void * data, int size, int count,
  FILE * file );
```

```
int fwrite ( void * data, int size, int count,
  FILE * file );
```

The first parameter is the data to be written or read, the second is the size of each data item, the third is the number of data items, and the final parameter is the file stream, opened with a call to `fopen`. The use of a `void` pointer in the first parameter is because it is not known what kind of data will be passed to the function until it is invoked.

In addition, because the first parameter is itself a pointer, it can be cast to any type, including a pointer (reference) to a single item of data.

The following is perfectly legal C code:

```
fread ( &nLength, sizeof( int ), 1, hFile );
```

This example reads a single integer from a file. In this case, you do not know how big the integer representation is at the time you write the code, nor do you need to know, because you use the `sizeof` function to reveal it at runtime.

You can also read in a string, using code such as:

```
fread ( (char *) szString, sizeof ( char ),
        nLength, hFile );
```

This code treats `szString` as a block of memory and is particularly useful for writing arrays of data. You'll learn in the next chapter just how useful this feature can be. For now, it means that you can read an entire string in one function call, as you can see, without having to worry about whitespace characters.

The variable-length string file-handling routines therefore become a little easier to work with. Writing becomes a two-stage process:

```
fwrite ( (int *) strlen ( szString),
         sizeof ( int), 1, hFile );

fwrite ( (char *) szString,
         sizeof( char ), strlen ( szString ), hFile);
```

Code Sample 11.5: Reading a Variable Length String from a File as Binary Data

Note that you need to make two function calls because the `fwrite` function cannot deal with formatted fields of data in the same way that `fprintf` can. Although this makes the code slightly more complicated than the formatted text version you saw previously, reading the data back in becomes a mirror image of this code:

```
fread ( &nLength,
        sizeof ( int), 1, hFile );

fread ( (char *) szString,
        sizeof( char ), nLength, hFile);
```

The previous coded segments assume that you have correctly allocated the `szString` parameter as a block of memory, using a call akin to:

```
szString = (char *) malloc ( sizeof(char) * nLength+1 );
```

In addition, you usually need to add the null character to the end of the string (which is why you allocate one character more than you need) once you have read the string from the file. This is straightforward:

```
szString[nLength] = '\0';
```

One final note. If you have a string containing 10 characters and a null terminator (11 in total), strlen will return 10. This is because arrays are accessed using a zero-based index. The array contains characters [0] to [9] with [10] being the null terminator. So when you write out the string, you write out characters [0 ... nLength-1].

This means that when you allocate the memory, you need to allocate an extra byte (nLength+1) for the null terminator, but it will actually be the character [nLength] of the resulting array. This may sound convoluted, but it quickly becomes second nature.

The same technique can be applied to data blocks containing any kind of data. However, it is vital to remember that if strings are to be manipulated with the string.h library, a null terminator (\0) must be added to the end. This is not provided by default, and if it is not there, the string.h library functions will produce incorrect behavior, sometimes leading to memory corruption and crashes.

Directory Management

I have tried to remain operating system independent throughout this chapter, but often there are some functions that are tied to a specific platform. Directory-handling functions are one such area—the Windows API has specific directory (and file) handling functions, as do other APIs.

However, the ANSI C specification does provide, in the io.h library, a number of useful functions for handling directories. Although there are many functions in io.h, in the interest of providing just enough information to enable you to achieve useful programming tasks, this chapter looks at three main areas:

- Creating and deleting directories

- Renaming and deleting files

- Searching for files and directories

Creating and Deleting Directories

You can create a directory with a very simple function call:

```
int mkdir ( const char * dir_name )
```

If the dir_name is not fully qualified, the directory will be created in the current working directory. You can find out which directory that is by calling the getcwd function:

```
int getcwd ( char * dir_name, int max_length )
```

The current working directory will then be returned in the dir_name variable. An error value is returned, and the dir_name is set to null if the call fails. You can also change the current working directory by calling chdir:

```
int chdir ( const char * dir_name )
```

Again, if the path is not complete, you assume that dir_name exists in the current working directory. To get a list of directories that are available, you need to search for them; this task is covered in the last part of this section.

To delete a directory, call the rmdir function:

```
int rmdir ( const char * dir_name )
```

Again, dir_name must exist and can be fully qualified. However, the directory must also be empty or the function call will fail. To check why the function call did not work and to return the appropriate error message to the user, it will be necessary to call chdir to check that the directory exists and search it to see if it is empty.

Note that you can call chdir with a double period to change to the parent directory for the current working directory:

```
chdir ( ".." ); // Change up a directory
```

So testing to see whether a directory exists can be done by changing to it and then changing back again to make sure that the current directory is not changed permanently.

Renaming and Deleting Files

If the program needs to rename a file (to create a backup, for example, before writing the new file), it can be done with a simple call to the rename function from stdio.h:

```
int rename ( const char * old_name, const char * new_name )
```

If a file with the new_name already exists, the return value will be an error. To check in advance, the program simply needs to call the fopen function with the r flag set. The same applies to the file referred to with the old_name parameter.

You can delete a file by calling the remove function:

```
int remove ( const char * filename )
```

Some compilers also provide an unlink function, which performs the same file deletion. File deletion will take place if the file exists and if it's empty. Some implementations, even on the Windows platform, will remove the file permanently without easy recourse, so it is a function that is best used with care, if at all.

Searching for Files and Directories

A selection of functions in io.h can be used to search directories for files. Again, the Windows API, for example, has specific functions to achieve this, but the standard ANSI C implementation has some cross-platform equivalents.

You have not yet read about abstract data types such as structure, yet the directory search functions require that you populate a structure containing file data. This file data provides a skeleton that can be filled by the file-finding functions; at the outset, you populate it with some basic information, and the file-finding functions will fill it with the details of each file found.

The basic process is as follows:

1. Find the first file (with skeleton data).

2. Find the next file.

3. Repeat Step 2 until no more files are found.

4. Close the file-finding process.

The structure is called _finddata_t (or similar), defined in io.h. This contains the following members that are of interest for populating the search skeleton:

```
attrib      the file attributes
name        the filename
```

The attrib member is a combination of several flags, which are combined using the OR operator (|). The most common attributes are as follows:

```
_A_NORMAL      normal files
_A_SUBDIR      directories
_A_RDONLY      read-only files
```

```
_A_HIDDEN        hidden files
_A_SYSTEM        system files
```

The three functions that use the _finddata_t structure are as follows:

```
int _findfirst ( const char * file_name, struct _finddata_t * find_data )
int _findnext ( int find_handle , struct _finddata_t * find_data )
int _findclose ( int find_handle )
```

The _findfirst function needs to be handed the filename (which can include wildcards and spaces) and a partially populated _finddata_t structure that gives additional information—usually just the file attributes. The handle returned is an integer that you can then use in subsequent calls.

When you call _findnext, you provide the find_handle and the find_data structure, which is then populated with the details of the next file to be found. If none is found, _findnext returns –1; if a file is found, _findnext returns 0.

If there are no more files left, the program must call _findclose. The only parameter in this case is the find_handle. Calling _findclose returns the resources associated with the file-finding process to the operating system.

Code Sample 11.6: Finding Files in a Directory

So if you want to find all the directories that are subdirectories of the current working directory, you can use the following code:

```
_finddata_t oFindData;
char szFindSkeleton[255];
int nFindHandle;

oFindData.attrib = A_SUBDIR; // Set the attrib to be directories
sprintf ( szFindSkeleton, "*.*" ); // All files
nFileHandle = _findfirst ( szFindSkeleton, &oFindData );
if ( nFileHandle != -1 )
{
     do
     {
            // Do something with the found file
            // The name is in oFindData.name
     } while ( _findnext ( find_handle, &oFindData ) == 0 );
     _findclose ( find_handle ); // Close the find operation
}
```

This code should be fairly self-explanatory. You first set the attributes to look for directories, and then set the filename to *.*, which means all files. You then look for the first file and process it.

One check that is done explicitly is the validity of the find_handle, and this check must be completed before trying to access oFindData.name or calling any other _find functions. At the end of the loop, the _findnext function is called with the find_handle to get the next file, should it exist. If it does not, the loop is exited and _findclose is called.

The only changes that need to be made to adapt this code to other situations are the attributes and filename. So to look for all read-only text files, you would set the attributes to _A_RDONLY and the filename to *.txt.

It's best to play with these possibilities before implementing this in a real application. However, the process is relatively easy to grasp.

Recap

In this chapter, you saw two kinds of file (stream-based) input and output. The formatted variants mirror the stream-oriented terminal reading and writing capabilities provided in the stdio.h library. This is useful for textual data and for instances where the format is well known and should be shared across applications (HTML or CSV files, for example).

Binary input and output have other advantages. They are easier to manipulate programmatically. However, they come with the added disadvantage that the binary files are harder to debug. They can, however, be more data efficient and provide a better closed binary system than text files.

Generally speaking, it's best to use formatted text for shared plain text data and binary formatting for shared binary files (pictures and compressed data, for example) or for private format, closed binary files (a Word document, for example).

Directory and file management can be carried out using ANSI C functions, but be sure to check with your operating system and compiler toolkit documentation to see whether any platform-specific variants also exist. Generally speaking, considering that there are additional security and other attributes available in most operating systems, it is probably a good idea to check for them.

For example, some attributes in the Windows filing system include compression, which are not reflected in the attributes listed in this chapter. However, no matter the operating system, as long as the libraries exist to be linked with the application when it is built for a given platform, the functions listed here should be portable.

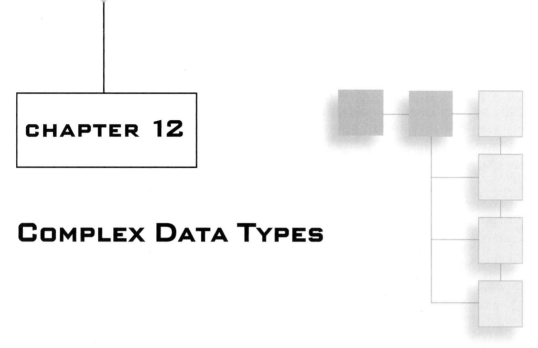

CHAPTER 12

COMPLEX DATA TYPES

The aim of this chapter is to introduce you to ways in which the standard data types available to the C programmer can be extended by using more complex data types. These are called abstract or user-defined data types.

These constructs are very useful in building a program that's capable of dealing with data in a logical fashion. Some of the pitfalls and caveats are pointed out along the way, and you'll see an example that should help you create your own complex data types.

After you work through this chapter, you should be able to model real-world data in a coherent manner. This is a vital part of being able to create useful applications.

There are a number of reasons why knowing about complex data types is so vital, chiefly among them being the ability to treat complex data types as chunks of memory that can be manipulated as pure data rather than as numbers, strings, or anything else. As you saw in Chapter 11, "File I/O," with the file-finding process, it also helps to keep complex data in a single object.

The `struct` and `union` Keywords

Superficially, `struct`s and `union`s work in the same way—they provide the definition of a single entity that can contain different kinds of data, and you can use that definition to create objects that are individual instances of that data.

However, there is a fundamental difference between the two in that a `struct` is fully populated, and a `union` provides a mechanism to selectively populate the data contained in the object. Thus, the definition will be different from the final implementation.

In terms of storage, an instance of a `struct` occupies a space in memory that is as big as the size of each individual data type inside it. So if the `struct` contains six integers, the memory space will be six integers wide. On the other hand, an instance of a `union` occupies a space in memory that is as large as the largest member it contains.

So each member in a `struct` is independent and can be independently referenced (and data stored), whereas in a `union`, the data members all overlap. Once you understand the subtle difference, using these complex data types is very easy.

The chapter looks first at the `struct` and then at the `union`. The way that the data members are accessed (in terms of the notation used) is similar, so much of the discussion pertaining to `structs` also applies to `unions`.

The `struct` Keyword

A `struct` is used to create a user-defined data type that can contain multiple items and yet be manipulated via a single variable name. It is akin to a `RECORD` in other programming languages, such as Pascal or Modula-2. For the uninitiated, imagine an address book entry. If the entry is a record, each piece of data is a field within that record.

Each member of the `struct` can be of a different data type, either a built-in type like an integer or an array of characters. The entire `struct` can be passed to functions but cannot be used directly in decision processes because it has an indeterminate type. You cannot even use an assignment or comparison operator between two `structs`, even if they are identically defined.

However, each field (or *member*) can be used in decision processes and assignments as long as they are referenced properly and as long as they are built-in data types. If they are not, the same caveat applies; they cannot be used directly. From this you might deduce that you can nest `structs` within `structs`.

A `struct` can be declared in different ways, but the following style is the most portable:

```
struct
```

```
{

    <type> <name> ...

} <struct_id>;
```

There can, of course, be multiple `<type> <name>` entries, depending on how many fields the record needs. By itself, this definition just states that you require a struct format to be available. To use it, like all other data types, you need to create a variable in which to store the actual data—an *instance* of the struct. This is declared as follows:

```
struct <struct_id> <variable_name>;
```

This is perhaps not as convenient as you might like, because each time you want to create an instance of the struct, you have to repeat the stanza struct `<struct_id>`. To use the struct as a type, which is much more convenient, you can create it as follows:

```
typedef struct
{
    <type> <name> ...
} <struct_id>;
```

Using the typedef keyword in this way, you can then declare a variable as follows:

```
<struct_id> <variable_name>;
```

Code Sample 12.1: Example of typedef struct

This description might seem a little abstract. Imagine an entry in an address book—you could construct a user-defined complex struct type as:

```
typedef struct
{

    char szName[50];
    char szStreet[50];
    int nNumber;
    char szPostalCode[12];
    char szPhoneNumber[25];

} sAddressEntry;
```

In the previous definition, each item is based on a built-in type. You could have implemented it slightly differently, having three sub-structs to hold complex data types for the name, address, and telephone number. This can sometimes over-complicate an initially simple data definition, but it is useful to bear in mind.

The size of the struct can be calculated by the compiler using the sizeof operator. This is useful when resizing memory blocks containing many different elements. For example, if you need an array of 100 sAddressEntry structs to be assigned at runtime, you could make a call to malloc with an appropriate variable and cast:

```
sAddressEntry * oAddressBook; // Variable declaration
oAddressBook = (sAddressEntry *)
          malloc( sizeof (sAddressEntry) * 100);
```

This snippet would create a block of memory large enough to contain 100 user-defined structs. The realloc function could also be used to change this, as you have seen in previous memory-management examples.

Having introduced structs as complex data types, you need to be able to manipulate them using some built-in C language features. Before you do so, note that, in the same way that the string.h library contains functions for processing strings (comparison, length, and so on), when you define a complex type, you need also to provide some similar functions to process them.

These functions will need to access the data, either passed by value or by reference. So, before you can do anything useful with the data, such as reading from or writing to files, you need to understand the ways in which you can extract the information from the object that is the instantiation of the struct.

The union Keyword

The union keyword is similar to the struct keyword in its notation. For example, the typedef variant takes the following form:

```
typedef union
{
    <type> <name> ...
} <union_id>;
```

Although there may be many <type> <name> data members, recall that they all occupy the same space in memory. This is both helpful and confusing. It's helpful because it enables you to change one item and have that change reflected through the other items. It's confusing because it is often difficult to tell from the use of the union that it is not a struct, because the data access method is so similar.

A concrete example should help to clarify the meaning of this. Assume that you want to define a union to represent a data type that can be accessed as a long integer or as four separate bytes (characters, in this case).

The definition of such an entity might take the following form:

```
union
{
    long l;
    char b[4];
} longword;
```

In this example, the memory occupied by longword.l and longword.b[0 . . . 3] is the same. Therefore, you might expect to be able to extract the individual byte components from the long value without resorting to bitwise operations. This is very convenient in programming because it enables you to set and access values directly.

Other than this, the same rules apply to unions as apply to structs—you can have an array of unions, set the array up as a type definition, and create pointers to unions. You can also embed structs inside unions, and they will still occupy the same area of memory.

So if you wanted to extend this definition to allow for access to the long value through a low and high word (integer), you could add a struct, as follows:

```
union
{
    long l;
    char b[4];
    struct
    {
      int low;
      int high;
    } w;
} longword;
```

The named struct w now overlaps the long and the char array, allowing access to the low and high words directly. Note that this is platform dependent, however, and should be used with care. Some systems will reverse the order of the words inside the long data type and will need a slightly different `union` definition (high word first).

You'll learn how to selectively compile sections of source code when you read about preprocessor directives, and this facility will enable you to choose which kind of `union` you define, depending on the platform.

It is also possible to embed a `union` inside a `struct`. The same rules apply, except that the data in the `union` overlaps, whereas the data in the parent `struct` does not. You could embed a `union` inside a `struct` for a variety of purposes, such as allowing the same data type to contain a floating-point value or an integer value, depending on other data members in the `struct`.

```
typedef struct
{
    int code;
    union
        {
          int nValue;
          float fValue;
        } amount;
} currency;
```

In this example, depending on the currency specified by the `code` member, you might want to assign a currency amount the integer or the floating-point version of the `amount` union. Some currencies (for example, US dollars) require a floating-point representation, whereas others (such as the Japanese yen) do not. This representation allows for both.

As an aside, it is also possible to introduce an anonymous `union`:

```
typedef struct
{
    int code;
    union
        {
          int nValue;
          float fValue;
        };
} currency;
```

Note that the `amount` name has been dropped from the definition. This allows you to access `nValue` and `nFloat` as if they were members of the currency struct, as you'll see later on. One caveat: The names must be unique so as not to conflict with other members of the struct that the anonymous union is contained within.

Accessing Data

Data stored in a struct or union is accessed member by member. So if you needed to copy one object to another, with both having the same type (a user-defined struct, for example), you would need to do so member by member. If one happens to be a struct, then it too must be copied member by member.

Accessing a member of a struct or union is accomplished in the following way:

```
variable_name.member_name
```

This code assumes that you have defined a variable of a specific type in variable_name, and that it is a struct or union. You'll learn about the specific concerns of union data member access later; for now, let's look at structs specifically.

You saw this originally in the definition of the data type tm for use with the various standard time functions and again in the file-finding function set. In both cases, the variable was defined directly, for example:

```
_finddata_t oFindData;
```

However, if the variable has been defined as a pointer to the struct, you can also use the following notation:

```
variable_name->member_name
```

The -> operator references a field in a variable that has been assigned to a struct by way of a pointer to the data in memory. By itself, this does not work, because you also need to allocate an appropriate memory block to put it in. The variable should be defined as:

```
_finddata_t * oFindData;
```

By itself, this code does not actually create an object of the _finddata_t type, it just creates a pointer that is compatible with it. If you want to store anything of use in the struct, you need also to allocate the memory and free it again afterwards using malloc and free. You'll see this in action in a moment.

Code Sample 12.2: Manipulating Time and Date *structs*

Using a pointer (or reference) to the variable in the declaration, rather than just declaring it as a normal variable, means that you can manipulate it more easily. For example, to print an ASCII representation of the current date and time, you use code such as:

```
time_t now;
struct tm * time_info;
        // Declared as a pointer to struct tm

time ( &now ); // Pass by reference

time_info = localtime ( &now );
        // Return pointer to struct tm

printf ( "Current date/time : %s\n",
        asctime ( time_info ));
```

Pointers are covered in detail in the next chapter. They are essentially just references to the places in memory where the data types are stored. If you had declared time_info in the previous snippet a regular struct, the last line would read:

```
printf ( "Current date/time : %s"\n",
    asctime ( &time_info ));
```

The reason for the change from pass by value to pass by reference is that the asctime function needs to be able to access values in the time_info structure. The definition of asctime requires that a pointer to that data be passed, so you need to use the reference operator, &.

Data based on structs can also be stored as arrays. In other words, you can create an array of structs in the same way that you can create an array of integers, characters, or any other built-in type. You can access each member of an element in the array using code such as:

```
variable_name[element_number].member_name or
variable_name[element_number]->member_name
```

In the first line, you must declare the array as an array of struct objects, while the second array is an array of pointers. Using the address book complex data type, the definitions would look like the following:

```
sAddressEntry oAddressBook[255]; // An array of 255 sAddressEntry
sAddressEntry * pAddressBook[255]; // Array of pointers to sAddressEntry
```

Again, in the second example, you still need to allocate memory to put the actual data in, because the array is just a collection of references (pointers). This allocation would look something akin to the following:

```
pAddressBook = ( sAddressEntry * )
    malloc ( sizeof ( sAddressEntry ) * 255 );
```

Using an array of pointers makes manipulation (such as changing the order of two or more items in the array) a very easy proposition. Because you are dealing only with references and not with the actual data, copying just becomes a case of swapping pointers around.

For example, to swap two items in an array, you might use code such as the following:

```
sAddressEntry * pTemp = pAddressBook[i];
pAddressBook[i] = pAddressBook[i+1];
pAddressBook[i+1] = pTemp;
```

This example assumes that you have declared a suitable sAddressEntry array of pointers and allocated a memory block to store the data in.

Although the swapping approach is easy enough for simple object manipulation (that is, swapping references), what you cannot do here is easily copy all the data from one struct to another. For example, straight assignation such as the following will not work:

```
target_variable = source_variable;
```

With this code line, even if target_variable is a struct of the same type as source_variable, you cannot copy from one object to another as if it were a regular built-in type. This is because there is probably no copy constructor available, as there is for all the C built-in types (char, int, float, double, and so on).

Instead, you can either define a copy function that copies each member, or you can treat the struct variable as a memory block. In the former case, you need to define a copy operation for each member of the struct. In the latter case, you can copy the data from one object to another only if they are in *exactly* the same dimension.

This last point is important. If a struct consists of a collection of pointers, you can copy the pointers but not the data that they point to. In other words, assume you had created the sAddressEntry as follows:

```
typedef struct
{
```

```
        char * szName;
        char * szStreet;
        int nNumber;
        char * szPostalCode;
        char * szPhoneNumber;
} sAddressEntry;
```

In this case, you could not copy data from one object to another. For the definition of sAddressEntry, you must provide a copy operation for each of the char * members, because you have no idea what size they are without explicitly finding out. The strings might be 100 characters wide or 10, and you cannot tell from the definition, unlike with sized character arrays.

Using sized arrays allows you to copy the object as a block of memory.

To do this, you simply need to allocate a block of memory big enough to contain one of the instances in the array and then copy the data across. This assumes that you have declared a suitable array of pointers to structs, with each struct having a constant and known data size. First, you allocate the memory:

```
sAddressEntry * pTemp =
    (sAddressEntry *) malloc (sizeof (sAddressEntry) );
```

Once you have the memory allocated, you can copy from one struct to the other using the memcpy function from string.h:

```
memcpy ( pAddressBook, pTemp,
        sizeof ( sAddressEntry ) );
```

The decision whether to define a struct as having members that are pointers to data (like strings) or arrays of data (of a known size) is always a trade-off between execution speed and memory usage. Choosing the best one will depend on the application being developed and is a choice that quite often only the programmer will be able to make.

As a final point, in some cases, a struct containing members that are just pointers to areas in memory (like pixels on the screen) may actually be the desired data representation. The typical incorrect use is when you declare a string as a pointer to an array of characters, forgetting that the only way to copy from one to the other and end up with two instances of the string is to use the appropriate string.h copying function.

Otherwise, all that will result is a copy of the two-byte pointer to the string, and not the string itself!

Accessing Data in `unions`

The previous discussion relates to `structs`, but the data access notation for members of `unions` is almost identical. Recall that because the members overlap, the result is rather different.

The original `union` example looks like this:

```
union
{
    long l;
    char b[4];
} longword;
```

This means that you have established a definition of a `union` that contains four bytes, represented either as a long integer or four characters. You can now access an instance of the `union` as follows:

```
union longword uLongWord;
uLongWord.l = 1000;
printf ( "%c:%c:%c:%c",
    uLongWord.b[0], uLongWord.b[1], uLongWord.b[2], uLongWord.b[3] );
```

In this example, you first create the instance uLongWord and then access it as a long integer, setting the value to 1000. You then display each of the four bytes that could be an alternative representation one at a time to show the value stored therein.

Taking the original definition of a `union` with a nested `struct`, you can also access the same four bytes as low- and high-order words (assuming a big endian machine architecture). The definition of the `union` and `struct` is as follows:

```
union
{
long l;
    char b[4];
    struct
    {
      int low;
      int high;
    } w;
} longword;
```

Accessing the low-order word is simple:

```
printf ( "Low order word : %d", uLongWord.w.low );
```

You can also use the same dotted notation to access the data member to set it, but note that you need to specify an additional dot between the struct name and data member. You can also introduce an anonymous struct, without the w name, and access instances of the same data structure without the additional dotted data member.

The definition would therefore be as follows:

```
union
{
    long l;
    char b[4];
    struct
    {
      int low;
      int high;
    };
} longword;
```

Given this definition, you can now access the high-order word (for example) as follows:

```
union longword uLongWord;
uLongWord.high = 100;
printf ( "%ld", uLongWord.l);
```

This is the only recommended use for anonymous structs. When sub-structs are treated as anonymous, it detracts from the goal of a sub-struct nested inside a parent struct; you might as well just define extra data members. On the other hand, in instances such as this one, it makes sense in a union definition.

What is more common is an anonymous union inside a parent struct. Recall the previous currency struct definition, complete with value representations contained in an anonymous union:

```
typedef struct
{
    int code;
    union
        {
          int nValue;
          float fValue;
        };
} currency;
```

When you access an instance of the previous definition, you no longer need to name the union—indeed you cannot because you have removed the name. So if you want to assign a floating-point value to the currency record, use code such as:

```
currency sCurrency;
sCurrency.fValue = 10.10;
printf ( "%f",sCurrency.fValue );
```

At this point, you might be asking yourself if you can access the nValue part in the same way, even though you have only specific a value for the fValue data member—the answer is yes. However, the result might not be what you expect.

The code would look like this:

```
printf ( "%d", sCurrency.nValue );
```

Try that one out, just to see what the result is, having set the fValue member to 10.10 as in the previous example. The difference is that floating-point and integer values are stored differently and are not directly compatible.

File Processing with Complex Data Types

One of the most important operations that needs to be performed on data types in a real application is file input and output. You learned about file handling in previous chapters, and the choices remain similar, namely:

- Member by member, formatted (text).

- Member by member, binary.

- Memory block.

The first choice usually yields a structured text file that can be edited with a text editor. The second yields a partially editable file—some of the items, such as integers, will remain in binary format. The final option yields a file that can usually be read only by the application that created it.

As you've seen, there are some advantages to all three options, but the most appropriate for user-defined complex data types is to treat them as a series of objects in memory. Rather than write out the data member by member, you can read or write each object in turn as a memory block.

Don't forget to indicate the number of objects in the file, so that you can allocate enough memory when reading it back in. It might also be a good idea to have a version number for the file available in case you create an enhanced application version some time in the future.

Writing out the data is an easy proposition. If you assume that you have defined a struct sAddressEntry, you could instantiate an object using a pointer to an instance of that struct and then write out the data as a memory block:

```
sAddressEntry * pAddressEntry;

// Code to fill up pAddressEntry->szName, etc.

// Now write it to an existing, open file:
fwrite ( pAddressEntry,
     sizeof ( sAddressEntry ), 1, hFile);
```

Had you defined a simple struct, you also would have the option of passing a pointer to the struct:

```
sAddressEntry   oAddressEntry;

// Code to fill up oAddressEntry.szName, etc.

// Now write it to an existing, open file:
fwrite ( &oAddressEntry,
     sizeof ( sAddressEntry ), 1, hFile);
```

Looking at these two snippets, notice the difference in notation for selecting members (. vs. ->) as well as the way in which the first parameter is passed to fwrite.

Code Sample 12.3: File I/O with structs as Memory Objects

When you read the data back in from the file, you can fill up an array or dynamically reallocate memory to store the entries in. Using a simple array, you could write code such as:

```
sAddressEntry oAddressBook[MAX_ENTRIES];

// Get the file length
fseek ( hFile, 0, SEEK_END );
```

```
long int lSize = ftell ( hFile );
fseek ( hFile, 0, SEEK_SET );

// Read until the end of the file
int nRef = 0;

do
{
  fread ( &oAddressBook[nRef],
       sizeof(sAddressEntry), 1, hFile );

  nRef++;
} while ( ftell (hFile) > lSize (hFile) );
```

This short snippet introduces a simple method that establishes the file size and then checks to see that you have not reached it. This allows you to know when you should end the file-reading loop—there is no more data left because you've reached the end of the file.

The actual file read operation is in bold text, and it is very similar to the write operation you've already encountered. You pass fread a reference to the item that you have allocated as an array of sAddressBook structs.

The alternative when reading back in is to use malloc and realloc to grow a block of structs, which can be accessed later in the same way as an array. The main differences in this approach are that the oAddressBook object is a pointer to the memory location for the structs, and each one is read in by passing a reference into the resulting array.

Code Sample 12.4: Reading structs into a Dynamic Memory Block

You retain the same file management (size and end-of-file testing) as before, and the file read operation also remains the same. Therefore, you arrive at the following code:

```
sAddressEntry * pAddressBook;

// Get the file length
fseek ( hFile, 0, SEEK_END );
long int lSize = ftell ( hFile );
fseek ( hFile, 0, SEEK_SET );
```

```
// Read until the end of the file
int nRef = 0;
int nRead = 0;

pAddressBook = NULL; // No objects at first

do
{
  if ( pAddressBook == NULL )
  {
    pAddressBook = ( sAddressEntry * )
    malloc ( sizeof (sAddressEntry ) );
  }
  else
  {
    pAddressBook = ( sAddress Entry * )
    realloc ( sizeof (sAddressEntry) * nRef );
  }

  nRead = fread ( &oAddressBook[nRef],
      sizeof(sAddressEntry), 1, hFile );

  nRef++;
} while ( ftell (hFile) > lSize (hFile) );
```

Note that as a safety mechanism, this code introduces a check for the number of records read (via the nRead variable). This will need to be checked post-file manipulation to return the last block of memory to the system, in cases where the read operation failed for some reason.

File Processing with unions

All of the preceding discussions pertain to file processing with complex data types related to structs. There are a few points about unions that you should be aware of. The first point to note is that a union is a single piece of data as large as its largest data member. It has to be, in order to store a value that fits into that data member.

So a union with a long and an integer data member will be the size of the long integer. When you write the union out to file, you can either:

- Write the union directly, as an object.

- Write the required union member, individually.

The UnionTest.c program on the companion Web site (go to www.courseptr .com and click on the Downloads button) illustrates the following discussion of these two possibilities. Before trying out the program, it's important to recall that if a member of a union is written out directly, the size of data will not necessarily be the same as the union itself.

Code Sample 12.6: Writing a union to File

In other words, although the memory requirement for a union is equal to the size of the largest data member, unless you write the whole union as an object to the file, the size taken will only be the same as the member you choose to write.

The following code snippet is taken from the UnionTest.c program:

```
    hFile = fopen ( "ulw.txt", "w" );
fwrite( &uLongWord, sizeof(longword), 1, hFile);
fclose(hFile);
```

Note that the size of the union is provided in the second parameter of the fwrite function call. So the whole four bytes of the union will be written out. This is an example of writing the instance of the union as an object.

Code Sample 12.7: Reading Individual Members of a union from a File

Conversely, consider the snippet for reading in data from the file:

```
hFile = fopen( "ulw.txt", "r" );
fread( &uLongWord.word.low, sizeof(int), 1, hFile);
fread( &uLongWord.word.high, sizeof(int), 1, hFile);
fclose (hFile);
```

In the previous sample, you can see that the members are read in individually as integer values. Subsequently, the result (as checked by a printf statement in the source code) is identical in value to the original, because the two-word union members overlap.

This brings you to a final example, and something that is useful for readers working with record data from operating systems that use a record structure that is not delimited. A common approach to record data is to precede it by the length.

This length then tells the readers how many bytes of data follow. You saw a similar approach in Chapter 11, when you looked at reading and writing variable-length strings.

The problem occurs when you receive a file from a little endian system and are working on a big endian system. If the length indicator is more than one byte wide (they are usually two or four), you face a problem because the order of high- and low-order bytes is swapped.

However, if you use a `union`, you can adapt the file reading to allow for this issue by asking the users whether the file to be read in is big or little endian and then selecting to read the bytes in a different order, depending on the users' responses. Because you are using a `union`, you can then treat the two bytes as a single integer value.

The definition for the `union` would be as follows:

```
typedef union
{
  int nLength;
  struct
  {
  short bLow;
  short bHigh;
  };
} record_length;
```

Assuming you have correctly defined the data block as an array big enough to contain the data, you can then proceed to read the data in as follows:

```
hFile = fopen( "ulw.txt", "r" );
fread( &uRecordLength.low, sizeof(int), 1, hFile);
fread( &uRecordLength.high, sizeof(int), 1, hFile);
fread( szData, sizeof(char), uRecordLength.nLength, hFile);
fclose (hFile);
```

If you need to change the "endien-ness" of the program to cope with data from a system that orders the bytes high/low rather than low/high, all you need to do is swap the file read operations, as follows:

```
fread( &uRecordLength.high, sizeof(int), 1, hFile);
fread( &uRecordLength.low, sizeof(int), 1, hFile);
```

Note that this example uses an anonymous `struct` to make the code slightly less cumbersome.

This complete solution to the endian problem is a useful technique and illustrates the use of complex data types. If you are ever in any doubt as to the order of bytes in an operating system, you can use a `union` to discover the ordering by setting nLength (from the previous example) to be a very low value (say 2), and then print the bytes in order.

If the low-order byte contains 1, it is, in fact, the high-order byte, with the high-order byte (actually the low-order byte) containing the 2. In order to verify this completely, you might try writing out the integer value to a file and then reading it back in. Then you can see how the individual bytes end up being ordered.

Recap

Complex user-defined data types are commonly structs but can be other supported data types. The most common way to introduce them for use in a C program is to use the typedef keyword. They can be declared in the same way as any other data type—as a variable, as a reference to a variable, in an array, or as a memory block.

Structs are special because they allow you to store multiple pieces of heterogeneous data. In other words, you can store data fields inside the record that have different data types. As long as the data elements are of a known size, the entire record can be treated as a memory block.

This makes reading and writing them to and from files much easier. If the size of each field is not known at compile time, each member needs to be read/written separately, incurring a processing time penalty. The balance of memory usage against this added inefficiency is left as a decision to be taken when the program is designed.

unions are generally used when you want to enclose data in a single object that can have various, sometimes incompatible, types. It makes programming complex data types easier because you need to refer to the object only with a single name.

However, be sure that you know which representation of the union has been initialized or you cannot retrieve the correct value from it. This is especially true when using member types that are intrinsically incompatible. Some errors will be caught by the compiler, but not all of them.

The notation used for accessing data members in structs and unions is almost identical, with the caveat being that the data members in a union overlap. Pointers to, arrays of, and definitions with the typedef keyword are possible for both structs and unions.

Anonymous uses of both are also possible as long as they are nested inside named data types.

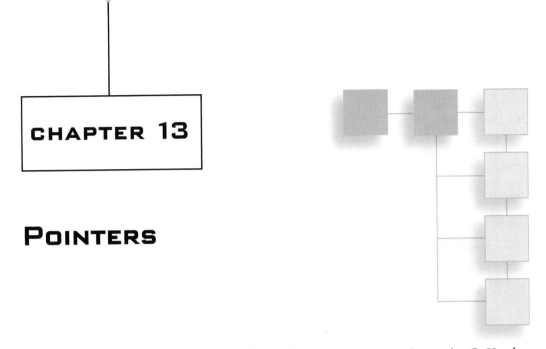

CHAPTER 13

POINTERS

The aim of this chapter is to provide an introduction to pointers in C. You've come across pointers in various guises slowly over the preceding chapters in the book, but the book has not yet scratched the surface of how pointers can be used.

After you finish this chapter, you will have covered enough of the C language to begin serious programming tasks in C. Pointers are useful in manipulating lists of information, memory blocks, and arrays such as strings.

In order to explain the way that pointers work and how they can be used, the chapter deals with them using two of the most common applications—strings and lists. It is easier to understand how to use pointers when you see them in action.

You've been dealing with pointers at various times throughout the book, most particularly in the last chapter. It is now time to pull the various threads together and look at pointers formally. They are an important part of programming.

Strings Revisited

A *string* is an array of characters. Each item in the array is a *dereferenced* pointer to an element in that array (in this case, a character). The array itself is just a reference to the first in the collection of characters. The difference between an array and a pointer to a piece of memory containing characters is that you generally know the size of the array at compile time.

In other words, you usually declare a sized array of characters as follows:

```
char my_array[255];
```

You could equally well define a pointer to the start of a block of memory containing an undisclosed number of characters:

```
char * my_array; // Or, char my_array[];
```

Think back to the `main` function and recall that it is generally defined as:

```
int main ( int argc, char * argv[] )
```

The last parameter, `argv`, is essentially a double array, or an array of arrays, defined as a pointer to a collection of character arrays. The `[]` notation indicates that at compile time you do not know the size of each array that contains the parameter data. This is because the users provide the parameters on the command line (and also the special `argv[0]` entry that contains the executable filename).

Generally, if you want to use a pointer to a collection of characters in memory, you need to make sure that the program knows how many characters make up the memory block, so that you can allocate enough memory. This memory allocation is usually done through the `malloc` function.

In the case of the `main` function, the stdarg.h library file populates the parameters at the entry point to the program. The implementation of this library will likely allocate the memory blocks when the program starts up.

The result of a call to `malloc` is a pointer to a `void` (no type), which you can cast to a pointer to a collection of anything that you like. In the case of argument processing, it is cast to an array of characters. You've seen this in the section on memory management.

Usually, when you manipulate strings in this way, rather than store a specific value for the length (or size) of the string, you use a null terminator \0 in the last position of the array. As long as you do so, you don't need to worry about knowing the size of the memory block, because you can call the `strlen` function, with the pointer to the string, and multiply the result by the size of a character on the target architecture.

The following line of code would achieve the desired affect:

```
long lMemoryRequired = sizeof ( char ) * strlen ( szString );
```

All you need to remember is that, when allocating the memory, you must allocate an extra byte for the null terminator. You last saw an example of this in Chapter 11, where you learned how to read and write variable-length strings from and to files.

So, a quick recap. A string is an array of characters, defined as a pointer to the memory block that contains the array. Assuming that you define the string as a pointer (char *), you can access individual elements using the subscript operator []. As long as you do not try to access an element beyond the end of the array in memory, this approach works conveniently.

The same goes for arrays of integers, floats, or even structs. You just need to know how big the block of memory is and how big each individual element is. So to determine the length of a string, you can obtain the size of the memory block and then divide it by the size of a character. Or you can call the strlen function, which will tell you the number of characters in the string.

The same approach, minus the call to strlen, can be taken for any array of individual objects, be they built-in data types or structs. Bearing this in mind, take a closer look at pointers and references and how they can be used in practice.

Pointers and References

A pointer can point to an instance of a variable, the start of a memory block, or even a function. It can also point to other pointers, but that topic is beyond the scope of this book. The most common example of this is an array of pointers—such as the argv parameter that you saw in the strings discussion.

In a program, you can refer to a pointer (the pointer itself) or the value in memory that it is pointing to. Operations on a pointer have a different effect than operations on the value that it refers (or is pointing) to. You can, for example, move through an array of integers pointed to by a variable by incrementing the pointer.

To access the value pointed *at*, though, you would need to *dereference* the pointer to reveal the actual value. This is the equivalent of putting an index in square brackets after an array name in order to access a given element in that array.

Dereferencing

The dereference operator is the asterisk *, and it is needed whenever you want to manipulate the value that the pointer points to. This allows you to access the value in memory rather than just the abstract reference to it.

This seems a little academic, but you can think of it in terms of the cooking analogy from the earlier chapters. If you have a recipe for baking and decorating a cake, it is likely to refer at some point to a recipe for icing. Because icing is a standard mixture that can be used on many cakes, it is usually not printed on each recipe.

Instead, in the book, it might refer to a section entitled "Cake Toppings," where the icing recipe is printed. You, the reader (the chef), then have to look up—*dereference*—the pointer to that recipe before you can use it. There might be a whole collection of recipes on toppings and you might have to flick through them one by one before actually finding the one you want for icing.

This is similar to what you might do in a C program when you have a pointer to the start of the information but do not know which item you need or the size of the memory block itself. You do know that it is an array, and you do know the size of the items.

Code Sample 13.1: Pointer Arithmetic and Arrays

So, for example, to move through an array of an indeterminate size that was created using malloc, you use code similar to the following:

```
int * nArray, ptArray;

nArray = (int *) malloc (sizeof (int) * 101);

// Some additional code here ...
//    ... to set values for items 0 to 99

nArray[100] = -1;
    // Set the 100th value to a default 'end of array'

ptArray = nArray;

while (*ptArray != -1)
{
    ptArray++; // Move through the memory block
}
```

Note that in the previous code snippet ptArray++ moves through the memory block (pointer arithmetic), and *ptArray accesses the actual value and tests it against −1. If the comparison succeeds, that value must be the last element in the array.

This allows you to create an `intlen` function, akin to the `strlen` function, to return the number of integers in the array. The difference between explicitly accessing each element and testing it for an end-of-array value is that you can return the number of used (or effective) items in the array.

If you take the size of the memory block and divide it by the size of an element, this will return the total number of elements in the array, whether or not they are used.

Pointers and Memory

The technique of using pointers to memory blocks comes into its own when creating lists of user-defined data structures and, in particular, a linked list of items. This is due to the nature of pointers as references that can be changed without needing to manipulate the data that they are pointing at explicitly.

In other words, you can sort an entire list of items just by swapping references to them, whether they are in an array or in a block of memory. If you're not using pointers, the same operation requires that a copy of the data be taken and stored and the contents of that item be overwritten with the contents of another, and then the stored data restored to a different place.

Pointers simply make life easier, and one example of this is in the definition of a linked list. Creating a linked list is possible by the use of pointers. Once you understand linked lists, data manipulation, a subject at the core of programming, is much easier to implement.

A linked list is a collection of nodes that point to each other. The last node points to `NULL`, a built-in type meaning *unassigned*. Each node can be linked to the next one, or a previous one, or both. When nodes are linked to the next and previous nodes, this is called a doubly linked list and should not be confused with a linked list that contains nodes that point to the start of other linked lists.

This can be quite hard to envisage, so I'll complete the discussion with a practical application of a linked list, as applied to command-line argument processing. The steps you use are the same for any linked list design.

Example: A Linked List of Command-Line Arguments

A linked list needs two kinds of structure—a node to hold the information pertaining to the list management and an area containing the data that is associated with this node. This example starts with the payload struct—the data that you want to store in each node of the list.

Assume for this example that you want to store pairs of values representing command-line arguments. So you can create a struct in C as follows:

```
typedef struct
  {

        char szParameterName[255];
        char szValue[255];

  } sParameter;
```

In Chapter 9, you learned how to parse the command line and saw an example whereby each parameter could be specified as a pair of strings:

```
-<parameter name> [["]<value>["]]
```

In parsing this example, each parameter type is assumed to start with a -, and any value having spaces in the string is enclosed in quote ("") characters. The value is, of course, optional, in which case the szValue member of the sParameter struct will be set to the constant "TRUE".

This exercise was partially covered in the original discussion of command-line processing. Because this section concentrates on using the parsing to create a list of sParameter structs, you can assume that the parameter name and value are available. The actual code is left as an exercise for you.

The linked list node structure will probably look something like the following:

```
typedef struct
  {

        sNode * oNext;
        sParameter oParameter;

  } sNode;
```

You will probably quickly identify that the oNext variable is a pointer to a memory location that contains an sParameter struct. In turn, the struct at that memory location will also have an oNext member pointing to another sParameter struct. In this way, a list of nodes, all linked to each other, can be defined in memory.

Creating the Linked List

To use the linked list, you just need to keep a track of the first node in a variable, commonly known as the *head* of the list:

```
sNode * oHead;
```

The first function that you need to define will initialize an sNode structure so that it can be added to the list—either as the oHead or at the end of the list.

Code Sample 13.2: Example Linked List Node Initialization

Because you know what data the sNode stores, you can define the function accordingly:

```
void InitializeNode ( sNode * oNode,
      char * szName, char * szValue)
{

    // Set the oNext member to NULL
    oNode->oNext = NULL;

    // Copy the data
    strcpy ( oNode->oParameter.szParameter,
        szName);

    strcpy ( oNode->oParameter.szValue,
        szValue);

}
```

As you parse the parameters, each pair is passed to the InitializeNode function, along with a block of memory to contain the new sNode structure. It is important to note two points:

- If you lose the pointer to the sNode structure, you lose the node.

- If you do not allocate memory for each node, all you'll do is overwrite the existing node.

Consequently, the initialization process is completed in two stages—allocate the memory and then assign data to that memory. This can be done in two steps or as part of the InitializeNode function. If the process is done outside the InitializeNode function, you could use code such as:

```
sNode * oTemp =
        (sNode *) malloc ( sizeof (sNode) );

InitializeNode ( oTemp, szName, szValue );
```

This assumes that you have already allocated the appropriate memory before performing the initialization. In some cases this is logical, but you might prefer to do it all in one function—allocate and initialize within a single function.

Code Sample 13.3: Improved Linked List Node Initialization

Were you to choose to perform the initialization of the memory block inside the InitializeNode function, you could arrive at code similar to:

```
sNode *  InitializeNode ( char * szName,
char * szValue)
{

  sNode * oTemp =
    (sNode *) malloc (sizeof (sNode));

  // Set the oNext member to NULL
  oNode->oNext = NULL;

  // Copy the data
  strcpy ( oNode->oParameter.szParameter,
            szName);

  strcpy ( oNode->oParameter.szValue,
            szValue);

  return oTemp;
}
```

In the previous snippet, the new code is in bold.

Code Sample 13.4: Argument Parsing with a Linked List of Command Parameters

If you assume the existence of a parsing function to process the command-line arguments, which can process optional values and so on, you could write the code designed to build the linked list. Minus some error-checking code, which you should include on your own, you could use a block of code such as:

```
int nArgPos = 1;

// The ParseArguments function updates nArgPos,
// retrieves szName and szValue, and returns
// a negative value when done.

while ( ParseArguments
     ( argc, argv, &nArgPos, szName, szValue ) )
   {
       // Create a new node
         sNode * oNewNode =
                   InitializeNode ( szName, szValue );

       // Add it to the list
       AddNode ( oHead, oNewNode );
   }
```

So far, so good. Note the new function, AddNode. It maintains the growing list without first showing its internals. Before you look at the internal workings, let's see how far you have come. So far, the code example performs these tasks:

- Reserves a memory block.

- Initializes the data storage.

- Populates the data structure.

- Isolates the node by pointing to NULL.

The result of these operations is a block of data that's ready to be added to the list. It exists in isolation, and all you have is a pointer to it. You also have a pointer to the start of the list, initialized to NULL.

Code Sample 13.5: Adding a Node to the Head of a Linked List

The AddNode function, then, needs to deal with two cases:

- An empty list.

- A growing list.

Being a singly linked list, this is a fairly painless process and could be coded as follows:

```
void AddNodeToHead ( sNode * oHead, sNode * oNode )
{
    oNode->oNext = oHead;
    oHead = oNode;
}
```

The previous code adds the current node to the head of the list by first assigning the existing head to follow the new node and then repointing the head to the new node. Thus, the list will grow at the head end.

Code Sample 13.6: Adding a Node Safely to the Tail of a Linked List

To grow the list at the tail end, you could use code such as the following:

```
void AddNodeToTail ( sNode * oHead, sNode * oNode )
{
  // If oHead is NULL, this is the first one
  if ( oHead == NULL )
  {
      oHead = oNode;
  }
  else
  {
      sNode * oTemp = oHead;

      // Traverse the list, until we get to
          // the end-1, and we'll add the node to
          // the end.

      while ( oTemp->oNext != NULL )
      {
```

```
        oTemp = oTemp->oNext;
    }

    // We're at the end
    oTemp->oNext = oNode;
  }
}
```

In the previous code, the linked list is *traversed* by repointing the oTemp variable until it would point to NULL. It is *vital* that you not lose the original value of oHead. Otherwise, you'll lose the entire linked list. An alternative to the previous code is to hold a value for the tail of the list as well as for the head.

Code Sample 13.7: Example Linked List Node Insertion

To insert a node, you need a function that can repoint the node directly before the insertion point to the new node and repoint the new node to the node directly after the insertion point. To avoid losing the reference from the before node to the after node, you need to use code such as the following and perform the operation in reverse:

```
void InsertNode ( sNode * oBefore,
 sNode * oAfter, sNode * oNode )
{
  // Point the new node to oAfter, so as not to
  // lose the reference to the rest of the list
  oNode->oNext = oAfter;

  // Now point oBefore to the new node
  oBefore->oNext = oNode;
}
```

This last snippet can be used to insert nodes in an organized manner—for example, sorted alphabetically. In addition, you might contemplate how checks for NULL pointers should be used to avoid inserting nodes into an empty list or trying to insert nodes past the end of the linked list.

Destroying the List

Finally, you come to the clean-up function. When you have finished manipulating the list, you need to dispose of it in a way that returns the memory that you allocated for the data and pointers back to the operating system. The standard companion function to malloc is called free.

You need to traverse the list and dispose of each node in turn. Naturally, there are a few different ways to do this, but this section concentrates on a recursive approach because it illustrates this important technique.

Code Sample 13.8: Recursive Linked List Destruction

Recall that you need a way to stop the recursion as well as a call to the function to continue until such a time as that condition is met. The following is a suggested approach:

```
void DestroyList ( sNode * oHead )
{
    if ( oHead->oNext != NULL )
    {
        DestroyList ( oHead->oNext );
    }
    // If the next node is NULL, we can
        // safely dispose of this one
    free (oHead);
}
```

You might need to study that code snippet a bit before you understand how it works. The stack size is kept to a minimum by not storing a pointer to each node anywhere. As the recursive stack unwinds, it releases each node to memory. However, for a very large list, the stack may grow to an unacceptable size, and so let's also consider a non-recursive, less memory-intense solution.

Code Sample 13.9: Non-Recursive Linked List Destruction

A non-recursive solution exists for most recursive solutions. The difference in this case is that you treat each node on its own, without stacking up multiple calls to the destruction function. The following function walks through the list, disposing of nodes:

```
void DestroyListNonRecursively ( sNode * oHead )
{
    while (oHead != NULL)
```

```
    {
        // Store pointer to next node
        sNode * oTemp = oHead->oNext;

        // Dispose of this one
        free ( oHead );

        // Re-assign head
        oHead = oTemp;
    }
}
```

In both of these snippets, note that they take care not to dispose of the node before the code has safeguarded the pointer to the next one. In the recursive method, it is on the stack; in the non-recursive method, the reference to the node is stored in a temporary variable.

This makes the entire process slightly more economic. Rather than pile up a stack of useless references, make sure that you have a reference to the most current part of the collection of nodes and destroy the node that should be disposed of.

Recap

Pointers are an integral part of advanced programming in C and string manipulation at every level. They are also an underlying part of understanding other C-based languages such as Java and C++. Using pointers is considered good practice, but you need to take care in order to use them effectively.

A pointer is just a reference to an area of memory. That area of memory has bounds only if a variable of a certain type is used to cast it into something that is understood by the program. This being the case, it is often easy to misinterpret the end of the memory block and then trespass into other areas by accident. This is the source of many bugs in C programs, the source of the most common of these being non-terminated strings.

Pointers are also good for creating linked lists, where the *link* is a pointer to the next node in the list. This makes more efficient memory and processor usage than an array. However, it comes with some caveats, including the possibility that the list-management code fails due to inadequate testing for conditions that would cause pointers to become invalid.

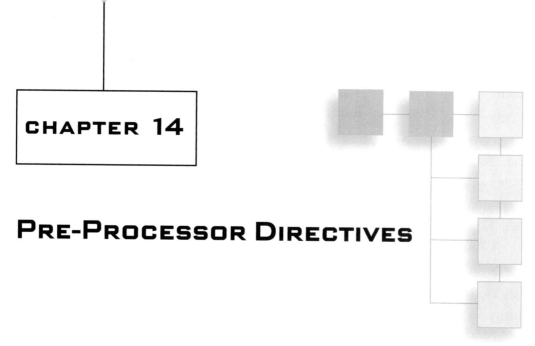

CHAPTER 14

PRE-PROCESSOR DIRECTIVES

You briefly encountered the idea behind a pre-processor directive before, in the very first chapters of this book. Essentially, a *pre-processor directive* is a piece of code that's processed by the compiler before the actual compilation takes place. In other words, pre-processor directives allow you to give the compiler some direction before it does its work.

The aim of this chapter is to provide an overview of the various C pre-processor directives and their practical uses. It is possible that there are some advanced or esoteric uses that fall out of the scope of this book; however, this chapter covers most of the C pre-processor directives you'll come in contact with.

You should be able to apply these techniques in creating your own projects, especially when you're building larger applications. The chapter also provides a solid foundation for more advanced uses of pre-processing in the C language.

One of the main aims of this book is to prepare you for when you must try to make sense of other people's code, and some programmers use pre-processor directives extensively. These directives can be confusing at first, but practice will eventually prove to be fruitful in understanding how powerful they can be.

The Pre-Processor Concept

If you think back to the first chapter, recall that the purpose of the compiler is to turn a C program into object code, ready for linking with other pieces of object code to form the final application. The C pre-processor is invoked before the compilation phase but is transparent to the user or programmer.

The C pre-processor exists for several reasons. First, it allows the programmer to reference (include) external files that are needed in order for the compiler to be able to produce the object code.

Second, the C pre-processor allows the language to be expanded in a user-defined fashion by the use of macros. A *macro* is just a set of instructions referred to by a single name. Each macro can be defined and then inserted into the C code, and the pre-processor will expand the macro before the final source is compiled.

This is an important facility because it allows you to keep your code cleaner by using short aliases for more complex operations. Macros are expanded by the pre-processor into the code handed to the compiler for compilation.

The third reason behind the C pre-processor is to allow conditional compilation of source code. This can be useful when a debugging or platform-dependent version of the software needs to be built. Code that should be included or excluded can be contained within a set of statements that are expanded by the pre-processor before compilation.

With all this power, it is easy for pre-processor directives and external files to become quite involved. You need to strike a balance between ease of maintenance and flexibility in the implementation. Macros, especially, can be hard for the inexperienced programmer to debug.

As a programmer gains proficiency, however, it is possible to make good use of the pre-processor and actually increase the readability, maintainability, and efficiency of the code. The rest of this chapter details the bare minimum that a beginning programmer should be aware of and versed in.

Pre-processing revolves around two keywords—#include and #define. The first is used to include an external file, and the second to define a macro or constant value. There is also an entire conditional language created around the #define facility. This allows you to test for definitions that might not have been made.

This, in turn, allows you to conditionally choose to compile specific pieces of code into the final application. More accurately, it allows you to choose which pieces of source code to build into the final source sent to the compiler for compilation.

One way to look at it is to consider the source code as one big block of text. The compilation process starts with a blank sheet. The pre-processor then goes through all the source files that the programmer has indicated from a part of the program.

In doing so, the pre-processor builds up the entire source code that is to be compiled, processing the directives, as you shall see, to substitute constants for values or conditionally include files and code. The compiler then processes the resulting code before passing it all to the linker to create the final application.

The #include **Directive**

The #include directive, as you might recall, indicates to the compiler that you want it to treat an external file as part of the file being compiled. The basic syntax for this directive is as follows:

```
#include <filename.h>
```

or

```
#include "filename.h"
```

Note that there is no semicolon at the end of the line, although you can make a comment after it using the // or /* comment */ markers for C commenting. The types of characters delimiting the filename are significant.

The first use indicates that you want to look for <filename.h> in the standard include directories. These are usually added in the environment of the compiler during installation and may be found in a folder on the path of the compiler set called include.

For example, if you will using the standard input and output functionality in stdio.h, this file can be included using the following form:

```
#include <stdio.h>
```

The compiler will then expect to find this file in a folder on the compiler's toolpath:

```
/include/stdio.h
```

Should you want to do some network programming, you might need to include the socket.h library header. This is usually located in the sys folder, so you would need to use the following form:

```
#include <sys/socket.h>
```

The file itself will therefore be located at:

`/include/sys/socket.h`

Besides the Standard Libraries, you also usually need to reference your own header files, which contain abstract data types or user-defined data types and functions. There might also be constants and macros (covered in the next few sections) that are required by the compiler, written by you, for inclusion in the project.

Because these files do not reside in the standard path but on the path belonging to the project, you use the second form of the #include directive:

`#include "main.h"`

You can, of course, put your code to be included in any file you choose (header or C code: .h/.c) with any name. Because the filename is in quotes, the compiler knows to look for the file down the current path, rather than on any predefined library paths. There are some rules for searching for a specific file, but these vary between compilers.

As a general rule, it is safe to assume that by putting the filename between quotes, the compiler will find any file that is on the source path. So if you have a specific set of files in a folder called my_networking that is part of the current project, you could include one of them using the following call:

`#include "my_networking/network.h"`

One caveat is that each file should be included only once per compilation cycle. In other words, if you have a file that contains definitions used in several source files, the compiler will try to include the file several times. This can lead to conflicts in type definitions and is known as a *multiple include.*

Avoiding multiple includes is very easy and is described in the next section.

The #define Directive

The #define directive is used for two purposes. Both purposes discussed here involve basic substitution—in other words, the pre-processor substitutes one constant value for another whenever it is encountered in a source file. The way to use #define is to define a constant value that will be replaced by the pre-processor.

The pre-processor is capable of substituting a named value with a real value or even performing some basic expansion and evaluation tasks. The four key #define keywords most commonly used in C programming are as follows:

`#define <constant_name> <coinstant_value>`

```
#ifdef <constant_name>

#ifndef <constant_name>

#endif
```

The #define statement defines a constant <constant_name> and associates it with <constant_value>. The pre-processor will then replace every instance of <constant_name> with <constant_value>. This is useful for defining constants that are used throughout a program, but that might change in the future. You can define a single named value and change that value only if need be by altering a single line.

So you could define values such as these:

```
#define UNIVERSE_WIDTH 25
#define PROGRAM_NAME "My Application"
```

The pre-processor will, for every instance of UNIVERSE_WIDTH that it encounters, substitute the value 25. For each PROGRAM_NAME it will substitute the string "My Application". In the application, you never use the value 25 or string "My Application"; you just use the constants defined here.

This makes the value easy to substitute as the application evolves. For example, for test purposes, 25 might be an adequate value, but when you move from test to real use, you might then decide that 250 is more appropriate. Because you have used the constant UNIVERSE_WIDTH in the code rather than the actual value 25, you need only change the single #define statement to use the new value throughout.

As seen, you can use #define with other scalar types and strings. In fact, any time that a value represented by a built-in type can be introduced into C code, it can be substituted by a constant definition.

The C language also provides some logic statements to test for the status of various constants. This allows you to build some reasonably sophisticated decision blocks that allow you to choose to include certain code statements in the program code. This is known as *conditional compilation*.

The #ifdef statement tests to see whether <constant_name> has been defined, and if it has, the C pre-processor will then process all statements up to the #endif statement. The #ifndef statement performs the same function but tests to see that <constant_name> has *not* been defined.

There is also an #else statement that provides alternate code to be processed by the pre-processor if the original #ifdef or #ifndef statement evaluates to false. This is useful for testing platform- or debug-dependent code.

Before you look at these in action, note first that conditional compilation is not the same as testing in an if statement during execution of the application. However, optimizing compilers might generate code that is equivalent, depending on how they approach the problem.

To help you visualize the differences, consider the following:

Conditionally Compiled Statement	Conditionally Executed Statement

`#ifdef _A_CONSTANT`
`    // Compile this code`
`#else`
`    // Compile this instead`
`#endif`
	`if ( _A_CONSTANT == 1 ) {`
	`    // Compile this code`
	`} else {`
	`    // Compile this instead`
	`}`

On the left side is a set of conditionally compiled statements. If _A_CONSTANT is defined, one set of statements will be included; if it's not defined, another set will be included. On the right side is code that, for values of 0 and 1 in _A_CONSTANT, is functionally equivalent, with a few caveats.

If _A_CONSTANT has not been defined, for example, the code on the right side will not compile. If _A_CONSTANT contains any number except 1, the alternative code will be executed. In the code on the left side, any value assigned to it causes it to be defined.

This is the crux of the difference between the two approaches—the code on the left side is conditionally compiled, whereas the code on the right side is conditionally executed. Now, a smart compiler will note that _A_CONSTANT is a constant value and not include those parts of the if statement in the application, thereby emulating the conditional compilation behavior.

However, the approach on the left side is generally held to be more appropriate for certain tasks, namely preventing multiple includes (files included more than once) and conditionally compiling debug code. It also typically produces more optimized target code, but this is compiler dependent.

Avoiding Multiple Includes

One useful way to apply the #define directive is as a mechanism for avoiding multiple includes. Compilers deal with including the same header file in different ways. To ensure compatibility, it's good practice to keep these cases from actually occurring in the first place.

The worst case is when a compiler cannot compile a project because it has several (albeit identical) definitions for the same constant or multiple identical function prototypes. More advanced compilers might be able to resolve these, but the most common approach is simply to prevent compilation.

When programming, this can be inconvenient, so it is better just to prevent it from happening at all by avoiding including the same header file twice. The steps are as follows:

- Check to see if the file has been included.

- If not, process it and indicate that it has now been included.

To do this, you need to #define a constant for that file. You can look at this constant as being a kind of identifier for that file. If the constant is defined, you do not need to process the file again. The following code implements this solution for a file called filename.h:

```
#ifndef _FILENAME_H
#define _FILENAME_H
        // This code will be processed only once
        // per compilation cycle
#endif
```

The naming convention for the constant name reflects the filename—in this way you can be fairly sure that the constant is unique. Filenames that are #included in the project should be unique, so incorporating the filename in the constant in this way helps to ensure that the definition is also unique.

You should create your own constant value for use with the #define and #ifndef macros. You are also free to discard the convention used here of _filename_ extension in favor of your own particular convention, but make sure that each constant is unique.

The way that the previous example works is simple. The first line checks to see whether _FILENAME_H has already been defined. If it has not been defined (#ifndef), the example goes on to #define the constant and process the remaining content of the file. The last line in the file is the #endif statement, which closes the conditional compilation.

This approach works perfectly well. However, there is an alternative that requires merely using #define to make sure that the constant is defined in the header file and then choosing whether to #include the entire file on the basis of testing whether the constant is defined.

The code to test for the definition of the constant looks akin to the following:

```
#ifndef _FILENAME_H
  #include <filename.h>
#endif
```

There are some caveats with this approach. The first one is that you need to know the name of the constant so that you can test for its definition. The previous approach contained the definition and the test for it in the same file, so all you needed to do is #include it.

Another caveat with the second approach is that you cannot selectively compile statements within the same header file—you are choosing to exclude the whole file at the point that you test for the definition of the constant. The first approach would allow you to build in a more robust and sophisticated mechanism for conditional compilation, such as platform- or usage-dependent mechanisms.

In the first case, you might want to choose between Windows, Apple Macintosh, and UNIX systems in the header file. A constant can be #defined in the main source file before any other compilation takes place that selects the platform required. This approach can also be used to select between debug and production versions of the same application.

Using Pre-Processor Directives for Debugging

You read previously that you can build a debug or production version of an application by using pre-processor directives to selectively execute debug features. This is different from selective compilation but requires that you use selective compilation with pre-processor directives to prevent multiple inclusion.

The idea is that users can invoke the debug code by introducing a flag on the command line, say "-debug", for example. This needs several stages to achieve the end result: You need to define a flag that is global to the whole project, define a debug flag to test against, and provide conditional execution statements to invoke the debug code.

The first two stages are easy—you introduce a static integer variable named g_nDebug in the program's main header file. Don't put this variable in the main.c file because you want it to be available to all other modules. Consequently, you have to put it in a header file that is common to all modules and source code files.

In order to do this without causing compile-time errors stemming from multiple inclusions, you need to create a file that prevents its own multiple inclusion. This file might look like the following:

```
#ifndef _DEBUG_H
  #define _DEBUG_H // Prevent multiple inclusions
  #define DEBUG_FLAG "-debug"
  static int g_nDebug;
#endif
```

This code sample can safely be included in all code modules and contains enough information for you to be able to set a global debug flag. Setting the flag requires that you identify the presence of the "-debug" flag on the command line. Provided that you have the aforementioned command-line parameter processing function, this is simple.

In fact, you've already seen the process in Chapter 9, "Command-Line Processing," as follows:

```
if ( GetParameterValue( argv, DEBUG_FLAG, argc ) != NULL )
{
  g_nDebug = 1; // Debug is ON
}
else
{
  g_nDebug = 0; // Debug is OFF
}
```

Of course, you can also selectively compile debug versions of the application using a similar approach. In this case, you don't have to ship a version of the application with the debug code included.

To do this, you just need to make sure that you #define a value that turns debugging on, and then test for its definition before each debug-oriented code block. One of the advantages of pre-processor directives is that they can be placed in .c source files as well as in .h header files.

So for each set of debug code statements, you need to enclose them as follows:

```
#ifdef DEBUG_ON
  // Debug statements
#endif
```

The static flag equivalent is, of course:

```
if ( g_nDebug == 1 )
{
  // Debug statements
}
```

Using all of these lines, you can choose platforms, versions, and whether to turn debugging on or off. This is only part of the power of pre-processing directives; the other part is in defining macros that can help perform some actual processing.

C-Style Macros

In C programming, macros are short pieces of code. You can use these macros as a shorthand for C code, with or without parameters. This enables you to create short, function-like code snippets designed to fulfill a specific task. These can then be used in the code proper and can help to increase readability, while reducing the possibility of mistyping complex code segments.

One common implementation problem revolves around defining a function that's capable of returning the smaller of two values. Let's call this function min. There are several ways in which you can implement the min function:

- Inline, as an if expression

- As a function returning a value

- As a macro

In the first case, you might write a condition test as follows:

```
int a, b;
...
  if ( a < b )
    {
      // If a is less than b
    }
  else
    {
      // If b is greater than (or equal to) a
    }
```

This would suffice for simple tests of inequality, and you might even extend it to cases whereby the two parameters might be equal. However, in the end, the value returned by the comparison is still true or false, and there will be cases when you'll want the actual value returned.

So you might create a condition test inside a function, designed to return the smaller of the two values:

```
int MinInt ( int a, int b)
{
    if ( a < b ) return a; else return b;
}
```

There is nothing wrong with this function. It fulfills the design exactly and could feasibly be extended to return a specific value should the two parameters be equal. However, it is cumbersome and inflexible—it can test only between two integers.

Suppose that you want to compare two floating-point numbers, two characters, or any number of user-defined scalar variable types. You would need a function for each one. You can probably imagine various ways to make a generic min function, but the C language gives you an elegant alternative:

```
int nMin = (nA < nB ? nA : nB);
```

The shorthand in this example is a useful trick that does nothing to enhance readability. Like anything else, however, it is just a question of using it until it becomes second nature. You can break it down into three parts:

```
<condition> ? <return if true> : <return if false>
```

The <condition> is tested, and the value returned is either <return if true> or <return if false>, depending on the outcome of the <condition>. The previous example returned values from the condition test, but equally, you could return arbitrary values:

```
int nMin = (nA < nB ? 1 : 2);
```

You could equally define other variations:

```
float fMin = (fA < fB ? fA : fB);
```

The goal, however, is to make your min function type generic, and so clearly another tack needs to be used. This is where the C-styled macro comes into play.

The C pre-processor works on the basis of substitution without paying any attention to the language structure. This means that you can make errors that will be picked up only when the program is compiled, but that you can also create generic function-like macros that are *polymorphic* in nature. In other words, they are able to process values of any data type.

The final generic min function, therefore, is actually a macro that takes account of the previous shorthand for the sake of elegance:

```
#define min(A, B) ((A) < (B) ? (A) : (B))
```

This code defines a macro min, which takes two parameters, A and B, compares them, and returns one or the other, depending on the outcome of that comparison. This macro can be used in place of the shorthand if statement or the MinInt function:

```
int nMin = min ( nA, nB );
```

Of course, it can also be used with any other scalar type:

```
float fMin = min ( fA, fB );
```

You might wonder why there are so many parentheses in the macro definition, and the answer is simple: to preserve operator precedence in compound statements. You want the operator '<' to take precedence no matter what the contents of the arguments A and B expand to.

By putting them in parentheses, you ensure that the value is expanded and evaluated before the comparison is made. This brings you to the previous statement—the min macro can be used with *any other scalar type.*

In fact, each of the arguments should *expand* or *evaluate* to a scalar value of the same type. It is perfectly legal to nest macros, because they will be expanded by the pre-processor before compilation. So you can use code such as:

```
int nMin = min ( nA, min (nB, nC));
```

This would return the smallest of the three values. The exact expansion is left as an exercise for you. If you want to test arrays in a similar manner, you need to be able to evaluate the entire array against another array.

In string handling, for example, the string.h library provides you with a useful function to compare a pair of strings—strcmp. It returns −1, 0, or 1, depending on whether the string on the left side is less than, equal to, or greater than the string on the right.

To create a simple `str_min` macro, all you need to do is take advantage of this simple behavior and create a macro that evaluates the *result* of `strcmp`:

```
#define str_min(X, Y) (strcmp(X, Y) < 0 ? (X) : (Y))
```

The obvious drawback is that you need to #include the string.h library beforehand; otherwise the compiler cannot evaluate the macro expanded by the pre-processor. Because the pre-processor has no knowledge of the C language, it will continue to expand the macro blindly.

So clearly macros are very useful but should be employed with care. More advanced code examples split macros across multiple lines, but at this point you should evaluate whether the reduction in readability outweighs any performance issues. In such cases, a function should be considered as an alternative.

Although many of the previous code examples center on comparisons, you can substitute any valid C code by a macro. Hence, it is possible to create an entire pseudo-language from macros that expand to C code that can then be compiled.

Conditional Compilation with #if

In previous examples, you used the #ifdef statement to test whether or not a constant is defined. You also looked at #else and #endif as well as #ifndef to test whether a constant is *not* defined. You will probably not be surprised to learn that pre-processor directives include a whole decision-making mechanism that mirrors the conditional execution mechanism (if .. elseif .. else).

So combined with the defined function, you can build code with the same functionality as the multiple-include-prevention mechanism using #if:

```
#if !defined (_FILENAME_H)
#define _FILENAME_H
    // This code will be processed only once
    // per compilation cycle
#endif
```

You can also use a similar mechanism to specify a debug level, as well as a debug flag. If, for example, you wanted to display messages depending on whether a certain detail level is set, you could use #if, #elif, and #else. Assuming that you set a debug level flag as follows:

```
#define DEBUG_LEVEL 3
```

You can then go on to evaluate it against various values in order to selectively compile various kinds of debug reporting:

```
#if DEBUG_LEVEL == 3
    // Most detailed reporting
#elif DEBUG_LEVEL == 2
    // Next most detailed reporting
#else
    // No debug reporting
#endif
```

It is also possible to nest these statements in the same way that regular if statements can be nested. Again, the difference between using these pre-processor directives and conditional execution is that only the code that needs to be there, based on the evaluation of the conditions, is included in the application file.

You can also use the conditional compilation method to select between code destined for different platforms. In particular, if there are low-level functions that differ between platforms such as Windows and UNIX—file and directory handling for example—then you can selectively include the libraries and selectively compile the usage statements.

The first thing you need to do is define constants for the two platforms:

```
#define WIN_32 1
#define UNIX 2
```

Next, you need to make sure that any platform-specific function calls are contained within conditional compilation statements. These can then test another constant against these defined values, as in:

```
#if PLATFORM == WIN_32
    // Win32 specific code
#elif PLATFORM == UNIX
    // Unix specific code
#else
    // Generic, we hope, code
#endif
```

To make sure that you compile the right code for use with the platform in question, you need to #define the constant PLATFORM at the beginning of the first source file (main.c or main.h) to set the correct platform type between WIN_32 and UNIX.

Recap

You use the #define family to declare named values (constants), which can then be included in your C program or tested by the #ifdef and #ifndef directives. You can also use snippets of C code, known as macros, in the same way, but because the pre-processor has no knowledge of C coding rules, the compiler is left to catch any syntactic misuse.

You can also provide parameters to function-like macros, which act in the same way as regular functions in C. However, any parameters that are passed can be made type-independent, which gives you a distinct advantage, provided you can live with the inevitable downside associated with an increase in code complexity.

There are other pre-processor directives, but they are beyond the scope of this book. When you use pre-processor directives, take care to avoid issues relating to the following:

- Nesting

- Recursive calls

- Operator precedence

One feature of many C pre-processors is that recursive calls are minimized by a mechanism that intervenes to disallow self-referential macros. Subsequently, if you wanted to define a recursive macro (to compare strings in an array, for example), you would not be able to do so because self-referential macros are permitted to expand only once.

This provides you some protection, but it cannot be relied upon. There are as many C pre-processors as there are compilers. Each one is likely to react differently to advanced cases such as this, so it's best for the "just enough" programmer to use only the most useful features outlined in this chapter.

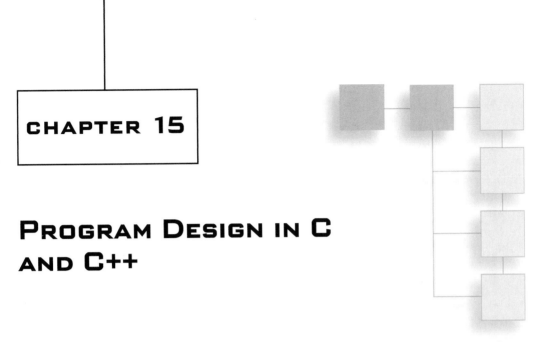

CHAPTER 15

PROGRAM DESIGN IN C AND C++

So far in this book, you have looked at code written in the C language. Everything that you have looked at until now can be used to create application programs that are reasonably robust, provided that care is taken to understand the nature of the problem, and that you understand how to break it down into appropriate data structures and algorithms.

For many people, the purpose of learning C, however, is to get a better grasp of a much thornier topic: C++. This is why so many programming professionals tend to look at C++ as a separate language and worthy of being understood as a language in its own right.

However, doing this does require some prior knowledge of programming and a will to become intimate with a reasonably challenging programming language. This is why I prefer, in the interest of providing "just enough" information to take advantage of the features of C++, to treat it as an extension of C.

Or, if you prefer, think of C++ as a language based on the syntax of C, with some added semantics to make object-oriented programming more accessible. The aim of this chapter, therefore, is to give you an introduction to the object-oriented paradigm and look at the way that C++ implements it.

First, you'll look at design in C, which I use as a basis for introducing C++. In other words, this chapter illustrates good design, implementation in C, and the guiding philosophy behind C++.

It is important that you understand that the material presented here teaches a pragmatic use of C++, rather than an all-inclusive use. In other words, it provides some of the best features of C++, while hiding some of the complexities that take time to master.

Those complexities, although valuable in the long term, are out of the scope of this book, which is aimed at helping you learn C++ as a programming language in a more general way. It will take years to become an expert in C++ programming, and much of that time will be spent absorbing whatever is possible from looking at other people's code.

The first stage in understanding that code is reading about the mechanisms that C++ provides that are an improvement on, or extension to, the C language. However, in order to go about writing your own code, it is also necessary that you understand how the description of the problem domain differs from the C programmer's view.

C++ is about writing better code—better organized, more robust, and probably more efficient in both maintenance and execution as a whole. It is possible to write any C++ code in C, something that's often mentioned when comparing the two languages, but C++ provides a better way to lay the code out in many cases.

That said, you first need to look at the problems you are trying to solve before considering C++ the solution. As always, you should start at the design level. This chapter stays clear of implementation details, instead concentrating on the theoretical details that will help you understand why the language is constructed the way this it is.

Object-Oriented Design

The principle behind object-oriented design is that it is so close to the real world that it is easier to create the virtual version of it. Design helps you get a clear view of the system under development, and object-oriented design helps you to break that system down into manageable intercommunicating parts.

Entire books have been written on the subject of object orientation, and many college classes specialize in teaching it at an abstract level. There are also pure OO languages that reflect very accurately the paradigm in all its glory. This, on the other hand, is a book about pragmatic programming without going into unnecessary detail.

Object Name

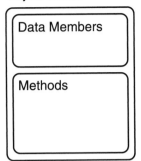

Figure 15.1
Object Definition

Therefore, you'll look at the area from the point of view of a C programmer, moving to C++ where necessary, and cover only topics that make implementation sense in these languages. This will necessitate a slight simplification of the paradigm, but it retains the broad principles that make it so powerful: the object space.

Each object in the object-oriented (OO) design space has, on the one hand, data that represents its internal space and methods that are used to operate on those pieces of member data. Even if it seems like a simple system that is being modeled, it is worth going through the steps that create the model of the problem domain. See Figure 15.1.

To help the design process, many programmers draw a diagram of some kind that helps them visual the description of the objects in the system. The exercise itself is helpful in enabling you to think through the system and organize it correctly.

This process is called mapping the problem domain. Whether you intend to implement the resulting system design in C or C++, the design steps are applicable in both cases. In C, you can implement each kind of object as a struct, with data members mirroring the design.

The methods that operate on the data commonly need to perform some basic tasks:

- Initialize data

- Retrieve data

- Copy data from one object to another

- Modify internal state data

Note that you can achieve these tasks by passing an instance of the `struct` to functions as a parameter passed by reference. Bearing this in mind, let's look at some basic tips on creating an object-oriented design of the problem domain.

The Problem Domain

In creating the description of the problem domain, the first step in producing an object-oriented design, you are mapping from the real world to the virtual one. In traditional programming paradigms such as structured methods, the emphasis is less on trying to mimic the real world and more on creating a program.

In order to maintain the OO paradigm, you need to retain a one-to-one mapping between the real-world objects and the objects in the system. So, if you are trying to create an OO design for a problem domain that contains a user interface for an address book, you have a clear list of possible objects based on observing a real-world address list:

■ Edit areas to view and edit details

■ Manipulation buttons (Previous, Next, Edit, and so on)

■ Something to store the data in (a file)

■ A menu

Note from this list that some of the objects will have multiple instances in the final program. For example, a certain entry will have a name, address, and probably a phone number edit area. Using the object-oriented design paradigm, realize that these share enough in common that you need to define only one type of object, called a *class*.

Sometimes it can be hard to achieve the correct level of *classes* in the system—and it is important to get the right level of granularity when designing the system. So, if you have a system in which you need to define a car, you might not need to go down to the level of wheels, nuts, and bolts; it might be sufficient to create classes to represent all vehicles.

What is important is that the various interactions that you are modeling between objects in the system should be the same as in the real world. As long as this is the case, you have usually found the right level of granularity. One of the reasons it is important to go through the design process is to ascertain whether you are building the system correctly, as well as whether you are building the correct system.

So, you need to define only those objects that have concrete examples in the problem domain. If you cannot describe an object based on something that you understand, it will be very hard to build a software version. This is one of the principle problems with software design and development—it is difficult to create something that does not really exist. This problem is known as the intangible nature of software development.

These objects that mirror the concrete objects from the real world may, however, need to be augmented in order to perform the tasks required. In the address book example, you need somewhere to store the data: a file. This could be mirrored by an actual address book (with paper pages and ink writing), but it could also be implemented in an object that has no real concrete example.

The ideas behind these other, non-concrete, objects is that they merely provide an easy way to interact between the objects that are reflections of concrete objects that do exist.

As in the discussion of programming in previous chapters, naming is very important. You have looked at some programming conventions that relate to the way that you implement the code in C, but you also need some that help you build the lists of objects and methods that form your object-oriented design.

For example, you use nouns or compound nouns to describe objects. A concept cannot be made into a class because there is no concrete representation to refer it to. Subsequently, using nouns as class names is perfectly in line with a description that mirrors real life.

By a similar token, interactions between objects or methods usually contain verbs in their name. This helps you describe more accurately what the method does. If the name is too long, perhaps it is trying to describe something that needs to be refined.

The methods need to be well named because they are the only way that the objects are allowed to interact in an object-oriented design. In other words, classes do not have access to each other's data members. The methods that you define give access to those members, and this is known as *encapsulating* the data.

Encapsulation and Messages

Also known as data-hiding, *encapsulation* is an important part of successful object-oriented design, both from the standpoint of creating the design itself and as an aid to design reuse. In other words, the more encapsulated the data is, the easier it will be to reuse parts of the design and, by extension, the implementation.

The principle of encapsulation is to keep all the data that pertains to the state of an object internal and not accessible by other objects. This means that if an object needs to know something about another object, you must give it the means to obtain that information without having access to the data.

In order to interact with the object, you need only know the interface requirements—what data must be given to the object and what data it will return—but you do not need to know anything about its internal state or how it processes input data into output data.

Recognize that this principle has also formed part of the "just enough" teaching process thus far. The book goes to some lengths, for example, to explain the interfaces to standard input and output (such as the `printf` and `scanf` functions), but the actual implementation is hidden from the programmer.

The interfaces are described in the header files, which provide some level of encapsulation. The internal representation of a file, for example, is hidden from the programmer and will change from platform to platform.

The stdio.h library, however, at an abstract level at least, is reusable. It is defined only once, although it might be implemented several times, depending on the platform mix supplied with the compiler.

Typically, in object-oriented design you look at the passing of data between objects in terms of their interface functions as *messages.*

Messages

An object message (a member or library function in C) fulfills several aims:

- Instantiates an object

- Passes data through objects (that is, in, out, or in/out)

- Elicits actions within the target object

So messages that provide interaction between objects exist to mirror real-world interactions. These messages obtain data from the object, causing a state change within the object, or hand some updated data to the object that might not effect a state change.

There is a fairly blurred line between messages and methods, as presented here, so these sections tend to talk in terms of methods generically and messages in cases when it's explicitly understood that you're using the method for communication with the object.

When you create the object-oriented design, you can then represent these messages as links between objects and begin to work out what the interactions between them will be. Again, this is best done in diagram form, but at this point you are probably tired of using bits of paper and might rather find a program to help you model the system.

Check out Chapter 20, "Web References," for some good starting points for learning a suitable diagramming notation (commonly UML) and tools to help leverage that knowledge. For large-scale applications, that is probably going to be a necessary exercise, but you can do much with simple tools, such as a pen and paper or text editor.

A Simple Example: Text Editor

Assume for this example that you want to model a text editor in an object-oriented design. You could produce a list of objects at a high level that includes the following:

- `EditWindow`
- `Menu`
- `File`
- `Printer`

These are all contained inside the main application object, which is what you are trying to build. Each one will have some internal data and methods, as illustrated in Figure 15.2.

Figure 15.2 lists only the most obvious methods and data items; were you building a complete application, you would need to refine this model further. For now, it is sufficient for you to be able to identify only the items that represent actual operations.

The notation used here includes the name of the object in bold, the data members in italics, and the methods in normal text. Different diagramming standards have different notations, of course, and you are free to choose your own notation method when drawing these diagrams manually.

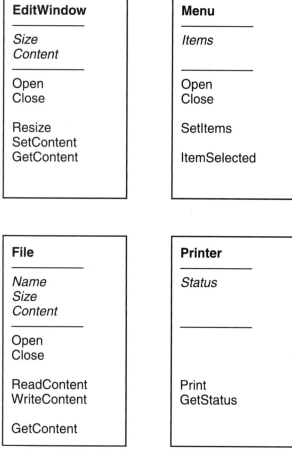

Figure 15.2
TextEditor Objects

The EditWindow object is fairly self-explanatory. It has size and content, which represents the size of the window on the screen and the text contained within it. You can obtain the text through the GetContent message and set it with the SetContent message, as well as open and resize it.

The File object is similarly uncomplicated. You will open it, probably by providing a name, and then read or write to it before closing it. You could add a GetSize method to query the file about its dimensions.

The Printer object is simplified, assuming that much of the work is done internally. All you need to do is pass it something to print and check its status on occasion. This is exactly like the operations you perform in the real world.

The Menu object is a little different. It is one of those objects that generates messages, seemingly on its own. As such, it is the starting point for any object-interaction diagram (some people refer to these as *use cases* in other paradigms). I encourage a single object interaction diagram per perceived operation at this level.

The Menu object itself is a direct mirror of the way that menus operate in a standard GUI-based operating system and, as such, reflects a concrete type of object. Menus provide a way for the users to interact with the application (along with buttons), and not much occurs until the users select an item.

Of course, EditWindow is also something of an exception, because you assume (rightly, in the case of Windows) that it contains the "typewriter" logic to allow text inside it to be edited. (In other words, it allows the users to type, select, delete, and insert text as if they were using a virtual typewriter.)

This simplification makes the object diagram easier to create and manage, but it would need to be expanded (probably in another diagram) if a suitable GUI element were not available.

So if you wanted to save the contents of the text window, the initial object interaction diagram might look somewhat unrefined, as shown in Figure 15.3.

Note that this is just one take on object-oriented design—it is a pragmatic helpful approach that centers around getting the job done, rather than following the paradigm in all its glorious detail. This approach is fine for small projects, but the bigger the project, the more sophisticated you would need to be in your modeling.

Essentially, all Figure 15.3 is saying is this—when the program receives an ItemSelected message that is equal to the Save File command from the Menu object, the WriteContent method of the File object will be invoked. In order to save the content, the File object will need to query the EditWindow object with a GetContent message.

You can assume that the logic to handle the filename, reading and writing, and all the error trapping occurs inside the File object, which is perfectly acceptable from an object-oriented point of view when you know the capabilities of the underlying language and operating system. The simpler you can keep your design, while retaining the ability to make it workable, the better.

You could actually write this object interaction slightly differently:

```
Menu::ItemSelected ( SaveFile )
    [→] File::WriteContent
            [→] EditWindow::GetContent ( File::Content )
```

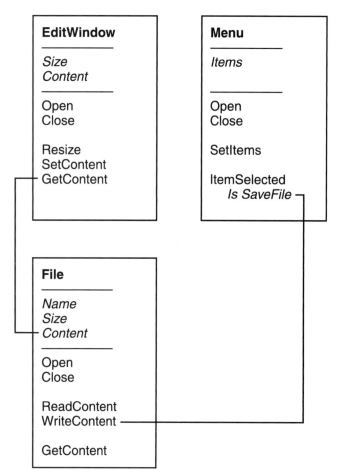

Figure 15.3
Save Contents Object Interaction Diagram

In this version, you chart the actual flow of control through the object space, noting the interactions as messages as you go. It is somehow easier to grasp for those used to writing programs in a sequential, procedural manner.

This is quite close to an actual implementation notation, so it is a good time to take a look at the other side of the coin—object-oriented programming.

Object-Oriented Programming

Moving from an abstract object-oriented design to an actual implementation requires that you understand some key concepts that relate to the way that C++ handles the transition. In the next chapter, you read about the language constructs that C++ provides to implement the elements discussed next, which are still in the realms of theory at this point.

Due to the approach, some of the following topics are classified as *programming*, where arguably, pure OO methodologies will put them in the *design* category. However, the goal here is to make an easy link between the design and the implementation, so I have chosen to express these concepts in a way that straddles the two areas.

If an OO design is an abstraction (or modeling) of the objects in a system, the OO programming paradigm seeks to implement these abstractions. In the meantime, you might find that you can group some of the objects together and turn them into a further abstraction, called a *class*.

So the first topic you'll look at really does straddle both the OO design and programming subjects. In a sense, you are treating the class mechanism as a kind of solution to an implementation problem. The OO design shows the complete object space, and where some of the object's definitions overlap, you might be able to create classes that provide the functionality.

An example of this design is the Windows operating system. Everything in the GUI is based on the Window class. This class provides the basic definitions that allow a widget to be positioned, activated, created, and destroyed, and contains information pertaining to its owner and behavior.

A button, for example, is a special kind of window object that has some attributes of the base class and also some specific features peculiar to buttons. An application can have many buttons, and an object diagram might have many examples of buttons inside it—each one having a separate function.

When you create the classes that are the embodiment of the system, so as not to be continually re-inventing the wheel, you can call upon the Windows API to help you out. It makes sense, therefore, when implementing these objects, to try to save valuable time and create classes that are abstractions of the objects involved.

Classes

A *class* is a precise definition of what an abstraction of an object should look like and how it should behave. There is a one-to-many relationship between objects and classes—in other words, many objects can potentially be based on a single class definition. For example, a car might have four wheels in an object diagram, each with its own interactions, but each wheel is based on a single wheel class.

The class needs to define the data that the objects store internally, the messages that they will react to, and the methods that can be used to obtain information from them, or change their internal state in some way.

You would typically create a class diagram that depicts these features in the same way that you create an object diagram to create an abstraction of the actual physical system. The class diagram can use similar notation as used previously; however, there are some vital differences in the way that the diagram is used.

In fact, you should aim to create a class hierarchy in which you can minimize the implementation workload by creating base classes and then deriving new classes from them that add behavior that makes them more refined. To return to the car and wheel analogy, wheels come in different shapes and sizes—different tires, different hubs, and so on.

If you create a wheel base class, you can treat it as a fairly abstract notion, safe in the knowledge that if you need a bicycle wheel, car wheel, or tractor wheel, you can use this wheel base class as a starting point and then create more specialized wheel classes as needs arise.

This is similar to the way in which an operating system such as Windows works—each widget is a specialization of a base widget class. In fact, some widgets are two or three classes into the hierarchy.

A combo box is a type of list box, which is a type of window. The combo box has special properties—an edit area, for a start—but is also a list box and has some attributes that can be defined by the base class—a window.

This is called *inheritance,* and you'll look at it in Chapter 16. In fact, the combo box goes one step further, because it needs to inherit from both the list box class and the edit box class. This is a special kind of inheritance called *multiple inheritance,* which you'll read about near the end of this chapter.

Before you look at the two areas of a class that define it, you need to understand that the properties and attributes of the class are usually considered public or private. Public things are exposed to the outside world, and private things are accessible only by the object itself.

Pure encapsulation requires that all the member data is kept private and that only the member functions that are needed to provide the interface to the behavior of the class are classified as public. However, some more pragmatic applications of the OO paradigm allow the two to mix; a private function is rare, but quite allowable; a public data member is even more rare and less forgivable.

Data

The properties of an object are often referred to as its data. These properties allow the object to maintain control of its own internal state. Therefore, data members are usually encapsulated, except in rare circumstances.

Incoming messages will cause changes to the object's data, which in turn will change its behavior when called upon to do something. You keep the data hidden so that, should the representation change in some way, other designs that might reuse it have no dependencies on that data representation remaining the same.

Functions

Otherwise known as methods, functions provide the interface to the class and any classes derived from it. They are the only way that the application and other objects can communicate with the class, and as such they need to provide ways to set and retrieve data stored in the private section of the class.

Not all data is useful, and so it is not generally thought necessary to provide a get/set member for every single piece of member data. Should this prove necessary, the design might call for a generic get/set all member data method, which is populated in the parameter list with a complex data type containing all member data to be updated.

This comes with its own specific drawbacks, especially in areas such as data encapsulation; however, it can also be the only viable way to perform a get/set of all data contained within the class. This is an issue that must be resolved at the design or implementation level.

Should it be solved only upon implementation, the design should be updated to reflect the approach chosen. This applies equally to all other implementation changes that differ from the initial design.

Instances

An *instance* is an embodiment of a specific class. In other words, it's like a variable that is based on a type. The type is analogous to the class, and the variable is analogous to the instance. This analogy works quite well when you consider the

= (equals) sign (or associated user function in the case of a complex data type) to be the get/set method and other operators to be modification methods.

Although an instance might exist, it might not yet be an object because it might not yet be instantiated. In other words, an object can exist but have no shape or have the default shape. This might be acceptable, depending on the kind of class and its limitations.

Objects

When this book refers to *objects*, it's referring to instances of classes that have been instantiated. They are the in-application equivalent of the concrete objects that you originally listed in the design for the application, with appropriate properties set to make them resemble those objects.

This brings you full circle back to the objects; if the application follows the design, the objects contained within it will have a one-to-one relationship with the OO design created in the first place.

Although this is unlikely to happen in the first instance, you should always strive to get as close as possible to this situation. It makes testing, debugging, and validating the system much easier.

Prototyping Revisited

Recall the term *prototyping* in Chapter 2 when you looked at separating C code into header files and source files. You also looked briefly at how you could provide the prototypes in the source file, before they are formally implemented, to allow forward references in the code.

A *forward reference* is simply the possibility to use a function before the implementation has been compiled. To do this, the compiler needs to have a prototype to work. This way, the compiler has the correct profile for the function calls to verify that they are being used correctly.

The implementation of classes as source code follows a similar pattern. The compiler will build the object code from the source independently of the main program. However, you need to tell the compiler what the classes contain so that it can successfully create the application. You do this through prototyping.

C++ Header Files

C++ header files store the following:

- Class definitions

- Class-independent data structures

- Application-specific constants

- Class-specific constants

In other words, anything that is not code goes into a header file. This means that you'll probably need to protect the files against multiple inclusion, as detailed in Chapter 14.

This example assigns the header files the standard .h extension, much as you would a normal C header file. Some implementations will use .hpp to associate the filename with C++ rather than C, but this is not necessary.

Try to keep OO code and application startup code as separate as possible, and limit each header file to prototyping a single class.

It is worth noting, because you'll likely come across an example that implements methods in header files. I do not advise it, because it makes future reuse, distribution, and debugging that much harder.

The one time that I might advocate this is when you're providing some initialization code for a default instance of a given class. This is sometimes necessary (for example, when creating a linked list node) so you can avoid doing something with the object before it has been correctly instantiated.

C++ Source Files

The C++ source files are used to implement the inner workings of the classes and to create the main application. They will need to reference the header files that will store the constants and macros needed to build the software, as well as the prototypes and class definitions that give information as to the interfaces to the classes.

You also instantiate objects, create instances of classes, and manipulate them in the C++ source files. Objects or class instances are never created inside the source files that are designed to contain the implementation of the classes, except in rare circumstances.

Again, a one-to-one relationship between the classes in the design, the header files, and the source files is advised. However, source files may include multiple header files if there is some inter-dependent code. On the other hand, the OO paradigm, which started with concrete real-world objects, should ensure that this is kept to a minimum.

Recall that I mentioned that prototyping in source files is possible. However, it will tend to hurt reuse, especially when you're building libraries. In other words, any prototype that exists in a source file and that is built into a static or dynamic library will not be shared with future projects.

The reason for this is that the header file contains the prototypes that are valid for a library. Extracting prototypes from the object code, or even from the library that is built for use in an operating system (such as a DLL or dynalink library), is a tricky procedure at best.

If you remain true to the idea that you prototype in a header file, the same header file that was used to build the source code into a library (be it static or dynamic) can then be supplied with the library for developers to use. In this case, the header file needs also to contain any constants that have special meanings to the objects in the library.

This is the approach that the Windows API programmers use and is also shared by many other commercial programmers.

Recap

This chapter is attempting to prepare you for the next stage in the C++ paradigm—implementing classes that are correctly designed. You have looked at the object-oriented mindset in a pragmatic fashion, which is as much a way of looking at the programming problem as a whole as it is about creating specific designs.

True to the "just enough" principle, you can also choose not to actually create design documents for small projects, as long as you understand how you are going to achieve the end result. For example, a small application that is destined only to ask the users for some basic information before doing a simple calculation can usually get away without a full design.

However, it is good practice to create a text document to act as a work in progress to hold class and data descriptions so that the best use can be made of any OO principles. After all, you might return to the code to enhance it in the future, and it is often hard to pick up where you've left off.

As an added benefit, you might find that you can reuse code and designs between projects, thus making more effective use of your time. Classes are not just a convenience, as many C-to-C++ programmer converts seem to think, they are an integral part of the way that the C++ language has been developed.

Classes aren't the only part of the language that improves over the original C. As you'll see in the next chapter, only part of C++ is about classes—an important part, but not the end of the story.

However, it is vital that you understand the thrust of this chapter first, because it will help you draw necessary parallels between C and C++.

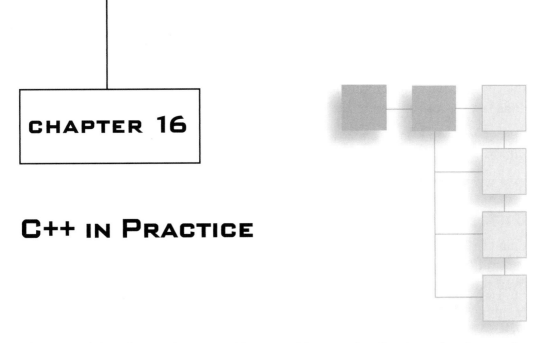

CHAPTER 16

C++ IN PRACTICE

The aim of this chapter is to provide you with enough of an introduction to the use of C++ so that you can:

- Make use of the new features of C++.

- Understand C++ source code and benefit from it.

- Benefit from the Standard Template Libraries.

C++ is a language in its own right, and large volumes have been dedicated to helping programmers get an in-depth view of it. The goal of the "just enough" approach is to help the readers use C++ in their own projects and make their coding time more efficient.

This chapter concentrates on the differences between C and C++, the language structure, and the new features that will help you achieve all of the tasks described previously.

Having worked through this chapter, you'll be well equipped to understand more advanced concepts, such as moving your C code to C++ via the C++ Standard Libraries and using the Standard Template Library.

It is perhaps worth mentioning at this point that the Standard Template Library consists of a large number of ready-made data structures (lists, for example) and the code needed to manipulate them. Unless you understand classes and C++ code layout, making use of the STL is almost impossible.

Even if you don't want to take advantage of the STL, the C++ Standard Libraries offer some useful extensions, and it is well worth reading through the next two chapters before deciding whether to use C or C++.

Differences in Code Organization

C and C++ differ in a number of places. Some of the major differences are in the declarations and scope of variables, which are slightly more flexible and logical from the programming perspective in C++.

In addition, there are some entirely new operators that simplify memory access and the way that functions are treated. In addition, there are two entirely new concepts to add to a working knowledge of C++:

■ Classes

■ Exception handling

You'll read more about these concepts later on in the chapter; they borrow on some of the new features discussed here. It is useful just to consider the various differences between the two languages before trying to understand classes or exception handling.

Declarations

The first difference you'll read about is something that you've been insulated from so far and has to do with void pointers. Recall, for example, that you can allocate memory blocks in C using the malloc function, which returns a void pointer.

In C, this means that you can, in theory, write code such as:

```
char * szString;
szString = malloc ( String_Length * sizeof(char) );
```

The discussion of memory management used an explicit, rather than an implicit, conversion from void * to char *. This leads you to write code such as:

```
char * szString;
szString = (char * ) malloc ( String_Length * sizeof(char) );
```

This second representation is required in C++, which largely does away with implicit type conversion in favor of improved type checking.

The range of built-in types is also extended with the Boolean type, allowing for TRUE and FALSE values. So, where in C you had to enumerate a Boolean type, now you have a type bool, which can be true or false. These last two are new C++ literals.

The true and false literals are automatically turned into 1 and 0 if they are to be used in numerical comparisons. This makes porting from C to C++ easy, as long as the Boolean type has been enumerated correctly in C as equating to 0 or 1.

In C++ declarations can appear anywhere in the code and not just at the start of a code block (source file, function, and so on), which is more convenient. Of course, there are drawbacks, because beginning programmers often attempt to redeclare variables by accident as the original declarations scroll out of view in the source code.

One of the common pieces of C++ code that uses this kind of declaration flexibility is in creating counted loops:

```
for (int x = 0; x < 100; x++)
{
   for (int y = 0; y < 100; y++)
   {
      int z; // Declare and do something with z
   }
}
```

Scoping follows more or less logical rules—z is visible inside the inner loop but not in the outer loop, because most compilers restrict the scope to the code between the braces. If there is another variable outside the loops also called z, this will only increase the confusion. The code will compile, but the execution will be flawed.

For example, you might have code such as:

```
int z = 42;
// some code here
for (int x = 0; x < 100; x++)
{
   for (int y = 0; y < 100; y++)
   {
```

```
      int z; // Declare and do something with z
   }
   if ( z == 150 ) // Oops; global z used!!
   {
      // Some code
   }
}
```

In this snippet, the z variable used in the if statement is not the same as the one used in the inner loop. Similarly, if you needed to test for premature exit of a loop, the following code would probably not even compile:

```
for (int x = 0; x < 100; x++)
{
   if ( rand() % 100 == x) break;
}
if ( x < 100 ) // x out of scope!!!
{
   // Some code here
}
```

Clearly, the flexibility to declare variables for use needs to be applied with some care. Good naming conventions and logical code structure help.

Finally, C++ allows you to pass values to functions by reference—using the & operator—instead of having to actually pass a pointer to the argument. In other words, you can define a function as receiving values passed by reference and then just pass the variable name in the code, instead of having to define the function as receiving pointers and using the reference operator to create the pointers from the variables.

As a concrete example, in C, if you declared the function as follows:

```
void some_function ( int * a, int b)
```

In the some_function definition, you expect to receive a pointer to an integer and an integer. So to call some_function with two values, you would use code such as:

```
int a, b;
// Some code
a = 1;
b = 2;
some_function ( &a, b );
```

The equivalent definition for some_function in C++ is:

```
void some_function ( int & a, int b)
```

This enables you to write C++ code to call the function with two variables as follows:

```
int a, b;
// Some code
a = 1;
b = 2;
some_function ( a, b );
```

The differences are that you have swapped the pointer in the function definition with the reference operator (&) and can call the function without using the reference operator explicitly. This makes passing variables through functions a little easier.

There are two side effects: one functional and one aesthetic. The functional drawback is that you allow the variable to be changed inside the function. This wouldn't matter but for the aesthetic drawback—you no longer have the visual reminder that the variable is being passed by reference and not as a value.

As long as you remember this, you will not face unexpected behavior.

Scope

Besides the change to variable declarations, there is another slight alteration to the way that scoping for function declarations is handled. In C++, all functions must be declared before use. This means that compiling files in the correct order becomes more important, as does the inclusion of header files.

Prototyping is, however, an acceptable form of declaration, and so it is quite common to find C++ programs that are structured in the following way:

```
#include ...
#define ...
function prototypes
main function
    {
    }
function implementations
```

By a similar token, the declare-before-use rules for variables means that sometimes they are not available outside a code block, as you saw previously. In other words, those variable defined inside loops, functions, and other code blocks might not be available outside of those blocks.

Finally, the use of constants in C++ is a little more sophisticated. The `const` keyword enables you to define a variable with a value that does not change. This keyword can be placed in a header file. For example, you might place a line such as the following in a main header file:

```
const int nConstant = 42;
```

This variable is not external by default. In other words, it is valid only for the scope of the file that explicitly included the file containing the constant. You can make the variable external by using the `extern` keyword:

```
extern const int nConstant = 42;
```

Wherever nConstant is defined, it will be available to all files being linked during the build process, because it is external. Of course, it should only be defined once. As a side note, the `const` keyword acts much like the #define keyword in C and has the same scoping rules as a variable.

The differences are that, unlike a variable, its value may not be changed, and unlike defining a constant with the #define keyword, it is not purely a textual substitution but an actual variable. This means that you can create references to it, for example, which you cannot do with a C macro.

New Operators and Features

There are a few items that are of importance to a beginning C++ programmer that qualify as extensions to the language. As mentioned, there are many intricacies of C++ as a language in its own right, but the following items are specifically aimed at those wanting to take advantage of C++ without all the baggage.

First, the C++ language introduces `new` and `delete` as replacements for `malloc` and `free`. In other words, memory management has become part of the language proper. It is no longer necessary to specifically allocate a sized memory chunk for a character string, because you can now use code such as:

```
char * szString = new char [255];
```

This is the equivalent to:

```
char * szString = (char *) malloc ( sizeof (char) * 255 );
```

This code will compile in both C and C++ but is not as convenient as the `new` keyword. In the same way that `malloc` has to be balanced by calls to `free`, `new` must be balanced by calls to delete. So, to deallocate szString, you use the following C++ code:

```
delete szString;
```

This code is the equivalent of the following:

```
free ( szString );
```

It is not advised to mix malloc and delete with new and free. In other words, the programmer should not malloc a memory block that is then deleted or attempt to free memory allocated with the new keyword. The reason behind this is simple. The new and free keywords provide memory management that is native to the C++ language. The malloc and free keywords provide C-based memory management. These two mechanisms might not be implemented in an equivalent and compatible manner.

So if you use new to allocate an array of characters and then try to free the memory block, there is no guarantee that it will work. Even worse—your system might crash.

The second useful feature is that you can provide default arguments inside function declarations. This allows you to set a default value for an argument when you have not provided a specific value in the function call.

However, it is not possible to have a default argument in the first position or middle positions of a function declaration. This would require some compiler sixth sense to work out which argument was supposed to be the default one.

So the following is incorrect:

```
void my_function ( int a, int b = 3, char c )
```

However, the following is perfectly legal C++ code:

```
int my_multiply ( int a, int b = a ) { return a * b; }
```

When called with only one argument, my_multiply will resort to the default behavior of squaring the argument that has been supplied.

Finally, there are two additional mechanisms that you'll come across in your exploration of the various libraries that are supplied with C++ environments. The first is the ability to process a variable number of arguments in a function call.

This enables you to declare a function in C++ with the following:

```
int my_add_numbers ( int nNumber, ...)
```

The three dots (...) at the end of the parameter list indicate that the function accepts any number of arguments. However, the issue of retrieving these arguments is not quite as straightforward as you might expect.

The standard header file includes some macros to help you retrieve the arguments from the list:

> va_start   Start the retrieval process
>
> va_arg   Retrieve an argument
>
> va_end   End the retrieval process

Before you can use these macros, you need to declare a variable of type va_list to store the list of parameters. Again, this is defined in the standard header file. So, you can expand your definition of my_add_numbers as follows:

```
int my_add_numbers ( int nNumber, ...)
{
  va_list arg_list;
  int nReturn = 0;

  va_start( arg_list, nNumber ); // start the retrieval process

  for ( int n = 0; n < nNumber; n++)
  {
    nReturn += va_arg ( arg_list, int ); // retrieve an argument of type int
  }

  va_end ( list ); // stop the retrieval process

  return nReturn;
}
```

So in the call to va_start, you give the macro the list of arguments and the address of the starting variable (that is, the last variable for which you know the name). Then you proceed to extract the variables one by one using the va_arg macro; you provide the list and the type of the variable to extract.

Finally, you call va_end when you're done. The user provides the number of arguments to expect in the first parameter of the function. If you had not insisted on this, you could instead have tested for an explicit termination value (such as −1), but this comes with its own issues.

The `sprintf` function works in this way, too. With the `sprintf` function, however, the format string gives the function the number of arguments; it just has to count the number of fields that the users provided.

The variable parameter list works only with built-in types. There are some tricks for using other types, but they require delving far deeper into the inner workings of the compiler than this book goes. It remains, however, a useful mechanism.

Last, but not least, you must consider the type safe checking that C++ offers. This means that every variable type is checked against what is allowed, be it a parameter in a function call, an assignment, or some other type processing.

As a consequence, the reliance on implicit type conversions is removed, and compilers tend to pick up more suspicious unsafe conversions than in the C language. It does encourage good coding practices, so it's a good thing.

Defining Classes

The C++ language also introduces the *class* mechanism. This provides you with an object-oriented mechanism for defining abstractions of objects. These abstractions adhere to OO principles such as data hiding (encapsulation), inheritance, and polymorphism.

In other words, you can define abstract data types where you know the exposed interface, but not the internals, and can only access the data in a way that is allowed by the class definition. Classes are ideal for a number of tasks and are useful in cases where you want to define a user-defined data structure coupled with all its processing functions as a single entity.

You'll no doubt find many uses for classes once you understand the mechanism that C++ provides. The basic structure of a class *definition* uses the `class` keyword:

```
class <name>
{
  private:
    // Data members and local functions
```

282 Chapter 16 ■ C++ in Practice

```
public:

  // Exposed member functions

}; // Trailing semicolon
```

In this snippet, note that the entire class definition is enclosed in braces, with a trailing semicolon. This code block will usually reside in a header file distinct from the code proper. It is a definition (prototype) to be expanded by C++ code at a later stage.

The `private` keyword details part of the class in which anything in the section (that is, after the keyword) is considered to be opaque. Data defined here cannot be accessed from outside, but it can be accessed from within the code that implements the class, via the `->` operator.

Functions can also be defined in the `private` section, but they will be available only to other functions inside the class (public or private). To expose a piece of data or a function to the outside world, it must be placed in the `public` part of the class.

The `public` section is where the constructor (setup) and destructor functions of the class are usually defined. They are responsible for creating and destroying the parts of the object that are based on the class needed for its operation.

Staying with the definition for the time being, the `public` section is also a good place to put any `get`/`set` operators (for access to data components) and the functions that can be called to ask the object to perform various tasks on itself. Generally speaking, objects will not operate on other objects, unless they are in a hierarchy.

This hierarchy allows you to also specify classes that inherit from other classes. In other words, they can become a specialization of a parent class, inheriting the `private`, `public`, or both areas of the class definition.

It is important to remember that the object does not exist until the constructor is called, which is triggered by the `new` keyword. For example, you assume that you have a class that is defined as follows:

```
class my_class
{
  private:
    // Data members and local functions
    int my_value;
```

```
  public:
    // Exposed member functions
    my_object ( int default_value = 0 ); // Constructor
    ~my_object (); // Destructor

    int get_value (int & value);
    void set_value ( int value );

}; // Trailing semicolon
```

This code should be stored in a file such as my_class.h. Assuming this to be the case, the accompanying source code file (called my_class.cpp by convention) would then implement the various operations.

You'll come to the actual implementation in due course. If all the code is in place, the main.cpp file can include the header file and use the class definition. Example code to do this might look like the following:

```
#include "my_class.h"

void main ( )
{
  my_class * my_object = new my_class(); // Defaults to zero
  my_object->set_value ( 3 );

  int nValue;
  printf ( "%d", my_object->get_value( nValue ) );

  delete my_object;
}
```

Note that this example uses new and delete to create and destroy the object that is based on the class. Subsequently, it uses the two access functions to get and set values, through the -> operator. You cannot access the variable directly, because it is in the private section of the class.

Compiling and linking will require that you:

- Compile the .cpp files separately.

- Link the various object files together.

This is more or less unchanged from the equivalent mechanism in C. You might note from your compiler documentation that this process can be simplified by the use of a makefile, which is outside the current discussion.

Constructors

A *constructor* is just a public member function that is called to create an instance of a class, known as an object. It is responsible for initializing private member variables and can receive parameters to enable it do so. The parameters work exactly as they do for any other function.

It is also possible to construct the object without a value being passed at all or to allow the calling code to optionally provide parameters. You can offer several constructors for the same class, each with different parameters, or none at all.

Be sure to set defaults for private member variables not explicitly initialized from the constructor call; otherwise the instance might not be properly instantiated. Just as variables don't have properly set default values when they are created, objects that are created have member variables that might contain invalid values.

You can also construct objects with a value. In such cases, it is common to provide some kind of default in case the programmer doesn't want to specify a value. Again, you takes on the responsibility to ensure that the constructor creates a fully instantiated instance, regardless of any supplied parameters.

Until the constructor is called, the class is still abstract and does not exist in any real sense. It cannot be accessed directly, and the member functions cannot be called through the -> operator until the object relating to the class has been instantiated with a call to new.

This call then returns a pointer to the object. The variable defined to provide access to the object is usually defined as a pointer to an object of the type of the class. This enables new to return a pointer and the programmer to access the object's member functions through the -> operator.

Destructors

The opposite of the constructor, the destructor is used to destroy the object and return any pieces of member data that have separately allocated memory to the system. The destructor is called when the delete keyword is used in conjunction with the variable name.

Having been called, the pointer is set to unassigned, and so the next line of code should assign the pointer to NULL in case it is accessed at a later line of code. The risk is that the program will crash if a line of code tries to use the unassigned pointer.

One use of destructors is in deleting a list. A list will contain a series of nodes, each pointing to the next. Part of the implementation of the destructor might be to delete the node pointed to. In calling this deletion, the next node will perform the same operation, deleting the node next to *it*, and the whole list will be destroyed as a chain.

This example illustrates stack behavior; the initial call will only return once all the objects have been destroyed. There is an alterative—you start at the top of the list and work your way to the bottom, deleting each node in turn. This is the approach used in "The List" example that follows, when you learn about the destruction function.

It is also possible to call the special this object, which refers to itself. So you can perform the rather unlikely operation:

```
delete this;
```

This is acceptable in some cases, but it should never appear in the destructor itself, because it would cause it to be called twice. However, if the setup (construction) of a node fails for any reason, it could feasibly be called as part of the constructor code.

Example: A Linked List of Command-Line Arguments (Revisited)

By way of a concrete example and as an illustration using something you've seen before, let's take a moment to create a simple linked list. This is perhaps one of the best ways to appreciate how classes can be used.

You'll look at four main areas:

- The node—storing the command and parameter

- The list—storing the nodes

- Adding a node

- Searching for nodes

Note that this not a complete implementation; it is just an example to cover some of the basics of using classes in C++.

The Node

In a linked-list implementation, the node commonly contains some data specific to the application under development and a pointer to the next node in the list. The next node variable points to an instance of the class; it can be slightly confusing, but recall that it is not actually pointing to anything until it is assigned to an instantiated instance of the class.

So the initial attempt at a class definition might look akin to the following:

```
class CArgNode
{
  private:
    // Data members and local functions
    char szCommand[255], szParameter[255];
    CArgNode * oNext;

  public:
    // Exposed member functions
    CArgNode ( char * command, char * parameter ); // Constructor
    ~CArgNode(); // Destructor

    void SetCommand ( char * command );
    char * GetCommand();

    void SetParameter ( char * parameter );
    char * GetParameter();

    void SetNext ( CArgNode * next );
    CArgNode * GetNext ();

};
```

Having defined the class, you can then implement the member functions in a C++ code file. Start with the constructor and destructor:

```
// Constructor for the Argument Node
CArgNode::CArgNode ( char * command, char * parameter )
{
  // Copy the information provided by the caller
  this->SetCommand(command);
```

```
    this->SetParameter(parameter);

    // Set any defaults
    this->SetNext(NULL);
}

// Destructor for the Argument Node
CArgNode::~CArgNode ()
{
    if ( this->oNext != NULL )
    {
        delete this->oNext;
    }
}
```

Note that the code immediately calls the member functions to set the appropriate member values. This is followed by a call to SetNext to make sure that the next node pointer is pointing to NULL.

This is important, because the node in the destructor will attempt to destroy the next in the chain, and if the resulting reference was pointing to an invalid value, it would cause the program to crash. So you must check that before you attempt to delete the object.

Note also that the way to denote a member function implementation is to use the notation <class_name>::<function_name>. Using this notation, you can define, by way of example, the SetCommand/GetCommand pair:

```
// Set command implementation
void CArgNode::SetCommand ( char * command )
{
    strcpy ( this->szCommand, "" );
    if ( command != NULL )
    {
        strcpy ( this->szCommand, command );
    }
}

// Get command implementation
char * CArgNode::GetCommand ()
{
    return (char *)this->szCommand;
}
```

The remainder of the set and get functions are left for you to develop. For now, take a look at the container class that is going to be used to manage the list of items.

The List

In order to provide an interface to the nodes as a collection, you can use a container class that manages the list of nodes from a central point. Self-managing lists are also possible and are defined as part of the Standard Template Library (Chapter 18). However, it serves to illustrate the discussions of classes to use a container class to hold the list.

The list of nodes is constructed so that each node points to the next, but you need to hold two reference points to the list—references to the first and last nodes, called the head and tail of the list. The list container class manages the head and tail, adds and removes nodes, and searches through the list.

So the list class might be defined as:

```
class CArgList
{
    private:
      // Data members and local functions
      CArgNode * oHead;
      CArgNode * oTail;

    public:
      // Exposed member functions
      CArgList (); // Constructor
      ~CArgList(); // Destructor

      void AddNode ( CArgNode * new_node );
      void DeleteNode ( CArgNode * node );
      char * FindNode ( char * command );
};
```

This code is placed in the same header file as the original node definition because it will need that class to operate on. When you create the list, you have the opportunity to set the head and tail to NULL. This is necessary to create an empty list:

```
CArgList::CArgList()
{
```

```
    this->oHead = NULL;
    this->oTail = NULL;
}
```

Likewise, the destructor gives you the opportunity to dispose of the list by deleting the first node in the list. The `CArgNode` implementation will then dispose of the list, node by node. First, however, you need to confirm that the first node has been allocated, as follows:

```
CArgList::~CArgList()
{
  if (this->oHead != NULL)
  {
    delete this->oHead;
  }
}
```

The implementation of these functions occurs in the same source code file as the original node implementations. To leverage this class, you need to create an appropriate variable as follows:

```
CArgList * oArgList = new CArgList();
//
// code statements
//
delete oArgList;
```

Besides the constructor and destructor, the example also defined an `AddNode` function, which you can use to add a node to the list. This is the next function that you'll learn about.

Adding a Node

To add a node, you have several options. You can:

- Add the node to the head.

- Add the node to the tail.

- Insert the node within the list.

This implementation simply adds the node to the head of the list—making it the head in place of any existing head. This requires that you check to see if the list is empty, add the node, and update the head and tail, if necessary.

```
void CArgList::AddNode ( CArgNode * new_node )
{
  if (this->oHead == NULL)
  {
    this->oHead = new_node; // Set the head
    this->oTail = this->oHead; // Tail same as head
  }
  else
  {
    // Set the head to be the new node
    new_node->SetNext( this->oHead );
    this->oHead = new_node;
  }
}
```

The interesting line of code is in bold. Having checked that the head is valid (or at least not NULL), the code can then proceed to assign it as the node *following* the new node. You could have added the node after the tail if you wanted to add the new node at the end of the list, using similar code.

Finally, it's time to consider how to *traverse* the list. In other words, you need a method by which you can access each node in turn and perform some operation on each one.

Searching for Nodes

Assume that you want to find a node that matches a specific command and return a parameter string (as you did in the original C implementation). To do so, you can check each node against a parameter supplied in the function call. You have to traverse the list and verify that one of the node members matches some criteria.

```
char * CArgList::FindNode ( char * command )
{
  // Initialize the temporary node pointer
  CArgNode * current = this->oHead;

  while ( current != NULL )
  {
    // Do they match?
    if ( strcmp ( current->GetCommand(), command ) == 0 )
    {
```

```
    // Return the parameter for this command
    return current->GetParameter();
  }
  current = current->GetNext();
}
}
```

Again, the new code is shown in bold. This code allows you to traverse the list until you reach the end. This assumes that the last node in the list has the next member conveniently set to NULL. Of course, because you have implemented the node class with that protection built in, it will be set to NULL by default.

Inheritance and Polymorphism

Another feature of object-oriented programming is the ability to reuse class definitions in order to simplify the creation of new classes. In other words, you can create more specialized versions of classes to deal with new types of object.

Because these derived classes share a number of features with existing classes, it makes sense to just extend the base, or parent class, rather than cut and paste the code into a completely new class. Added to this, if you change the underlying functionality of the base class, it is reflected in any classes that *inherit* from it.

There are a few points to remember when designing a class for inheritance:

- Assignment operators are not inherited.

- Constructors are not inherited.

- Private members are not accessible.

The last item might seem to be a problem at first sight, but C++ provides a keyword, protected, that allows you to get around the limitation. Anything that is in the protected section of a parent class can be inherited by its children, whereby it has the same properties toward the outside world as private members.

The general form for creating an inherited class is as follows:

```
class <child_class> : public <parent_class>
{
  protected:
    // Protected data and functions
```

```
public:

  <child_class> ( [ parameters ] ); // Constructor
  ~<child_class> ( ); // Destructor
};
```

When you create the implementation code, you can reuse the parent class constructor by using code such as:

```
<child_class>::<child_class> ( [ parameters ] )
  : <parent_class> ( [ parameters ] )
{
    // Construction code
}
```

In this implementation, the construction code should process data members only that are not processed by the parent class. This might seem a little abstract, so consider the classic example of an employee database, where you might start with the base class CEmployee.

This base class would need name and salary information, for example:

```
class CEmployee
{
  protected:
    char szName[50];
    long lSalary;

  public:
    CEmployee ( char * name, long salary); // Constructor
    ~CEmployee(); // Destructor

    long GetSalary();
    void SetSalary( long new_salary );
};
```

Now, if you assume that all these have been implemented in a way that makes sense—such as the object being correctly initialized with the parameters from the constructor—you can create an object using code similar to:

```
CEmployee * oEmployee = new CEmployee ( "Jonh Smith", 10000 );
```

In this hierarchy, you might have management personnel who have additional perks, such as a personal travel budget, for example. To add these perks to a class

CManager, you have two choices. You can create a new class, or you can derive an inherited class from CEmployee.

The second option leads to a class definition similar to:

```
class CManager : public CEmployee
{
  protected:
    long lTravelBudget;

  public:
    CManager ( char * name, long salary, long travel_budget); // Constructor
    ~CManager(); // Destructor

    long GetTravelBudget();
    void SetTravelBudget( long new_travel_budget );
};
```

This example adds a data member to the protected section and adds some data access functions for it in the public section, along with an extra parameter to the constructor. Note that you need to specify only the *new* items. Everything else is *inherited* from the CEmployee class.

When you implement the constructor for CManager, you do it as follows:

```
CManager::CManager (char * name, long salary, long travel_budget)
  : CEmployee (char * name, long salary )
{
    // Construction code
    this->lTravelBudget = travel_budget;
}
```

You do not need to instantiate the shared data members; the parent class implementation does that for you (if it has been implemented correctly to instantiate its own members). As you can see here, you can extend the functionality of a class by adding different behaviors to existing behavior.

However, you can also use polymorphism to handle functions in a different way, depending on the owner's class. In other words, polymorphism allows you to declare a function in a child class differently than in the parent class and force the compiler to choose the right form for the function based on that class.

To indicate that you intend to redefine the function, you must name it as a virtual function. For example, you might want to handle salaries differently, depending on whether the recipient is a CEmployee or a CManager (that is, hourly versus monthly reporting).

So you might redefine the appropriate function in the CEmployee class as follows:

```
virtual float GetSalary( int hours );
```

The implementation would then return the current salary divided by the number of hours. Because it is a virtual function, you can then provide a different definition in the CManager class:

```
long GetSalary( );
```

Notice that this example drops the parameter and the virtual keyword from the definition. It assumes that the function will just return the current salary information for the CManager. Similar mechanisms would then be necessary for the SetSalary function.

A virtual function that has no base class implementation is called a *pure virtual function* and must be overridden in classes inheriting from the base class. If it is not overridden, a compiler error will probably be generated.

Overloading

Operator overloading is a special kind of polymorphism that adds new functionality to existing operators for inherited classes. Recall from the discussion of inheritance that operators are not inherited. Because of this, you need to specify behavior for operators to work with the data associated with the new class.

You have not yet read about operators in classes, so now is a good time for a little refresher on operators in general. Essentially, a class definition can include definitions for all the mathematical and logical operators.

These operators can then be overloaded as if they were functions. This enables you to define a class that contains an overloaded assignment operator, which would assign one set of data to the other, just like with a built-in type.

First, let's define a class that holds two integers and overload the assignment operator =:

```
class CNumberPair
{
  public:
    int nFirst, nSecond; // note data in public section; not always good
```

```
    CNumberPair ( int first, int second );

    ~CNumberPair ();

    CNumberPair &operator = ( const CNumberPair & number_pair );
};
```

Note that when you're using operator overloading in a class, you need to add the class name to the definition and make the operator part of the public area of the class. The general form for the assignment operator is as follows:

```
<class> & operator= (const <class> & right_hand_side)
```

The implementation of the previous code would follow the general form:

```
<class> & <class>::operator=(const <class> & right_hand_side))
```

The assignment operator = allows you to directly assign the value from the object on the right side to the object on the left side. Both objects must exist, and you must take it upon yourself to handle any memory management associated with the copying operation.

There are also some special tasks that you need to perform in the implementation of the overloaded assignment operator that are not needed with other operators. First, you need to check that you are not trying to assign an object to itself, because this can create problems in the execution of the program and is not picked up by the compiler.

Next, you have to deallocate any memory that the object is using and reallocate enough memory to hold the data from the object you're copying from. Then, you copy across the data and return a pointer to the newly modified object.

```
CNumberPair &operator = ( const CNumberPair & number_pair )
{
    // Check that you are not assigning to yourself
    if ( number_pair == this ) return *this;

    // Copy the data
    this->nFirst = number_pair->nFirst;
    this->nSecond = number_pair->nSecond;

    // Return pointer to yourself
    return *this;
}
```

You can also overload the compound assignment operators (+=, –=, and so on) using exactly the same style of operation. However, you do need to make sure that there is enough space to hold the new data after it has been manipulated. Otherwise, the code is quite straightforward. For CNumberPair, the += operator can be overloaded as follows:

```
CNumberPair &operator += ( const CNumberPair & number_pair )
{
    // Check that you are not assigning to yourself
    if ( number_pair == this ) return *this;

    // Copy the data
    this->nFirst += number_pair->nFirst;
    this->nSecond += number_pair->nSecond;

    // Return pointer to yourself
    return *this;
}
```

The comparison operators (==, <=, >=, <, >, and !=) can also be overloaded, in which case they should return a value of type bool. So if you wanted to create a simple test of equality for the CNumberPair class, it would be implemented as:

```
bool operator == ( const CNumberPair & number_pair )
{
    if ( this->nFirst == number_pair->nFirst &&
        this->nSecond == number_pair->nSecond)
            return true;

    return false;
}
```

Finally, the binary operators (+, -, and so on) can also be overloaded. These are a little special, in that they return a new instance of the class being used. In other words, you need to create a new instance of the class, place the result of the operation in it, and return a pointer to it, all in a single operation.

The generic definition for the overloaded + operator, for example, is as follows:

```
const <class> <class>::operator+(const &<class>right_hand_side) const
```

The const keyword helps avoid programming mistakes and catch them at compile time. Because you have already created overloaded assignment operators, it makes sense to implement the overloaded function in three steps:

1. Make a copy of the instance, with the assignment operator.

2. Use the compound assignment operator to perform the operation.

3. Return the new object.

The actual implementation is left as an exercise for you, but the generic definition looks something like:

```
const <class> <class>::operator+(const &<class>right_hand_side) const
{
  <class> new_object = *this; // i.e. me
  new_object += right_hand_side; // assuming +
  return new_object
}
```

Of course, for other operators, the + can be substituted accordingly. The assignment operator and compound assignment operators all need to be correctly defined. Otherwise, this approach simply will not work.

There are many other facets about C++ that will become apparent upon reading other people's code, which is one of the best ways to learn how to fully leverage the language.

Exception Handling

The final new part of C++ that you read about here is the ability to trap errors in the code so that you can perform processing to deal with the error. There are some errors, such as memory-allocation issues and incorrect usage of types, that can be trapped using an automated mechanism, and some that you need to cater to explicitly. After all, the latter ones are those that your program raises itself.

C++ has a collection of exceptions that it can *throw,* which deal with some specific cases. To throw something means to cause an exception. For example, trying to allocate more memory than is available causes a bad_alloc exception to be thrown.

So you need a mechanism to *catch,* or trap, these exceptions. You can do so by defining two code blocks. The first is called the try block and is simply a named block of code (contained between { and } characters) named with the keyword try.

Within the try code block, you can perform any C++ code statements. Should one of them fail, you can identify the error by using the throw keyword, followed by an identifier. Theoretically, that identifier can be of any type, but usually you use a numeric, constant, or character value.

The general form for a try block is as follows:

```
try
{
    // Some code here
    throw my_execption;
}
```

Usually, the exception is thrown only when something untoward happens. You need to have a mechanism that can catch the exception and continue processing. Note that the processing will happen after the catch block, which should follow the try block. This looks akin to:

```
#define my_exception 1 // This in a header file
try
{
    // Some code here
    throw my_execption;
}
catch (int the_exception)
{
    // Handle the exception
}
```

The catch keyword must be followed by a parameter, which gives the type of the exception to be caught—int, char, and so on—and the code in the block will be executed when the exception is thrown. You can catch exceptions of multiple types by adding other catch blocks that specify different types in the parameter.

The exception value can then be accessed through the variable associated with it (the_exception, in the previous case). If you want to be able to handle any type, you use the ellipsis, as follows:

```
catch (int the_exception)
{
```

```
    // Handle INT exception
}
catch ( ... )
{
    // Handle any exception
}
```

Note that in the second block, the actual exception cannot be determined, because no variable is associated with it. This is sometimes known as the *default exception handler.*

You can use exception handling to track runtime errors by placing critical code inside try blocks. Each one has to be followed by a catch block, which will usually perform different reporting functions for regular or debug processing.

For example, you can print the contents of the exception, because you know what type it is, or you can determine what message to print based on the constant value used. Some of these are predefined as part of the C++ exception class.

These predefined exceptions do not need to be thrown explicitly by the program, because they are part of the underlying functionality. In brief, the most commonly used supported exceptions are as follows:

bad_alloc	Memory allocation issue
bad_cast	Cannot cast from one type to another
bad_exception	Exception type not handled elsewhere
ios_base::failure	Thrown by stream classes

The last exception will become clearer when you look at the C++ Standard Libraries in Chapter 17, of which the class ios is a part.

You can catch any of these exceptions using code such as:

```
catch (exception& e )
{
    printf ( "%s\n", e.what()); // Print exception
}
```

So if you were trying to allocate a new memory block of characters using the new operator, you might put it in a try block to be sure that you could catch any exceptions thrown resulting in bad_alloc.

You can also derive your own exception-handling code from the base `exception` class, in the same way that the standard ones are derived. If you do this, you need to override the `what()` function to return a string of meaningful data.

Finally, you can also nest `try` blocks as long as you remember to put the `catch` block inside the outer `try-catch` code segment. It is a useful mechanism, although not recommended as excessive nesting tends to obfuscate code and potentially renders it harder to maintain.

Recap

You might be surprised to learn that, although it's a good start, this chapter only scratches the surface of C++ programming. However, the chapter covered the most useful differences between C and C++, along with the best of the new features for object-oriented programming and creating robust code.

The salient points of C++ features are as follows:

- Remember that functions are declared before use.

- Variables can be declared anywhere.

- Scope is restricted to code blocks.

- The `new` and `delete` keywords can be used to create memory blocks.

Then, if you need abstract data types in your C++ code, you can use classes:

- Classes are defined in header files.

- Classes must be implemented in source files.

- Class code is compiled file by file.

The advantages of classes are many. You can use inheritance to create hierarchies of classes that share functionality. You can also create polymorphic functions that handle calls to themselves differently, depending on the type of class they belong to.

If you need to use operators with the classes that you define, you can overload the standard operators, rather than creating member functions with possibly cumbersome names (such as `Compare`, `GreaterThan`, `EqualTo`, and so on).

Finally, the exception-handling mechanism provided by C++ lets you handle issues found during program execution in a more robust manner. Correct handling of exception cases can also help you debug and trap errors in your development cycle.

In order to take advantage of everything that C++ has to offer, you should also take code that has been specially created to solve common programming problems. These include the Standard Libraries and STL (Standard Template Libraries).

Because both of these libraries use classes, abstraction, polymorphism, and overloading, not to mention inheritance and exception handling, you need to be aware of all of these mechanisms. It is a lot to take in at first, but it will quickly become second nature once you start to ply your trade.

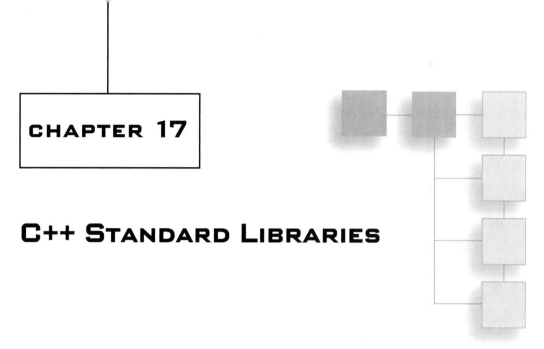

CHAPTER 17

C++ Standard Libraries

The aim of this chapter is to provide you a working overview of the Standard Libraries that are supported under C++. In the same way that the book covered the C Standard Libraries, the aim is to allow you to use this part of the book as a kind of reference. The concepts are, however, introduced in a pragmatic manner.

The three basic categories of library that are supported are the C language libraries (albeit in a special way), libraries for input and output, and data type-specific libraries. Each library is implemented as a system of classes, which means that you cannot only access the functions directly but also derive functionality from them.

Introduction to the C++ Libraries

Keeping my promise not to overcomplicate your life as a programmer, this chapter contains only the most basic of the available functions. This chapter presents a useful minimum of functions that you can use to create useful applications.

This chapter doesn't cover some of the more esoteric functions, but it does provide enough reference and learning material here for beginner programmers to find out what possibilities their own copy of C++ offers.

For more definitions, check the header files that shipped with your development environment. In doing so, you'll find (usually commented) function prototypes, classes, and other pieces of code that you may find useful in later programming tasks.

Chapters 19 and 20 have valuable insights into what, exactly, you need to do to turn a hobby into a profession. This is only the first step—you will be able to do useful tasks and create useful programs, but the power of C++ can be unleashed only with experience and practice.

The C Language Library

All the definitions that you've seen for C libraries are also included under C++, so most programs that work under C can be easily ported to C++. To differentiate the old C header files from the newer C++ versions, the newer versions are renamed in ANSI-compliant C++ build environments.

The header files can be accessed by looking for files with the old name, except with the character c in front—that is, stdio.h becomes cstdio.h. Other than that, the function names inside remain the same—sprintf is still `sprintf`—but most of the functions have been replaced with pure C++ equivalents.

As much as possible, you should use the C++ Standard Libraries with C++ programs, rather than reuse the old C functions. Part of being able to do this requires that you understand some of the mechanisms behind the C++ Standard Libraries, as follows in this chapter.

Using Namespaces

Namespaces allow you to create groupings of identifiers that exist within a specific scope. This mechanism is incredibly useful because it allows you to include identifiers within a subprogram without worrying about duplicating them with code outside of that namespace.

So if you have a header file that defines a collection of routines and data types, you can contain them inside a namespace that refers to the purpose that they fulfill, without having to create a `class` specifically for them.

The namespace Keyword

You start a namespace with the `namespace` keyword. Everything in the code block that follows the keyword is considered to be a part of that namespace. So you might create a namespace in a header file as follows:

```
namespace my_namespace
{
    int nMyVariable = 42;
}
```

This means that, within the scope of my_namespace, nMyVariable is always equal to 42. If you want, you can also extend the namespace across multiple source code units and even across different header files by repeating the namespace stanza.

Each new addition then becomes part of the namespace, rather than replacing it. Unlike class definitions, the namespace mechanism is open but cannot have public or private sections. Everything is visible from the outside.

However, there is a special notation set aside for accessing the items in the namespace—you cannot access them immediately. To do this in code, you write:

```
namespace my_namespace
{
   int nMyVariable = 42;
}


// Start main program
void main ( )
{
   int nNumber = my_namespace::nMyVariable;
}
```

Although this code might look cumbersome, it allows you to build up some sophisticated hierarchies and sets of identifiers:

```
namespace my_parent_namespace
{
   int nMyVariable = 42;
   namespace my_child_namespace
   {
      int nMyVariable = 4242;
   }
}
namespace my_other_namespace
{
   int nMyVariable = 4200;
}


// Start main program
void main ( )
{
   int nParentNumber = my_parent_namespace::nMyVariable;
   int nChildNumber = my_parent_namespace::my_child_namespace::nMyVariable;
   int nOtherNumber = my_other_namespace::nMyVariable;
}
```

Note that, if you have nested namespaces, you need also to nest the namespace identifiers between sets of double colons to be able to access sub-namespaces. This can become a little cumbersome, so C++ provides you with a special keyword to tell the compiler that, from this point forward, you are using a specific namespace.

The *using* Keyword

There are times when you need to tell the compiler to interpret your use of identifiers as local to a specific namespace, and the using keyword—within the scope of the code block or file in which it is active—does just that. In other words, you can use statements such as the following:

```
using my_parent_namespace::nMyVariable;
int nParentNumber = nMyVariable;

using namespace my_other_namespace;
int nOtherNumber = nMyVariable;
```

Using the using keyword, this example creates a direct alias to nMyVariable. In the second instance, this example declares that you want to use the entire namespace, my_other_namespace, and then can access anything in it as if it were local.

This last use of the using keyword is especially useful when you want to access an entire namespace such as the std namespace provided as part of the C++ language.

The *std* Namespace

All of the Standard C++ Libraries have been defined as belonging to a specific namespace, called std (standard). Contained within the header files for these classes, you'll see that the std namespace is being continually extended with new definitions.

There are some points to note. Note that you still need the #include statement at the start of the source code file to tell the compiler which library you will be using. Note also that the filename no longer has a trailing .h.

This gives rise to code that looks like the following:

```
#include <iostream> // iostream.h
using namespace std;
```

```
int main ()
{
  cout << "Hello World" << endl;

  return 0;
}
```

Without the `using namespace std` line, you would have to specifically name the `cout` class, which is derived from the base streams library. The namespace allows you to simply import all the identifiers in one line of code.

IO Libraries

All input and output functionality in C++ is based around the concept of *streams*. Each stream maps to a physical device in an abstracted fashion. It can be a keyboard, printer, screen, or file. The `<iostream>` header file contains all the definitions required to use the library.

This includes some basic classes, types, manipulators, and standard stream objects for use in derived programs. The standard stream objects usually included are `cin` (input) and `cout` (output), as well as `cerr` and `clog`.

In addition, there is a class for manipulating files (`fstream`) and one for treating strings as if they were streams (`stringstream`). There are also some variations of these for unidirectional streams that can perform only input or only output, but not both.

Stream Classes

Generally speaking, the stream classes all operate in the same manner. They can be used to extract data from or to a stream by parsing a collection of tokens. These tokens are one or more of the following:

- Constants

- Variables

- Modifiers

Each item in the stream is separated by an operator, which indicates the direction of the extraction. In this way, you can read from and write to streams of data in a very flexible manner. Because the various streams are represented by classes, you can also derive your own stream classes from the base stream classes to handle user-defined data.

Note that `cin` and `cout` are actually objects; they are instances of the `iostream` class. The most useful stream classes are as follows:

istringstream	Parsing strings into variables
ostringstream	Parsing variables into strings
stringstream	Parsing strings both ways
fstream	Files as streams

There are also two classes, `istream` and `ostream`, that can handle input and output, but the examples shown here use the objects `cin` and `cout` instead.

To illustrate a concrete example of these classes in use, you can write data to the screen using the following code:

```
int nNumber = 3;
string szString ("My Text");

cout << nNumber << szString << endl;
```

In this example, you define an integer and a string and then write them to the standard output stream, ending with a carriage return. The `endl` parameter is an example of a manipulator that can be used to change the subsequent output.

Using the standard input string stream to assign data to a series of variables is also easy. Here's a good illustration of the input stream class:

```
istringstream myInputStringStream (" Text");
myInputStringStream >> skipws >> szString;
```

The `skipws` parameter is another manipulator; it tells the class that you want to skip any whitespace when parsing (tokenizing) the stream. This can be equally well applied to the `cin` stream as it can to a string stream.

Manipulators

As you have seen, manipulators are useful mainly for output manipulation in formatting streams during extraction. They can also be used for input manipulation, although when such input relies on interaction with the users, you might not always get the expected result, because you can't control what the users actually type.

The first set of manipulators acts like switches that turn features on and off. In the following list, the (no) reverses the action of the manipulator. So noskipws is the opposite of skipws, meaning that the class will treat whitespace as significant if noskipws is specified.

The basic switch-based manipulators are as follows:

(no) boolalpha   Display Booleans as text, rather than as 0 or 1

(no) showpoint   Show the decimal point

(no) showpos   Add the + sign to non-negative numbers

(no) skipws   Skip whitespace in the stream

You can also perform numerical base manipulation to change the way that numbers are displayed. You can use these three switches:

dec   Decimal

oct   Octal

hex   Hexadecimal

Using one of these switches will apply the base manipulation throughout the remainder of the stream access. In addition to base modification, you can also switch between two modes of floating-point display:

fixed   Displays with decimal point notation

scientific   Displays with scientific notation

So you can write code such as the following:

```
cout << scientific << 42.442 << endl;
```

This code will display the value as 42.442e+000 rather than as the default 4.442, which is the decimal point notation.

Base Class Functionality

This section summarizes the base class functionality that is available to all classes derived from ios_stream. It includes formatting, manipulation, and exception-processing implemented as part of the C++ Standard IO Libraries.

Formatting

In addition to using manipulators in the stream, you can use flags that are contained in the definition of the streams library. These are set using the following member function:

```
ios_base::flags ( <collection of ios::flags> );
```

These flags offer the same possibilities as the manipulator switches and have the same names, but they can be combined to set a collection of flags at once. So you could write the following code, for example:

```
cout << showpoint << showpos << scientific << 42.42;
```

The equivalent to this method, done by setting the flags through `ios_base`, is as follows:

```
cout.flags ( ios::showpoint | ios::showpos | ios::scientific );
cout << 42.42;
```

The list of flags is identical to those listed previously. You can also set and unset specific flags using `setf` and `unsetf`, also members of the base class. For example:

```
cout.setf ( ios::showpos );
cout << 42.42;
cout.unsetf ( ios::showpos );
cout << 42.42;
```

In addition to the flags, you can also change the formatting using width and precision manipulators, either in the parameters supplied in the stream or by setting the appropriate values in the base class.

For example, you can set the field width to 10 using the manipulator `setw`, as follows:

```
cout << setw(10) << 42;
```

The equivalent to this method, using a call to the base class member function `width`, is:

```
cout.width(10);
```

```
cout << 42;
```

Both of these methods pad on the default side, depending on the variable being output. To control exactly where the padding occurs, use the `left` and `right` manipulators. Again, you can set these in the stream call or as flags. First, in the stream parameter list:

```
cout << right << 42.42;
```

This would pad on the left in order to right-align the field. The left modifier has the reverse effect, aligning on the left and padding to the right. You can set the flags using the setf member function, as follows:

```
cout.setf ( ios::adjustfield, ios::right );
```

Besides setting the width, you can set the precision in a similar fashion. To set the precision to two decimal places in the stream parameters, you use code such as:

```
cout << setprecision (2) << 7.759;
```

This would output 7.76 after rounding. The equivalent to this, using a member function call to the base class, is:

```
cout.precision(2);
```

```
cout << 7.759;
```

There are other more advanced options, but these are the essential formatting options available when processing streams.

Stream Output with <<

As you might already surmise, the << operator is used to pass data into a stream. When you use it in conjunction with an output stream such as cout, it writes data to the stream. The underlying target of the stream is defined by the object. You do not need to know, when you make the call, where it is being directed.

This means that the way you use << does not change according to the stream being accessed. The following examples assume that you are outputting to the screen, but it could also be an object instantiated from the ofstream class that writes to a file.

The basic usage is as follows:

```
cout << <item>
```

The <item> can be a variable or constant data. You can also chain together << operators to build up a more complex stream, including modifiers and other parameters:

```
cout << <modifier> << <item>
```

In addition to these structured (formatted) data processing possibilities, you also have some lower-level access possibilities. These allow you to write character data directly (among other things). Of most interest are the two functions `put` and `write`.

The `put` function allows you to print a single character of data to the stream:

```
cout.put ( cCharacter );
```

On the other hand, `write` allows you to write a buffer of data to the stream:

```
cout.write ( char * pBuffer, int nSize );
```

Because you have given the `write` function the size of the buffer, it does not have to be null terminated. It could also feasibly be binary data that can be represented as a character stream.

Stream Input with >>

The partner to <<, which is >>, allows you to extract data from a stream. In other words, when used in conjunction with `cin`, it allows you to read data from the keyboard. Again though, like <<, it can be used with any other input stream, including file and string streams.

The generic form for `cin` is:

```
cin >> <item>
```

Where `<item>` in this line of code can be any variable. As with the output, you are also free to add manipulators in the parameter list to modify the incoming data:

```
cin >> manipulator >> <item> >> <item>
```

The association runs from left to right, so input coming from the keyboard (for example) follows the path keyboard [→] `cin` [→] manipulator [→] variable.

By way of an example, you can remove whitespace from typed input by using the following line of code:

```
cin >> ws >> myString;
```

Other than this, manipulators will not be of much use, as they tend to restrict the data that can be read from the stream. The exception might be when reading fields from a file when you know what the field size is, because you wrote the data to the file in the first place.

There are also functions that you can use to retrieve unformatted data. For example, you can use the get function in one of two ways:

```
cin.get ( c ); // Where c is a char
cin.get ( pBuffer, nSize ); // Where pBuffer is a char *
```

If you want to read a whole line, regardless of length, you have a number of possibilities, all of which use the getline function, which has various parameter sets:

```
cin.getline( char * pBuffer, int nSize)
```

This variation reads the line into the buffer until the end of line is reached (until the user presses Enter) or until it has read up to nSize-1 characters. If you want to use a character other than the end-of-line to denote where reading should terminate, you use the following form:

```
cin.getline(char * pBuffer, int nSize , char cDelim)
```

This variation will stop reading when cDelim is encountered or, again, when nSize-1 characters have been read.

The last member function you'll look at is the read function. Its basic form is as follows:

```
cin.read ( char * pBuffer, int nSize)
```

This code will read from the stream until it can read no more or until nSize-1 characters have been read. You can then call the cin.gcount() member function to ascertain how many characters have been read. No null terminator is added when the read function is used.

File Access with iostream

One of the most useful streams that is derived from the iostream class is used to handle files. Although it exists in input file, output file, and input/output file variations, this section covers only the two-way fstream class.

The code in the following discussion always shows the class name and member function as follows:

```
<class>::<function>
```

Recall that, in order to actually use the class, it is necessary to take the appropriate steps to construct an object of that class before accessing the member function.

For example:

```
<class> <object>;
<object>.<function>;
```

To open a file, you need to specify the name and the mode. The general definition is as follows:

```
fstream::open ( char * pFilename, <mode> );
```

In this code, pFilename is a regular C string, and <mode> is a specific value taken from the following list (defined as part of fstream):

fstream::in	Input file only
fstream::out	Output file only
fstream::app	Append at each output; read from anywhere
fstream::ate	Open and move to the end of the file immediately
fstream::trunc	Open and empty the file (overwrite)
fstream::binary	Use binary mode, not text, for operations

If you want to test whether the file is open, there is a specific function to do so:

```
bool fstream::is_open()
```

The is_open function returns a value of true or false, and the logic is similar to that of the C Standard Library. If you attempt to open a file as read only and it is not opened successfully, you might assume that the file does not exist and proceed accordingly.

When you are finished with the file, call the close() function:

```
fstream::close()
```

Putting all of the pieces together, the following attempts to open a file for reading and then create it if it does not exist before proceeding with the read and write operations, and then finally closes the file.

```
fstream hFile;
hFile.open ( "myfile.txt", fstream::in );
if ( !hFile.is_open() )
   hFile.open ( "myfile.txt", fstream::in | fstream::out | fstream::trunc );
// do read/write operations
hFile.close();
```

The actual read and write operations occur exactly in the same way as with other streams, because the fstream class is derived from the base. So you can use the << and >> operators to write to and read from the file, respectively.

For example, you can write code such as the following:

```
hFile << "Hello File" << endl;
hFile.seekg(0); // Put file position to start
hFile >> myString;
```

In addition, you can use any of the members inherited from istream and ostream introduced previously, with the discussion of cin and cout.

Finally, you can also get the size of a file using a combination of various member functions that are unique to file streams. The following code retrieves the size of an open file:

```
hFile.seekg(0,ifstream::end);   // Go to the end of the file
long lSize = hFile.tellg();     // Get the file position (size)
hFile.seekg(0);                 // Return to the start of the file
```

This illustrates the seek and tell member functions. Be sure to recognize this general approach, as it was used when you learned how to find the length of a file in C earlier in the book.

As an exercise for you, think about how the file length could be retrieved in such a way as to not lose the current position of the pointer in the file. Such a file-length algorithm is non-destructive because it retains the information that it was called with (the current file position).

String Libraries

The string class is used to create and manipulate strings, removing the need to use char * and memory management to do it. The various functions that the class supplies replace and extend those that are available in the C string.h library.

The definition of the string class is found in the <string> library header file, and the header file contains many variations on the basic constructor. These range from empty constructions to ones with initialized strings of characters.

This chapter covers only the basic constructions here, by assigning a constant value, but it is important for you to remember that other possibilities exist. When you look at templates in Chapter 18, you will see some more advanced construction algorithms.

To define a string variable in the simplest way, you use code such as the following:

```
string pString, pCharString;
```

```
pString = "Test string: ";
pCharString = 'x';
```

Note that you can initialize the string with either a single character or a full string. Either way, the result is a string class that can be appended to other string classes using the overloaded + operator.

This makes appending strings much easier than using the `strcat` function from the standard C string library. For example, you can use code like the following:

```
string pNewString;
pNewString = pString + pCharString;
```

Recall from the previous discussion of classes that overloading the + operator requires that the class implementation deal with aspects such as resizing the memory allocated for the new object. You can determine the length of the resulting string by calling the `size` or `length` function.

From this example, you can determine the length of `pNewString` as follows:

```
int nSize = pNewString.length();
```

The result of the `size` and `length` functions are the same, namely the length of the string. Should you need to resize the string, `resize` allows you to grow or shrink the string, with or without padding.

So of you wanted to extend the string by 10 . (period) characters, you might combine the `size` and `resize` functions. The resulting code might look something like this:

```
pNewString.resize ( pNewString.length+10, '.');
```

Calling `resize` without the . in the second parameter will just extend the string by 10 characters, without adding any padding.

Finally, there's an additional function to set all the data to `NULL`, leaving it with a size of zero. The `clear` member function performs this operation, and you can call it like so:

```
pNewString.clear();
```

In order to test for an empty string, you can use the is_empty function, which returns a Boolean value—it returns true if the string is empty and false otherwise. An empty string has a length of zero, with no data in it.

For strings that do contain data, you can access the characters in it in one of two ways. The first way to access the characters is as if they were an array (such as a char[] or char *). This method uses the subscript operator with a zero-based index. So to access the first character, you would use this code:

```
char cFirst = pNewString[0];
```

This is the same as using the at function, which performs the same operation, thus:

```
char cFirst = pNewString.at(0);
```

Besides accessing the characters in the array that represents the string directly, you can also search it for character substrings in a variety of ways. Again, there are many variants, but two uses are the most common ones.

The first method takes a substring and a starting point inside the string and then returns a zero-based index into the array that represents the string. This zero-based index is the start of the first occurrence of the substring inside it. Using this index, you can then find the next occurrence of the substring.

The code to do this might look something like this:

```
size_t nIndex = pNewString.find ( pSubString, 0 ); // Find first
if ( nIndex != pNewString::npos )
{
    nIndex = pNewString.find ( pSubString, nIndex );
}
```

You can also use the find member function without the index parameter, in which case the search always starts from the first position—index 0 in the array. In addition, you can add a final parameter to the list, which specifies the number of characters in the substring to search.

The basic form for this looks akin to the following:

```
size_t nIndex = pNewString.find( pSubString, 0, 3); // For example
```

There are also collections of functions that work in the same way as the basic find function but that look for an occurrence of any one of the characters in the string.

For example, to return the first vowel in a string, you could use code such as the following:

```
size_t nIndex = pNewString.find_first_of( "aeiou" );
```

You can also use other parameters to start your search beginning at a different index, or you can search a specific substring, just as you can with the basic find function. The most common variations of the find_..._of function set are the following:

string::find_first_of	Find the first match
string::find_last_of	Find the last match
string::find_first_not_of	Find the first non-match
string::find_last_not_of	Find the last non-match

So to remove everything except the consonants from a string, you might use a loop such as the following:

```
size_t nIndex = pString.find_last_not_of ( "aeiou" );
while ( nIndex != pString::npos )
{
   pString[nIndex] = ' ';
}
```

One last point to note is that you use the member npos to test for an invalid index. It is part of the string class.

To obtain a pointer to a substring, you need to specify the position that the substring starts at, followed by the length. This is done through the substr member function:

```
string pSubString = pString.substr ( 3, 2 );
```

The object that is returned is constant—it is not a copy of the string; it is an actual pointer to the substring and therefore cannot be changed. If you need access to the substring in order to alter it afterwards, you must use the overloaded copy member function instead:

```
char * pBuffer = new char (10);
pString.copy ( pBuffer, 0, 10 );
```

The copy member takes a pointer to a character buffer, the starting position, and the length of the substring to copy.

Following on from this, you also can use comparison functions with return values that mimic the strcmp function. Recall that these comparison functions are 0 for equality, 1 for greater than, and −1 for less than.

The general definition for this use is as follows:

```
int string::compare ( string comparison_string );
```

There are also two other common uses. The first takes a position, length, and string to check against a substring:

```
int string::compare ( size_t pos, size_t length, string comparison_string );
```

You can also check a substring against a substring, using the third common use:

```
int string::compare ( size_t pos, size_t length, string comparison_string,
                      size_t substring_pos, size_t substring_length );
```

Again, there are more variations, but these are the most useful when you're starting out.

You have already encountered the overloaded + operator, but you also have an append function at your disposal that can append copies of a substring to another string. The generic form for this function is as follows:

```
string::append ( string & source, size_t size, size_t position );
```

This function takes a substring of source, as defined by its size and position within the array of characters that source represents, and appends it to the data in the calling string class. Another useful variant of this is as follows:

```
string::append ( int quantity, char character );
```

This code will append a quantity of character to the calling string. Naturally, the string will be resized as necessary to accommodate the new array.

Besides appending, you can also insert string data, substring data, or a number of characters into another string. If you have two strings, you can insert one into the other as follows:

```
string pFirst = "Hello";
string pSecond = "p!";
pFirst.insert ( 3, pSecond );
```

The next variation allows you to insert a copy of a substring inside the calling string:

```
string::insert ( size_t pos, string & substring, size_t start, size_t length);
```

This code takes the `substring` parameter and extracts the character data starting at `start` and ending at `start+length`. It then inserts the character data at `pos` position inside the calling string. You can also use the following code to insert a number of characters into a string from a given position:

```
string::insert ( size_t pos, size_t length, char character);
```

So you could prepend the previous string with a string of characters, using code such as the following:

```
pFirst.insert ( 0, 5, '*' );
```

To replace the characters, you can use the following `replace` function, which will overwrite the characters in the string, rather than insert characters into the string:

```
string::replace ( size_t insert_pos, size_t length,
            const string& str, size_t substring_pos, size_t substring_length );
```

Finally, you can swap two strings with the innovative `swap` function. All the data, including the length, is swapped. This means the contents of the strings are exchanged completely.

This function is defined as follows:

```
pFirst.swap ( pSecond );
```

The string library also provides overloaded operators for all of the standard comparisons (==, !=, <, >, and so on), available in three versions. They each return a Boolean value true or false, depending on the outcome.

The three variations are as follows:

```
bool operator <operator> ( const string & left_hand_side,
                           const string & right_hand_side )

bool operator <operator> ( const char* left_hand_side,
                           const string & right_hand_side )

bool operator <operator> ( const string & left_hand_side,
                           const char * right_hand_side )
```

The `<operator>` can be replaced by any of the standard comparison operators. The first variation compares two objects that are instances of string classes. The second one compares a character array with an object that is an instance of a string class. The third variation compares a string object with an array of characters.

These overloads all follow the usual rules for operator overloading in classes as seen in the previous chapter.

Recap

You might now see the similarities between the C support and C++ implementations of input and output (console and file) and strings. It pays to remember that the C libraries are still supported under C++ (so you can still use `sprintf` rather than `iostream`), but the C++ versions are considered superior, and in many cases, are more elegant.

What you cannot do with C easily is support overloading, so it becomes much more convoluted to create your own specializations of the base library classes. It is often said that anything C++ can do, C can be made to do, too, and this is borne out by the fact that C++ can be "converted to" C and then compiled by a C compiler.

So you might be tempted to treat C++ as merely C with classes, but that would mean missing out on all the standard C++ libraries and their templates. Templates are particularly useful in extending C++ for your own use and are a logical follow-up from using the C++ Standard Libraries discussed here.

The template equivalent of the base classes that you can derive (inherit) from that are part of the C++ Standard Libraries for I/O and string handling (for example) are contained in the STL (Standard Template Library). Choosing between the two approaches will depend on the exact application.

So bearing this in mind, now is the time to look at the last C++ topic for this book—templates and the STL.

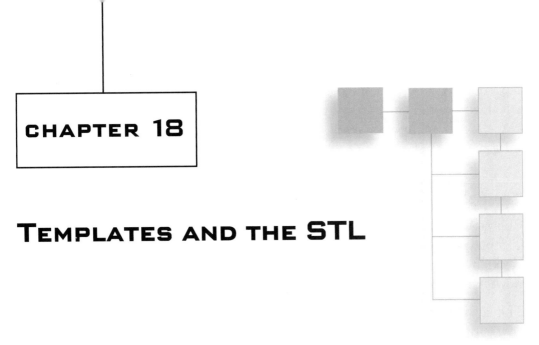

CHAPTER 18

TEMPLATES AND THE STL

This chapter introduces the C++ concept known as *templates,* which promote the use of reusable code by allowing you to create generic versions of useful functions. Each template can be used with a variety of different data types—both built-in and user-defined—and reused in different situations.

Part of the reason this chapter introduces templates is to also cover and discuss the Standard Template Library (or STL). This library contains some useful generic definitions of classes and functions to manipulate them.

This chapter is divided into two sections:

- Templates
- The Standard Template Library

The first section discusses template functions and template classes, whereas the second looks at specific classes and functions that the STL contains. The aim is not to cover every single possible use of the containers and algorithms, but to give you a workable introduction.

In addition, this chapter is intended to be a reference guide for your future use. You'll find examples for each class and function, rather than their definitions. The original definitions are available in the STL Header Libraries, and you'll be well equipped to decipher the information contained therein.

Each of the examples is designed to help you equate the header files to the way in which you would like to use the functions and classes in your own projects. This is the last C++ topic covered in this book, and will provide you with enough information to start programming in an efficient way.

Templates

The goal here is to help you understand the mechanisms behind the STL. Templates are a complex subject, and it is only through using them and reading through other people's code that you'll fully begin to appreciate exactly how powerful they are.

This section doesn't provide a real grounding in using templates as such, it just covers the way that they can be leveraged through the STL. However, you'll be able to appreciate their use, deploy them, and learn more about them from reading the STL header files.

Templates are good because they allow you to create generic versions of the following:

- Functions

- Classes

The same code is written once, and once only, and can then be reused with other data types. For example, if you have a comparison function that takes two parameters and returns the largest of them, you would need to write one for each data type that you wanted to process.

However, if you use a template function, you need only write the function once, as long as you can create a specific comparison that returns the appropriate parameter. You can take the same approach with classes, too. You can create an entire class that has a number of functions (comparison, operators, and so on) and reuse it for each type of data that you want to process.

Assume, for example, that you are building a stock control application, but you want it to be generic enough to cope with quantities in floating-point and integer notation. You might have amounts in integer notation (one item, for example) with a weight or currency expressed in floating-point notation (1.5 kg or $1.95).

The C++ language can handle a lot of the math, but you also need some comparison and sorting functions. If you have a list of items where some are in integer format and some are in floating-point format and you use one of the built-in comparison functions, you are potentially going to run into problems.

On top of which, if your own function is required to perform some kind of operation that receives an integer or floating-point number (such as adding sales tax, calculating postage based on weight, and so on), you could conceivably need one function for integers and one function for floating-point numbers.

What happens if you then introduce another data type (double precision or long integer)? Suddenly, you need a whole new set of functions to process these new possibilities. When you write a template function, though, these difficulties disappear to a certain extent.

A step further and you can create a template class instead, which will replace any built-in numerical classes, and can still deal with a wider range of objects. This would be appropriate if you stored the items in a list and wanted a solid list-manipulation class instead of using a template function to iterate over the list (applying the function once per list item).

However, some code in the owner class might have to be rewritten in order to allow future types to be correctly manipulated. This includes operator overloads, for example, to allow assignment, comparisons, and so forth. Recall from the last chapter that operator overloads involve giving new functionality (overloading existing functionality) to built-in operators such as =, <, >, +, -, and so on.

The reason that some code has to be rewritten is that some operations involve algorithms performing operations on the parameters supplied. Although the reason might sound straightforward, or even obvious, it can become more complex when you try to derive your own classes from the templates.

First, however, you need to understand how the template feature works in C++, using template functions as an example.

Template Functions

A *template function* is an abstraction of a function that fulfils a specific task. It is a function that accepts generic types, or, rather, it is a function that is defined with a placeholder name instead of a type that can adapt, at compile time, to any type that the programmer needs.

The general principal is that the types are determined by the compiler by examining the code. The compiler will then substitute the types into the function at the appropriate places, and as long as the operations are compatible with the types supplied in the function call, the code will compile correctly.

The parameters of the template function are generic, not the function itself—a common misconception of newcomers. The mechanism allows you to create polymorphic functions.

In some ways, it is a better technique than simple overloading, because you define only one function to work with many data types, rather than having to redefine overloads of operators; one for each data type.

However, function templates can work only with types (classes) that have overloaded operators when comparisons are involved. In other words, if you have a template function that compares two parameters, they must be either built-in types or have an overloaded operator defined as part of the class.

For example, if you wanted to find the larger of two items, you might create a template function such as the following:

```
template <class T>
T GetMax (T first, T second)
{
   return (first>second?a:b);
}
```

In the first line of this example, note that the programmer wants to create a template that will use class T. The T is simply a placeholder and can be any name you choose.

You then define the function, in the second line, as returning a value of type T and taking two parameters, each of type T. These types can be built-in types (which C++ implements as classes) or user-defined classes.

The *ternary operator*, ?, needs a little explanation. In the body of the function, you want to return the larger of two values. To do this, C++ provides a shorthand operator that can return one value of a set of two depending on the outcome of applying a comparison operator, in this case >.

Essentially, the ? tells C++ to take the first parameter and compare it with the second parameter using the > operator, and then return the first parameter if the result is true or the second parameter if the result is false.

To explore this a little further, you could write another function IsGreaterThan, for example, that returns a Boolean value:

```
template <class T>
bool IsGreaterThan (T first, T second)
{
  return (first>second?true:false);
}
```

This return statement compares the first and second parameters, again with the > operator, and returns a constant value, true or false.

Code Sample 18.1: TemplateTest1.cpp

Of course, you can also use the longhand if construct, but the ? operator does provide an easy-to-read alternative, once you get used to it. To call either of the previous functions, you'd use code such as:

```
#include <iostream>
using namespace std;
template <class T>

// Is greater than returns true if true
bool IsGreaterThan (T first, T second)
{
  return (first>second?true:false);
}

// Max returns the maximum
template <class T>
T GetMax (T first, T second)
{
  return (first>second?first:second);
}

// Min returns the minimum
template <class T>
T GetMin (T first, T second)
{
  return (first<second?first:second);
}
```

```
// Test IsGreaterThan and Max
int main ( )
{
   int nOne = 10, nTwo = 1;
   float fOne = 9.95, fTwo = 9.955;

   cout << GetMax ( nOne, nTwo );
   cout << " is bigger than " << GetMin( nOne, nTwo );
   cout << " IsGreaterThan returns ";
   cout << boolalpha << IsGreaterThan ( nOne, nTwo ) << endl;

   cout << GetMax ( fOne, fTwo );
   cout << " is bigger than " << GetMin( fOne, fTwo );
   cout << " IsGreaterThan returns ";
   cout << boolalpha << IsGreaterThan ( fOne, fTwo ) << endl;

}
```

Recall that it does not matter what you call the class in each template function. This example uses T, a common convention, but it could equally be any other value. In addition, the various uses of T do not become confused, because they are applied only when the template is used.

In fact, the T is swapped out by the compiler and the templates are compiled upon use—they are not precompiled and so the type names never conflict. When the compiler encounters the use of a template function in the code, it automatically generates the non-generic version of the code as it is needed.

When you call the template function from within the code, you do not need to tell the compiler which types to use, because it will assume the type from the parameters that you use. You're allowed to tell the compiler what type you are using, but you cannot mix them without taking steps to tell the compiler that the function can accept mixed types.

If you want to use mixed types, you need to use two class identifiers, one for each of the parameters that the function will accept. A revised example of the previous functions shows how to do this:

```
// Max returns the maximum
template <class TOne, class TTwo>
TOne GetMaxParameter (TOne first, TTwo second)
{
   return (first>second?first:second);
}
```

Note that you now have two classes: TOne and TTwo. You can now mix the types used in the comparison. However, the template function will return a value of type TOne, casting it as necessary to fit the class supplied in the first parameter.

As an example, the TemplateTest2.cpp source file on the companion Web site shows how this works with two parameters—a floating-point number and an integer—that are compared in the GetMaxParameter and GetMinParameter template functions.

If you want to create collections of functions that operate in a specific way, but want them to be useable with different types, you need to use a template class, which can logically group them together.

Template Classes

Rather than make a collection of generic functions to process data types, it is usually more efficient to create a class that performs a given set of related operations on a data type. In the STL, for example, there are classes that provide abstractions of various containers.

Each class offers methods that are generic in their definition but can be specialized by the compiler to handle any kind of data. These are called *template classes* and are very powerful, and very easy to use, with some caveats, which you'll read about along the way.

The class itself is then generic and can be used with any type. As with function templates, you denote the various type variations that you want to make available by a system of placeholders. Each type that might be different has a new placeholder name.

The functions within the class are then defined in terms of these placeholder type names, making them similar in operation to function templates. Again, though, some of the standard operators might need to be overloaded (built-in functionality extended) when used with user-defined types. This is because the compiler might not know how to evaluate complex types and will need to be told.

The following code defines a Triplet template class:

```
template <class T>
class Triplet
{
    T items [3];
```

```
public:
  Triplet (T one, T two, T three)
  {
    this->items[0] = one;
    this->items[0] = two;
    this->items[0] = three;
  }
};
```

In the first line, you specify that the definition that follows is a template, and will be using the placeholder T. You could have more types in between the chevrons, but for now let's just specify the one; all data in this class will be of the same type.

In the second line, you name the class, much like you would with any other class definition, and then define the private and public areas for the data and access methods. This is another bonus of using class templates over function templates—you can use object-oriented techniques such as data hiding to improve the readability of your code.

Note that wherever you would normally name a type for the data to be processed, you use the placeholder T. Other than this, the class is the same in construction as any other class that you've already seen.

You can use the Triplet class as follows:

```
Triplet <float> FloatTriplet ( 1.2, 2.3, 3.4 );
```

In this line of code, note that you need to tell the compiler which type you want to associate with the class. You can also write a line of code such as the following:

```
Triplet <int> IntegerTriplet ( 1, 2, 3 );
```

This line tells the compiler that you want to use an integer specialization this time, and that it should be associated with the variable IntegerTriplet. It is important to note that you do not derive a new class from the template, but that you cause the compiler to create a variable instance of a specialization of the template class that it creates *on demand*.

You can also force the compiler to choose a specialization of the class that might have specific overrides for the generic functions that you define in the template. Using the Triplet template, this would look something like the following:

```
template <>
class Triplet <int>
```

```
{
    int items [3];
  public:
    Triplet (int one, int two, int three)
    {
      this->items[0] = one;
      this->items[0] = two;
      this->items[0] = three;
    }
};
```

In this code, note that there is no type (class) or placeholder name in the chevrons. Instead, this code indicates to the compiler that you want this class to be chosen when processing the int type.

Then, when you specify an integer in the usage code, the compiler uses the specialization that you've defined, rather than any other generic template. There is no inheritance, however, so you have to supply definitions for all the members.

This is due to the fact that the compiler picks the best-fit specialization on demand and has no knowledge of any other template class for the Triplet (in this case) that might exist.

This illustrates the underlying difference between class inheritance coupled with operator overloading and template classes. It is also possible to explicitly inherit a template class, shown in terms of Triplet, here:

```
template <class T>
class NewTriplet : private Triplet<T>
{
  // Class code...
  // Can call methods directly
};
```

From this new class, you can access the Triplet class and define it in terms of the original template. The compiler will pick up the template and use it, replacing the T placeholder as required with no further programming. You need to appropriately overload any operators and redefine any interface methods that the new class needs.

An alternative approach is as follows:

```
template <class T>
class NewTriplet
```

```
{
  private:
    Triplet<T> data;
  public:
  // Class code...
  // Needs to call data.<method>
};
```

The principle difference between the two approaches is that the second approach uses the template class directly as a data member. So, you need to call each method that is required to interface with the data explicitly. In the previous approach, you actually inherited the functionality from the base template class.

Because this is a pragmatic guide and not a definitive scientific text, this explanation will suffice. There are proponents of both approaches, and technically the arguments for and against both are referred to as *inheritance versus containment.*

The second approach contains the template class inside a new class, thus you have to redefine everything from constructors to operators. The first approach inherits the base functionality, which means you must redefine any additional interfaces.

The STL

The C++ Standard Template Library is part of the ANSI standard for the C++ language, and extends the built-in types with a variety of features. The two most important and the ones discussed here are:

- Containers

- Algorithms

Together these mechanisms make it possible for you to use all manner of supplied common containers, along with suitable algorithms for searching, sorting, and managing the objects stored within them. The standard implementations can also be used as a starting point for your own classes.

This allows you to be more efficient and produce more correct code, because you don't have to reinvent the existing solutions. Careful design is a must, however, and you need to be sure that you are choosing the correct mix of STL components in order to model the data structures and algorithms that you might need in your project.

STL Containers

The STL containers are holder objects that hold other objects of a given type. Because they are template classes, they can hold any type and type selection is performed at compile time. An example of a container is an integer array; this is actually a built-in type in C but defined as a class in C++.

The data contained within the container class is a collection of elements. As in an array, where you refer to each item as an element, you also refer to each item in a container as an element and the class allows you to access them through specific interface methods.

Some examples of containers that are provided in the STL are as follows:

- Dynamic arrays

- Queues

- Stacks

- Linked lists

These have been given specific template class names in the STL, which occasionally differ from the names in the list. So a vector class is actually a dynamic array—it is an array that manages its own memory and can be resized by calling an interface method.

This section covers specifically these four types of commonly used non-associative STL container classes. There are associative versions that you'll be able to find by looking through the STL header files, but they are more complex and out of the scope of the "just enough" principle.

An *associative container* can hold a key as well as a data part for each element. The key can then be used to identify the element, as well as, or in place of, its position in the container.

This can be useful, but the same behavior can be obtained through using two parallel container classes and manipulating them using the various STL algorithms that are provided for manipulating data in a generic fashion.

STL Algorithms

The STL algorithms exist to offer functions that can operate on ranges and single elements in a way that is type-nonspecific. Each function that makes up the algorithms collection is designed to be used to iterate through a range, select from a range, modify a range, or provide miscellaneous single-element generic functions.

STL algorithms can be used with the template classes (vector, queue, list, and so on) or they can be used with built-in types that support ranges (arrays, for example). Some can also be used with individual elements based on user-defined classes, built-in types, or elements obtained from STL container classes.

This discussion classifies the STL algorithms into the following areas:

- Non-modifying

- Modifying

- Searching and sorting

There are additional categories and functions within them that are not discussed here—the aim here is to give you the most useful ones. Once you understand these, you can use the examples and prototypes in the STL headers to learn about variations that are initially out of reach for the "just enough" programmer.

STL Headers

The STL headers are arranged into two groups of files—one for the containers and another for the algorithms. The container class header files have the following naming convention:

```
<class-name>
```

Using this convention, you can include the headers in a file by using the line:

```
#include <vector>
```

Note that this line specifies the default compiler include search path for the libraries, which should be located in the \include directory or one of its subdirectories. These files have the .h extension, even though it's not included here.

The STL algorithms can be found in the algorithms.h file, which is included with this code:

```
#include <algorithms>
```

Again, its location may vary depending on the compiler setup being used.

Container Classes

The STL container classes provide useful templates for developing containers for any type of element. The built-in types (classes) can be used without any need to write supporting member interfaces.

However, when user-defined types are introduced, it might be necessary to provide correct instantiation (constructors) and operators with which the compiler can substitute the default behavior. For example, if you are storing elements on an array and attempt to call a method that requires that the == operator is overloaded, the compilation might fail if no overload is available.

In the vast majority of cases, however, the container classes themselves do not require that overloads exist because they generally work on pointers to the elements rather than the actual elements.

Vector

A vector is a type of dynamic array. It acts more or less in the same way as a regular array, except that it can be dynamically resized and contains more operators and functions to help manage the elements in the container.

A vector can be constructed in the following ways:

```
vector<char> my_string; // an empty vector

vector<char> my_string ( 10, '.' ); // a string of 10 x '.'

vector<char> my_other_string ( my_string ); // a copy of my_string
```

There are also the following operators, which all deal with various aspects of the size of the resulting array:

```
int nLength = my_string.size(); // how many characters?

my_string.resize ( 100 ); // make bigger

my_other_string.resize ( 5, '*' ); // make smaller, init. to '*'

bool bIsEmpty = my_string.empty(); // empty or not?
```

There are two ways in which you can access a specific element, and both methods return the type that was used to construct the vector (in this case, a char):

```
char cElement = my_string.at ( 10 ); // element at 9th position
```

```
char cElement = my_string[10]; // same as above
```

The at function throws an exception if the array is overstepped, whereas the [] operator does not. There are also operators that give you the extremities of the vector:

```
char cFront = my_string.front(); // the first element
```

```
char cBack = my_string.back(); // the last element
```

If you want to add or remove elements to the end of the vector, you can use code such as the following:

```
my_string.push_back ( 'a' ); // add an 'a'
```

```
char cBack = my_strint.pop_back(); // give me the last item
```

Note that in the last case, the item is *removed* from the vector completely. More complex insert operations are also possible:

```
my_string.insert ( my_string.begin(), 'b' ); // insert 'b' before start
```

```
my_string.insert ( my_string.end(), 4, 'e' ); // add four 'e' before the end
```

```
// insert my_other_string before the first element of my_string
my_string.insert ( my_string.begin(),
                   my_other_string.begin(),
                   my_other_string.end() );
```

Note that these examples introduce the concept of an iterator, used in this case to retrieve a reference to the start or end of the various character vectors. It is also possible to refer to a specific point using code such as this:

```
my_string.insert ( my_string.begin()+1, 'b' ); // insert 'b' just after start
```

In addition to these insertion operators, you can also erase elements with the following code:

```
my_string.erase ( my_string.begin() ); // delete the first element
```

```
my_string.erase ( my_string.begin(), my_string.end()-1 ); // all but the last
```

Finally, there are two useful operators that work on an entire vector:

```
my_string.swap ( my_other_string ); // my other now in my string
```

```
my_string.clear (); // clear all data
```

There are other operators and functions that the vector supports, but the ones presented here are a representative set of its functionalities.

Deque

The *deque*, or double-ended queue, is an array that's constructed in the same way as a vector and uses many of its same functions and operators. The deque can determine the array's size, resize it, and empty it. In addition, deque defines functions to obtain an indexed value—deque::at(int nIndex)—and offers the same front and back operators as a vector.

You can add to the deque at the front or back, as the name suggests. You can also remove from the front or back of the deque. Assume that have defined a deque as follows:

```
deque<char> my_string ( 10, '.' ); // a string of 10 x '.'
```

Given this new string definition, you can then use the push operations as follows:

```
my_string.push_front ( 'a' ); // add an 'a' to the front
```

```
my_string.push_back ( 'a' ); // add an 'a' to the back
```

Similarly, you can use companion functions for popping elements:

```
char cBack = my_strint.pop_front(); // give me the first item
```

```
char cBack = my_strint.pop_back(); // give me the last item
```

Finally, the insert, erase, swap, and clear operators work in the same way as for the vector.

List

The list container is a linked list and is constructed in the same way as a vector and deque. The resizing and empty test is the same as for a vector (or deque), and you also have access to the front and the back of the list using the same operators as the deque.

Where the list is different is in the various splicing operations that it can support. These splicing operations allow you to move elements from one list to another—no elements are created or destroyed, but the lists grow or shrink in order to accommodate the changed data.

The basic use for the `splice` operator is as follows:

```
list<char> my_string; // an empty list
list<char> my_other_string ( 10, 'a' ); // a list of 'a'

splice ( my_string.begin(), my_other_string );
```

This code splices `my_other_string` into `my_string`, at the beginning. You can also specify that only a single item be spliced using this code:

```
splice ( my_string.begin(), my_other_string, my_other_string.end() );
```

The previous code will move a single element from the end of `my_other_string` to the start of `my_string`. This is equivalent to the last form:

```
splice ( my_string.begin(), my_other_string,
                      my_other_string.end(), my_other_string.end() );
```

You can also remove elements with a specific value, as follows:

```
my_string.remove( 'a' );
```

The previous code will remove all the a characters from the string. The value needs to be of the same type as the data stored within the list. If you want to use a slightly different variation, you can also remove all characters that are not a in the following manner:

```
bool IsEqualToA ( char source )
{
   return (source=='a'?true:false);
}
// other code here
my_string.remove_if( IsEqualToA );
```

In addition, you can remove duplicates with code similar to:

```
my_string.unique();
```

If there is no sensible built-in test for equality, you can provide one by adding a predicate function (which takes two parameters and returns a `bool`). The use of such predicates is explained more fully in the "STL Algorithms" section.

There are also two merge functions—one to merge two lists irrespective of the individual element contents and another to merge two lists by leveraging a comparison function. This function should return a `bool` with the equivalent return logic of the ≤ operator.

This is necessary because the resulted merged list is sorted with respect to the operator ≤:

```
my_string.merge( my_other_string ); // sorted merge
```

```
my_string.merge( my_other_string, > ); // sorted merge, the other way
```

You can explicitly sort the list using one of the following forms of the sorting function:

```
my_string.sort(); // straight sort
```

```
my_string.sort( Predicate ); // sorted merge, assumes Predicate returns < logic
```

Finally, to reverse a list, use this code, which will simply reverse the element's order in the list:

```
my_string.reverse();
```

Stack

A stack is a vector that you can address only from one end, known as the *top*. You usually create it without data, push elements onto the stack, and then pop them off again. This is so similar to the vector that the following code should give all the necessary explanation:

```
stack<char> my_Lifo;
my_Lifo.push( 'a' );
my_Lifo.push( 'b' );
my_Lifo.push( 'c' );

char cLook = my_Lifo.top(); // sneak a preview into cLook

char cTake = my_Lifo.pop(); // pop the top off the stack
```

You can also use the `empty` and `size` operators to determine whether the stack contains data, and how much. You do not have any other operators for clearing the stack or interacting with it in any other way.

Queue

The queue is the first-in-first-out version of the stack. In other words, you add to one end and take off from the other, rather than pushing and popping of the same end. Consider the following code sample:

```
queue<char> my_Fifo;
my_Fifo.push( 'a' ); // queue contains 'a'
my_Fifo.push( 'b' ); // queue contains 'ab'
my_Fifo.push( 'c' ); // queue contains 'abc'
```

```
char cLook = my_Lifo.front(); // cLook contains 'a'
char cLook = my_Lifo.back(); // cLook contains 'c'

char cTake = my_Lifo.pop(); // cTake contains 'a', queue 'bc'
```

Finally, you have the usual operators for testing emptiness and size. Again, you do not have any other operators for adding to, removing from, sorting, or otherwise indexing the data contained inside the queue.

Algorithms

The STL algorithms are designed to make working with the STL containers and other data types easier by abstracting many useful programming tasks as functions. This section covers the algorithms in terms of the STL containers introduced in the previous section of this chapter.

In all of the following examples, *iterators* refer to a specific item in the collection— using a reference to the current item in the collection. This reference can be increased or decreased, depending on whether the iterator is a forward or backward (or bi-directional) iterator. Most of the STL algorithms work with collections contained in containers.

So, if the collection is based on the vector template class, you can access items in the collection using the `vector::begin` and `vector::end` iterators. Other containers offer `::front` and `::back` member functions to perform similar tasks.

The processing starts at the `::begin` (`::front`) iterator and can end at the `::end` (`::back`) iterator. This means that you can use them in a `for` loop, as you'll see later on in this section, to move through the collection, one item at a time, without having to know the size of the collection or having a direct pointer (reference) to an item in it.

You will remember from Chapter 13 that you can create a linked list using pointers and traverse it with calls to class members such as `::GetNext` (where such members are available). Iterators are like that, but without the necessity to create a reference explicitly.

Where specified, functions can be used as parameters, as long as they can process the base type of the template class. These functions can be used in place of binary predicates and operators to adapt the behavior of some of the algorithms.

A vector that is defined as containing a collection of `int` values can only be operated on with functions, comparison operators, and predicates that can operate on `int` values. Where specified, these predicate functions must return `bool` values, because that's what is often expected by the algorithms.

The following list is not exhaustive, but is an overview of the most useful algorithms available as part of the STL algorithms:

- Non-modifying—algorithms that cannot change elements.

- Modifying—Algorithms that can (and do) change elements.

- Searching and sorting—Algorithms to search and sort data.

- Merging—Algorithms to merge data sets.

Rather than just define these algorithms, this section uses examples to show the behavior in action and illustrate the various parameters that make up each function call.

The first vector is set up using code such as the following:

```
vector <int> FirstVector (10, 2);
generate (FirstVector.begin(), FirstVector.end(), Random);
```

In this code snippet, you first set up a vector (as you saw earlier in the chapter) and then use one of the modifying algorithms to populate the container. In the function call, Random is a function that `returns rand() % n`. This is an example of using a function inside the algorithm implementation, and is defined, in this case, as follows:

```
int Random () { return rand() % 100; }
```

The second vector is set up using code similar to this:

```
int nArray = { 1, 20, 300, 4000, 5 };
vector <int> SecondVector ( nArray, nArray + 5);
```

This shows an example of initializing a vector of integers from an array of integers, one of the uses mentioned in the discussion of the STL vector container class. The definitions of all of these are in the STL headers.

As mentioned, you can also have predicates and operator functions that can take a number of arguments, and these are taken from the elements in the container in a predefined manner. You cannot specify arguments to the functions that you use in the algorithm function calls that are not taken from the elements in the container.

Each one is just a user-defined function, the name of which is provided as a parameter in the function, without any additional information. If the algorithm expects a function with two parameters (be it an operator or predicate), it will supply the arguments itself.

As a general rule, predicates usually return `true` or `false`, whereas operator functions can return `bool` values or the type that they are being used with. It will usually be obvious from the aim of the function what return values are expected.

Each algorithm function takes ranges as inputs. There are a variety of ways you can access ranges and provide them as parameters. For example, you might have a simple array defined as follows:

```
int nArray = { 1, 2, 3, 4 };
```

You can supply this as a range to any of the algorithms that expect a range by supplying `nArray+0` as the starting point and `nArray+2` as the ending point. The algorithm can then iterate over the range using built-in array handling.

Vectors and other containers apply the same logic. For example:

- `vector::begin()` is the first element.

- `vector::end()` is the last.

- `vector::end()-1` is the second-to-last element.

Any other specific items that are needed are described as you progress through the various examples. Otherwise, this discussion has set the scene for each of your individual algorithm function calls.

Non-Modifying Algorithms

The `for_each` algorithm applies a user-defined function to a range of elements within a container class, whereby the function returns a value that is compatible with the class that each element was defined as being an instance of. For example:

```
for_each ( FirstVector.begin(), FirstVector.end(), Random );
```

The basic find algorithm looks through a range and returns the first element in the range that matches the user-provided argument. The return value can then be used to search the rest of the range. For example:

```
find ( FirstVector.begin(), FirstVector.end(), 42 );
```

If nothing matches, the algorithm returns the last element. This means that you need to determine whether the last element really matched or whether it was returned because nothing matched.

A more refined version of this algorithm is the find_if algorithm, which allows the users to provide a predicate function rather than a specific value. For example:

```
find_if ( FirstVector.begin(), FirstVector.end(), PredicateFunction );
```

The PredicateFunction is a user-defined function returning a bool value and accepting an element from the range. It must be able to handle the types that form the type associated with the elements in the container.

The count algorithm counts the number of elements that match a given constant programmer-supplied value of the same type as used in the container's elements. For example:

```
count ( FirstVector.begin(), FirstVector.end(), TestValue );
```

The return value is an integer count of the number of elements that match the TestValue, using the equality operator attached to the class.

The count_if algorithm counts the number of elements in a range for which a predicate function returns true when evaluated. For example:

```
count_if ( FirstVector.begin(), FirstVector.end(), PredicateFunction );
```

The PredicateFunction can be a programmer-defined function returning bool and is *unary* (it takes a single parameter).

The equal algorithm tests whether two ranges are equal. The first version expects that the classes used for the elements in the container class have an appropriate comparison operator defined for them. The form is as follows:

```
equal ( FirstVector.begin(), FirstVector.end(), SecondVector.begin() );
```

In this case, SecondVector can be pointing to any starting element, as long as it is of a comparable type, and as long as there are enough elements in the second container for the comparison to take place. If you want to supply your own predicate function, the second form is as follows:

```
equal ( FirstVector.begin(), FirstVector.end(),
        SecondVector.begin(), PredicateFunction );
```

The `PredicateFunction` is *binary*, meaning that it takes two parameters and returns `true` if they are considered equal. The parameters will be supplied by the compiler when the substitution for the standard comparison operator is made.

The `search` algorithm finds sequences in ranges where the elements match according to a comparison function—either the class-specific one or a predicate function supplied by the programmer. The return value is a range that contains the sequence. The first form is as follows:

```
search ( FirstVector.begin(), FirstVector.end(),
    SecondVector.begin(), SecondVector.end() );
```

The returned range is of the same class as `FirstVector` and can be operated on using the various iterators from that container class. The second form, using a programmer-defined predicate function, is as follows:

```
search ( FirstVector.begin(), FirstVector.end(),
        FirstVector.begin(), FirstVector.end(), PredicateFunction );
```

The `PredicateFunction` is binary, taking two parameters supplied by the compiler (defined in the function by the programmer), and returning `true` if they are considered equal.

Modifying Algorithms

These algorithms change the output in favor of the input and return the output iterator class where appropriate.

The `copy` algorithm copies a range of elements from one range to another. The use is as follows:

```
copy ( FirstVector.begin(), FirstVector.end(), SecondVector.begin() );
```

The `swap` algorithm takes two elements from two ranges (which could be the same range) and exchanges them. The first example is as follows:

```
swap ( FirstVector.at(1), SecondVector.at(1) );
```

The second example, with the same range specified in both parameters, is as follows:

```
swap ( FirstVector.at(5), FirstVector.at(10) );
```

If you want to swap entire ranges of elements—rather than just single elements—you can use the `swap_ranges` algorithm. For example:

```
swap_ranges ( FirstVector.begin(), FirstVector.end(), SecondVector.begin() );
```

There should be enough elements in the second range to allow the swap to take place, given the size of the range specified in the first two parameters.

The `iter_swap` algorithm exchanges values of elements that are pointed to by two iterators, rather than explicit element references. For example:

```
iter_swap ( FirstVector.begin()+2, SecondVector.begin() );
```

If you want to change values within a range, you can use the `transform` algorithm in one of two variations. The first variation applies a unary operator to elements from the first range and then puts the result in the corresponding element in the second range, starting where the third parameter (second iterator) points.

For example:

```
transform ( FirstVector.begin(), FirstVector.end(),
        SecondVector.begin(), UnaryOperatorFunction );
```

The second variation takes an element from the first range and an element from the second, and combines them with the programmer-supplied binary operator. The result is then placed in the appropriate element of the third range.

This could be a separate range, correctly allocated with, for example, `::resize`, or one of the original ranges. For example:

```
transform ( FirstVector.begin(), FirstVector.end(),
        SecondVector.begin(), ThirdVector.begin(), BinaryOperatorFunction );
```

The `replace` algorithm takes a range and two values. The first value, in the fourth parameter, is the value to search the range for, and the second value is the value to replace it with. For example:

```
replace (FirstVector.begin(), FirstVector.end(), 3, 5 );
```

This example assumes that you have a vector of integers. The algorithm will then replace all the number 3s with number 5s.

Rather than use a static value to look through the ranges, the `replace_if` algorithm uses a predicate function. This looks like the following example:

```
replace_if ( FirstVector.begin(), FirstVector.end(),
             PredicateFunction, 5 );
```

The predicate function is unary and returns `true` if a given condition is satisfied (defined by the programmer). The value in the last parameter then replaces the value pointed to by the iterator (between `FirstVector.begin()` and `FirstVector.end()`).

You can use the `fill` algorithm to iterate through a range and fill each element with a programmer-supplied value. For example:

```
fill ( FirstVector.begin(), FirstVector.end(), 42 );
```

This code will fill an integer vector from start to end with the value 42.

You can use a function to populate a range by using the `generate` algorithm, as you did in the opening part to this section. For example:

```
generate ( FirstVector.begin(), FirstVector.end(), GeneratorFunction );
```

The result of the `GeneratorFunction` is placed into the vector item currently being pointed at, which will be in the range specified, in this case, between `::begin` and `::end`.

Using the `remove` algorithm, you can scan a range for a given value and remove the element containing it. For example:

```
remove ( FirstVector.begin(), FirstVector.end(), Value );
```

The `remove_if` algorithm works in a similar way to the `remove` algorithm; however, rather than look for a static value, it evaluates each element using a programmer-defined predicate function that should return `true` or `false`. For example:

```
remove_if ( FirstVector.begin(), FirstVector.end(), PredicateFunction );
```

You can use the `unique` algorithm in one of two ways. The first method simply scans the range and removes consecutive values that are identical. For example:

```
unique ( FirstVector.begin(), FirstVector.end() );
```

The second method allows you to specify a binary predicate that takes two items—consecutive vector entries—and returns `true` if they are identical. For example:

```
unique ( FirstVector.begin(), FirstVector.end(), BinaryPredicateFunction );
```

If you want to reverse the elements in a range, you use the reverse algorithm. This takes a range as follows:

```
reverse ( FirstVector.begin(), FirstVector.end() );
```

This algorithm uses bidirectional iterators—a double reverse puts the range back into the same order as it was originally.

You can use the random_shuffle algorithm to change the order of the range based on the outcome of a random number generator. This algorithm exists in two forms. The first uses the standard random number generator and looks like this:

```
random_shuffle (FirstVector.begin(), FirstVector.end() );
```

If you want to supply your own number generator, which might not be random, you can place it as an additional parameter to the algorithm. This second form looks like this:

```
random_shuffle (FirstVector.begin(), FirstVector.end(), RandomFunction );
```

Searching and Sorting Algorithms

A simple sorting operation uses the sort algorithm. This algorithm has two forms, one that uses the standard built-in comparison function taken from the class belonging to the elements that make up the range, and one that takes a programmer-defined comparison function. An example of the first form is as follows:

```
sort (FirstVector.begin(), FirstVector.end() );
```

The second form allows you to specify a comparison function, which is a binary predicate taking two parameters supplied by the compiler. An example of this is as follows:

```
sort ( FirstVector.begin(), FirstVector.end(), ComparisonFunction );
```

The comparison function in both cases should mimic the behavior of the < (less than) operator in order for the sorting algorithm to arrange the elements appropriately.

To perform a search of the range, you use the binary_search algorithm. This has two forms. The first form takes a range and a value to search for, and an example of it is as follows:

```
binary_search ( FirstVector.begin(), FirstVector.end(), SearchValue );
```

The second form of binary_search has a comparison function that takes the current item and the value and compares them. Its use is similar to the following:

```
binary_search ( FirstVector.begin(), FirstVector.end(), SearchValue,
                ComparisonFunction );
```

The return value of the algorithm is a bool in both cases, and the comparison function should return true if the parameters are equal.

Merge Algorithms

The merge algorithm takes two ranges, merges them, and places them in a third range, starting at the iterator provided in the function call. The resulting range is sorted according, in the first usage, to the standard operator <, and in the second, using a programmer-supplied comparison function.

The first form looks like this:

```
merge (FirstVector.begin(), FirstVector.end(),
       SecondVector.begin(), SecondVector.end(), ThirdVector.begin() );
```

The second form takes an additional parameter, which is a function to use in place of the < operator. The second form looks like this:

```
merge ( FirstVector.begin(), FirstVector.end(),
        SecondVector.begin(), SecondVector.end(),
        ThirdVector.begin(), ComparisonFunction );
```

The includes algorithm tests whether one range includes another range and returns true if it is the case. There are two forms, one without a comparison function supplied by the programmer, which uses the class defined test for equality, and one with the comparison function. First, the simple form (without the comparison function) is as follows:

```
includes (FirstVector.begin(), FirstVector.end(),
          SecondVector.begin(), SecondVector.end() );
```

The second form, with the comparison function, is as follows:

```
includes ( FirstVector.begin(), FirstVector.end(),
           SecondVector.begin(), SecondVector.end(),
           ComparisonFunction );
```

The programmer-supplied comparison function returns true if the two items provided are equal. The comparison might not be the same as provided by an overloaded comparison operator for the same class, but this will affect the result of the algorithm.

To obtain the union of two ranges, you can use the `set_union` algorithm. This function takes two ranges, specified in the first two parameters and the second two, with the last parameter of the first form receiving a range that equates to the union. This first form looks like this:

```
set_union ( FirstVector.begin(), FirstVector.end(),
          SecondVector.begin(), SecondVector.end(),
          ThirdVector.begin() );
```

The second form works in the same way as the first, but allows you to supply a comparison function. It looks like this:

```
set_union ( FirstVector.begin(), FirstVector.end(),
          SecondVector.begin(), SecondVector.end(),
          ThirdVector.begin(), ComparisonFunction );
```

The comparison function returns `true` if two values taken from the first and second ranges, respectively, are considered equal.

To obtain the common points between two sets (the intersection), use the `set_intersection` algorithm. This is available in two forms. The first form takes two ranges and a third to receive the result. The second form adds a programmer-supplied comparison function.

The first form:

```
set_intersection ( FirstVector.begin(), FirstVector.end(),
                 SecondVector.begin(), SecondVector.end(),
                 ThirdVector.begin() );
```

The second form adds a comparison function that returns `true` if the two elements taken from the first and second ranges are considered equal. It looks like this:

```
set_intersection ( FirstVector.begin(), FirstVector.end(),
                 SecondVector.begin(), SecondVector.end(),
                 ThirdVector.begin(), ComparisonFunction );
```

In order to obtain the difference between two ranges (to return the elements that are not the same), you use the `set_difference` algorithm. Just as with the previous set operations, this is available in two forms—with and without the comparison function.

The first form, without the function, is as follows:

```
set_difference ( FirstVector.begin(), FirstVector.end(),
                SecondVector.begin(), SecondVector.end(),
                ThirdVector.begin() );
```

The second form, which allows the programmer to supply a comparison function, is as follows:

```
set_difference ( FirstVector.begin(), FirstVector.end(),
                SecondVector.begin(), SecondVector.end(),
                ThirdVector.begin(), ComparisonFunction );
```

The comparison function in this case returns false if the two items are not equal. The third range (starting at the iterator ThirdVector.begin()) receives the set difference, represented by a range. The set difference represents those items that appear in the first range (FirstVector.begin() to FirstVector.end()), but not in the SecondVector range.

Min and Max Algorithms

The min algorithm operates on two values, without or with a comparison function provided by the programmer, and returns the lesser of the two arguments. Rather than operating on ranges, it operates on single values.

The first form looks like this:

```
min ( 3, 5 );
```

The alternate form, which can be supplemented with a programmer-defined comparison function, looks like this:

```
min ( 3, 5, ComparisonFunction );
```

The comparison function should return an appropriate value if the first value is considered to be less than the second.

The max algorithm is similar to the min algorithm, except that it returns the greater of the two supplied parameters. The first form looks like this:

```
max ( 3, 5 )
```

The alternate form, as with the min algorithm, allows you to supply a comparison function that should mimic the behavior of the > operator.

```
max ( 3, 5, ComparisonFunction )
```

If you need to retrieve the smallest element in a range, you can use the min_element algorithm. This is available in two forms, one with and one without a comparison function. The first form, without the comparison function, looks like this:

```
SecondVector = min_element ( FirstVector.begin(), FirstVector.end() );
```

The algorithm will search the range and return a reference to the smallest element in the range. The alternate form looks like this:

```
SecondVector = min_element ( FirstVector.begin(), FirstVector.end(),
                             ComparisonFunction );
```

The companion to `min_element` is `max_element`, and it returns a reference to the largest element in the range. The first form for this is as follows:

```
SecondVector = max_element ( FirstVector.begin(), FirstVector.end() );
```

This algorithm uses the > operator to establish the relationship between the two elements in the range currently being compared. The alternate form allows the programmer to supply a function to use in its place. It looks like this:

```
SecondVector = max_element ( FirstVector.begin(), FirstVector.end(),
                             ComparisonFunction );
```

The comparison function should mimic the behavior of the > operator, and will take two parameters provided by the compiler, which will match the class of the elements in the range supplied.

Iterators

Most container classes have iterators supplied with them that allow you to move through the range and obtain successive references to elements contained within it. You've seen iterators all through the discussion of the STL algorithms, but they are also available to the programmer.

The main iterators are `begin`, `end`, `rbegin`, and `rend`. These iterators provide the functionality to specify the end points of the range that you want to examine. You can move through the range of elements without knowing anything else about either the range or the elements.

One example of this uses a `for` loop that starts at `::begin` and goes to `::end`, returning the container class type at each step. For example:

```
for ( element = my_string.begin() ; element < my_string.end(); element++ )
    cout << " " << *element;
```

This snippet uses the `element` variable to hold the reference to the range, as it moves through it from start to end by incrementing the pointer until it is equal to the `::end` iterator.

User-Defined Classes and the `using` Keyword

Usually you want to use STL with classes and types other than the built-in ones—`int`, `char`, and so on—because you need to manipulate user-defined types and classes. For example, you might want to create a linked list of `struct` data elements.

To do this, you need to derive your own classes from the templates or at least add your own data to the container definition. This allows you to provide functionality that does not rely on built-in predicates and operators.

This implies that you need to overload some of the operators, or at least provide your own operators to perform some of the vital functions that the underlying built-in types use when you create the ranges.

Generally, these overloads will be construction, assignment, and comparison operators—operators that are required for many of the algorithms that you read about in this chapter, as well as the member methods of the classes themselves.

Recap

This chapter looked at templates from a high-level point of view. It doesn't cover every detail of every feature that template functions and classes are capable of, but you should now have a working knowledge of templates, after having read this chapter.

Although you can use templates, the best use is to apply the knowledge of using the STL to perform common programming tasks. The STL has containers, which are models of various storage facilities such as dynamic arrays that allow you to avoid constantly reinventing the wheel when you program.

The STL also has a collection of functions to apply to those containers, as well as some that can be used with single types. It also defines some iterators that you can use to move through the items in the containers.

The chapter is designed to be kept as a reference to the STL, in the same way that the C library function can be used as a reference to C programming.

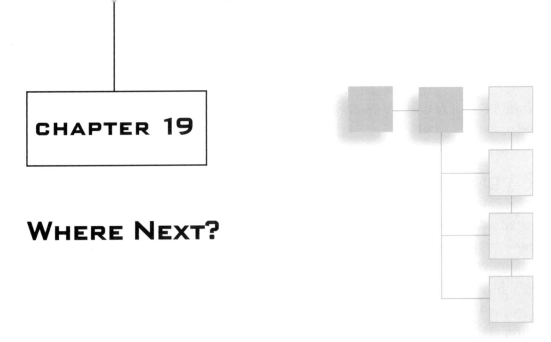

CHAPTER 19

WHERE NEXT?

This book has provided you with the basics. Beyond these concepts, there are many directions in which you can take your C and C++ programming expertise.

For those who have enough to get working on private, or commercial, projects, all that is needed is practice. The intricacies of the language itself will become apparent as each program developed pushes the boundaries of the programmer's knowledge a little further.

Treat this book as a stepping stone into other areas—software engineering, design, and other programming languages such as Java, PHP, and even Perl. If you've made it this far, you have a good handle on most programming concepts. However, there are some concepts we didn't cover, in the interest of getting as many readers up and running as quickly as possible.

This book serves as good preparatory text, and you should now feel comfortable following a college course in programming. This is a wise step forward if you're beginning a career from programming, because there are academic topics not covered here.

This chapter covers two topics that will be of interest to readers who want to apply their newfound knowledge in their own projects immediately. If you want to get down to the fun task of putting together a program, this chapter can help.

This chapter teaches you a few pointers before you embark on your own project; after all, experience will teach a lot of valuable lessons, but there is no harm in getting a head start.

Programming for Reuse

There are many good reasons to approach each project as if it is a part of a larger set of solutions that can be used and reused. The programming readership might now break into two camps—the professional programmers and the programmers who are reading this because they just need to know enough about C and/or C++ to help them solve a particular problem.

On the one hand, the professional programmers might assume that they can jump straight in and start working on a project and not worry about reuse. After all, they can always write the code again, and next time it might even be better.

On the other hand, the casual programmers might be asking themselves whether the extra effort is really worthwhile. Isn't programming for reuse just for the professionals?

Both types of programmers can reap enormous benefits from the philosophy of reuse. It will save the professionals many hours of programming time in the long run, making them more efficient. For causal programmers, the code base will serve to remind them of key language points that they might forget—after all, they are not usually programming every day, and the human mind can sometimes become preoccupied with other things.

Reuse in Design

The book has mentioned the concepts that are close to the core of object-oriented design. Programmers of all levels are encouraged to take the advice to heart, and concentrate of producing designs that are based on:

- Reusable coded components.

- Reused designs.

The chapter covers reusable coded components in a bit. Reusing designs relates to a software design paradigm known as *design patterns.* The core theory behind design patterns is that they provide template solutions that can be reused in different projects and languages.

Programmers who create object-oriented designs will find that there may be some commonality between projects that they create. If those designs are easily indexed and identified, they can be reused.

The advantage of reusing designs is that implementations based on them can also be reused, as can the designs themselves. Even if the "just enough" programmer finds that, initially, this creates more work, in the long term it will reduce the complexity of projects.

Reuse in C Programming

The mechanisms for reusing C code are very simple—you can break up the source code into separate files containing user-defined data types and functions that manipulate them, thus ensuring that the modules are kept separate.

Another option that you have is to create libraries that can be dynamically or statically linked. This requires a little more work and some additional research, but is also a feasible approach.

These libraries should also be designed and programmed in a reusable fashion. This includes being able to properly document them—meaning both notes *and* inline comments—so that they can be located and understood.

Of course, every programmer that uses the C Standard Library Functions is participating in reuse, so extending that to your own projects is not a large step out of usual practices. It just means that you are taking a more professional and efficient attitude to programming.

Reuse in C++ Programming

Of course, the template mechanism, the Standard Template Library, the classes, and other object-oriented principles that underpin C++ make it the perfect platform for reuse. All programmers should make use of the STL, as it contains tried-and-tested objects, containers, and algorithms.

From the implementation side, you have the same facilities as C programmers; with the added bonus that the class hierarchy mechanism gives you a better platform for it. In other words, where the C code needs to be forever extended with new functionality to solve a new problem with existing code, a class can be derived from a base class.

The derived class can then be specialized for a given application, with only the required code passing back into the parent class as necessary. It does mean that you need to maintain a very strong grip on the class library—and change reused base classes only when absolutely necessary.

All of these reuse principles might take time to absorb and put into practice. Good programming does not *require* reuse, but good programmers should try to use it whenever possible.

Open Source and Glue Code

One incredibly good source for reuse is the open source community. So long as you respect the terms of the license under which the code is released, open source is free to use and can save you valuable programming hours. After all, if someone else has developed an encryption library, why not leverage that rather than develop one from scratch?

However, complete solutions are not usually available for every project that you might embark on. Often what is needed is to create code that takes what is available and rearranges it slightly. The logic that is then required to solve the actual problem can be implemented as *glue code*.

Again, however, you must ensure that you comply with the conditions of the license of any source code that they include in your projects. The reason for this is that some projects may fall into a category known as a *derived work*. In this instance, the code becomes subject to various terms stipulated in the license under which the component parts have been issued. Of course, this usually applies only to projects that have a commercial goal.

Above all, it is polite to return any improvements to the code to the open source community, credit the use of source code correctly, and thank the original author. After all, the author has performed a great service.

To adopt this approach, it is necessary to identify the parts of the design (see the section "Reuse in Design") that could be contained as sub-projects independent of, but integrated with, the main project. For example, a text editor might be part of a development IDE, but it could also stand alone in its own right, as could the file-handling portion of the editor mechanism.

Many projects, then, can be represented as a collection of modules that are interconnected, at the design stage. Performing this part of the design, no matter how loosely, will be beneficial in the eventual creation of a system that is much more than the sum of its parts.

Leveraging open source and glue code in this way—by using existing solutions and bending them to fit new projects—is an effective way to kick-start a development effort, even if the eventual open source components are swapped for more customized solutions in the long term.

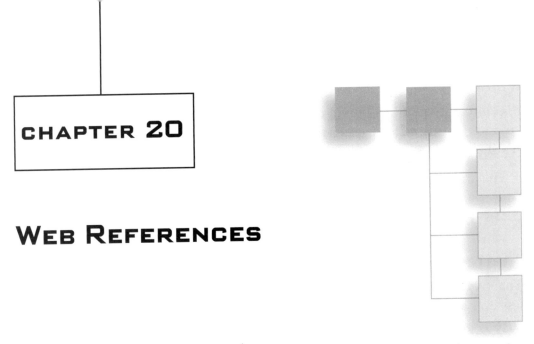

CHAPTER 20

WEB REFERENCES

This chapter contains a collection of some of the best places to visit when you're coming to grips with the topics in this book. The first place that you should go to is the "Compilers" section in order to download the latest IDE (integrated development environment) for your platform.

Compilers

Different platforms have different compilers, ranging from command-line to fully GUI IDEs. Some IDE providers wrap up existing command-line compilers (like gcc) into their IDE to provide a reasonably seamless complete development environment.

The weakest link in the tool chain tends to be with the debugging facilities. Debuggers can be quite difficult to set up and use without an easy GUI interface, and for that reason, paying for an environment can be worth it. Everything works as expected, right out of the book, and comes with a paper reference manual.

However, because Microsoft made Express Editions of their excellent development tools available to Windows users for free, that platform, at least, now has a definitive easy option. It is, on the other hand, very Windows-centric in the way the C and C++ languages are compiled.

Linux

All Linux distributions have a compiler, gcc, that can be optionally installed in addition to the other packages. It is a command-line compiler that supports ANSI C and C++.

There are plenty of open source development tools and add-ons found at SourceForge (http://www.sourceforge.net) that can be used alongside gcc and its related tools, such as the debugger gdb.

TheFreeCountry.com

TheFreeCountry is a Web site full of compilers and supporting tools for more or less every language that you can think of. Of particular importance here is the collection of compilers for C and C++. See http://www.thefreecountry.com/compilers/cpp.shtml.

Microsoft

Express Editions (free) of Microsoft's Visual Studio tools are now available, and provide a truly excellent platform for Windows users.

See http://msdn.microsoft.com/vstudio/express/visualc/ (see Figure 20.1).

Note that the Express Editions refer to a package that is usually a little behind the curve in terms of the current product line. In 2007, for example, the current Express Edition of the Microsoft Visual Studio carries the 2005 moniker. This is merely a convention and does not reflect the quality of the product.

Borland

A long-time leader in compilers and IDEs, Borland made its flagship compiler and tools free for use—subject to certain conditions—a while ago. They added to this free list recently with an Explorer version of their Turbo IDE (see Figure 20.2).

This is an excellent alternative to the Microsoft environment, again principally for Windows users. See http://www.turboexplorer.com/cpp.

Apple Macintosh

Apple made the gcc tool (see Linux) available for free for OS X users. It had some initial issues, but now seems to be widely appreciated. See http://developer.apple.com/tools/xcode/.

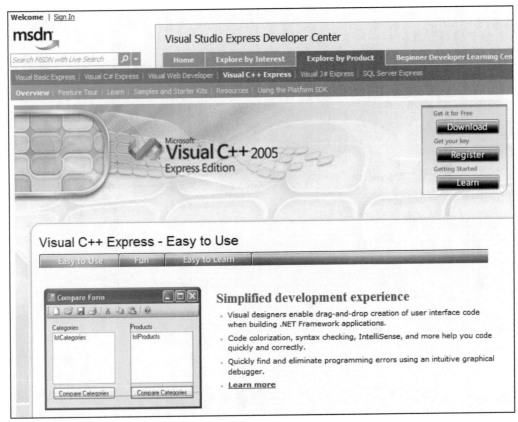

Figure 20.1
The MSDN Visual C++ Express Edition Page

An alternative is the Eclipse IDE with the C/C++ environment installed. See http://www.eclipse.org.

Source Code

You might often find that other developers have already developed a solution to a problem that you are trying to solve. As you saw in Chapter 19, there is little sense in continually trying to reinvent solutions, so the best approach is to see what other programmers have done before you attempt a solution.

The Code Project

This site is divided into several areas and navigation is through a hierarchical menu system (see Figure 20.3). There are articles that describe specific solutions (with source code) and general approaches.

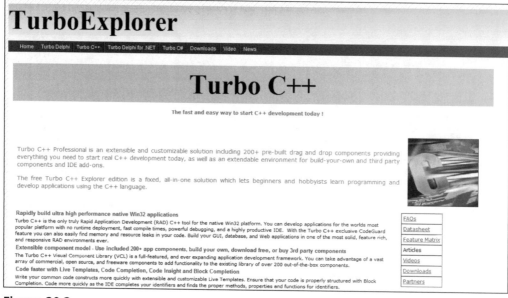

Figure 20.2
The Borland TurboExplorer Web Site

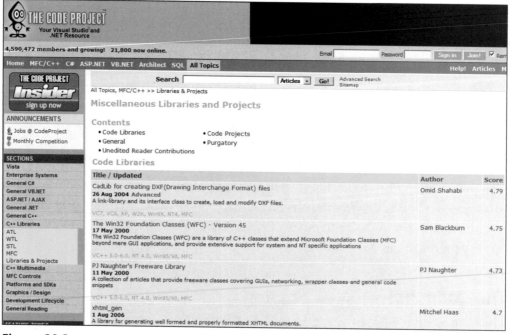

Figure 20.3
The Code Project Web Site

A peer voting system is in place to help you decide the level of value that a given solution provides.

It is often the first place to look when you're trying to implement a specific solution, and the search facility allows you to restrict the results returned by language and category, as well as the search terms. Highly recommended.

See http://www.codeproject.com.

SourceForge

If you're looking for complete libraries, works in progress, or hints on how to formulate solutions, SourceForge is a wonderful resource. It contains open source solutions in all languages, across platforms, for all kinds of programming problems.

There are complete environments, libraries, applications, and even small snippets of solution-oriented code. See Figure 20.4.

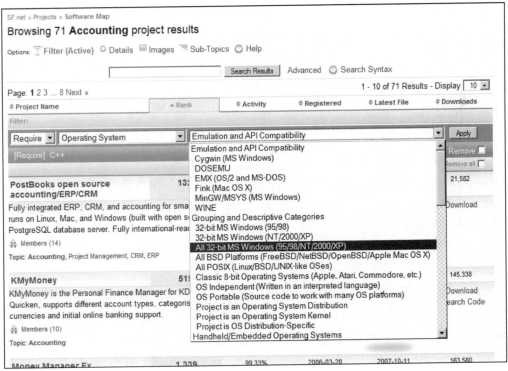

Figure 20.4
Browsing and Filtering SF.net Projects by Language and Platform

The search and browse system is not for the faint hearted, and it will take a little time to get used to. However, the improvements that have been made over the original site make it accessible to programmers of all levels. See http://www.sf.net.

C and C++ Programming

The following is a collection of Web sites and USENET groups that cover C/C++ and programming in more detail.

C/C++ at About.com

This is a reasonably complete reference site and the C/C++ section is no exception. It has a good collection of tutorials, but they tend to be relatively scant and have a heavy emphasis on advertising revenue. It can take some digging to find the information that you are looking for. See cplus.about.com.

The C++ Resources Network

Great quick reference section. This site provides good ANSI compatibility information for the standard function libraries. The forums provide open discussion; this is a great starting point if you have slightly esoteric questions.

The C++ STL and Standard Libraries are also well covered here—it's a great place for those who get slightly stuck when trying to implement some of the container classes or derive new ones from them. See www.cplusplus.com.

Cprogramming.com

A very complete set of resources. Possibly the best site out there for those getting started, and a good reference site for the more advanced. If you want to take programming in C to the next level, this is the place for you. See Cprogramming.com.

The C Programming Language Wikipedia Entry

A potted history of C, some of the important concepts, and a look at C-like languages await you at the Wikipedia entry for C programming. Ever expanding collection of links to resources, some better than others, and some interesting diversions from the core topic complete the picture. See Figure 20.5.

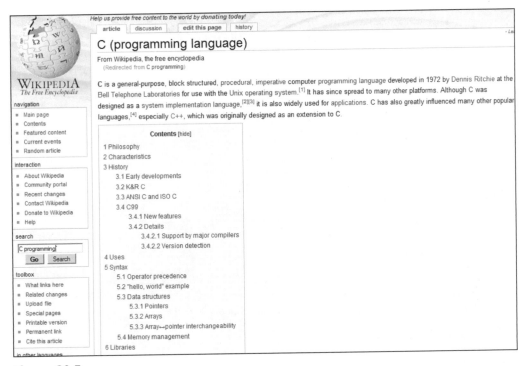

Figure 20.5
The Extensive Wikipedia C Language Entry

Go to www.wikipedia.org, choose your language, and then type **C programming** or **C++** into the search box.

Programming User Groups

There are many user groups dedicated to the art of programming, some language-independent, and some language related. User groups come and go, to a certain extent, but the following are fairly stable and very, very useful.

The groups are accessed via a third-party service such as Google Groups (groups.google.com) or a piece of newsreader software. See Figure 20.6.

comp.lang.c and comp.lang.c.moderated

Un-moderated and moderated versions of a discussion group dedicated to the C programming language. The moderated version has fewer members and gets less traffic, but can be more useful for those just starting out because of it.

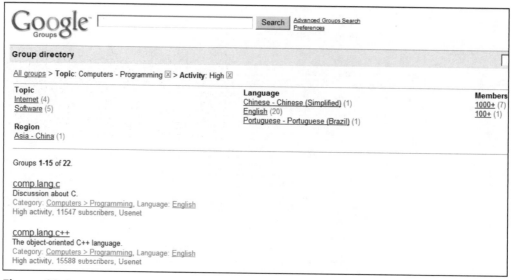

Figure 20.6
Usenet Groups via Google Groups: C Language Is the Highest Activity

comp.lang.C++ and comp.lang.C++.moderated

Un-moderated and moderated versions of a discussion group dedicated to the C++ programming language. The moderated version has substantially fewer members and gets less traffic, which means the content is less time-consuming to sift through.

comp.programming

General programming themes. Great for those needing some help with the theory and practice of programming in general.

comp.programming.contests

Sometimes the best way to learn is to do or observe what other programmers have done. The contests in this group will give programmers at all levels a useful insight into the way that solutions can be crafted.

INDEX